Integrating Spirituality into Counseling

Integrating Spirituality into Counseling uses the Christian tradition as a starting point for developing a universal frame of reference and is predominantly based on an existential approach to counseling, one that is applicable to several faith traditions as well as spiritual but nonreligious audiences.

The chapters of this book proceed from the theoretical toward the more practical, in a logical fashion, allowing a clear distinction between different topics, starting from meta-reflection and finishing with practical applications. The design of the book allows students to focus on whatever is of importance to them; each chapter is self-contained and can be read independently of the others.

Integrating Spirituality into Counseling is designed for students of counseling, pastoral care, spirituality, theology, and chaplaincy. It will provide readers with the tools they need to work with spiritual issues across traditions. Students will also find advice for when to refer clients to religious leaders or ministers, and they'll also deepen their understanding of the ways in which spirituality influences one's life.

Andrzej K. Jastrzębski, OMI, is a professor at Saint Paul University in Ottawa. He has a keen interest in promoting a holistic understanding of the human experience through research on spirituality, philosophy, psychology, and neuroscience.

Integrating Spirituality into Counseling

Methods and Practices

Andrzej K. Jastrzębski

Routledge
Taylor & Francis Group
NEW YORK AND LONDON

Cover image: © Getty

First published 2023
by Routledge
605 Third Avenue, New York, NY 10158

and by Routledge
4 Park Square, Milton Park, Abingdon, Oxon, OX14 4RN

Routledge is an imprint of the Taylor & Francis Group, an informa business

Library of Congress Cataloging-in-Publication Data
Names: Jastrzębski, Andrzej, 1973– author.
Title: Integrating spirituality into counseling : methods and practices / Andrzej K. Jastrzębski.
Description: New York, NY : Routledge, 2022. |
Includes bibliographical references and index.
Identifiers: LCCN 2022015548 (print) | LCCN 2022015549 (ebook) |
ISBN 9781032200194 (hardback) | ISBN 9781032200187 (paperback) |
ISBN 9781003262145 (ebook)
Subjects: LCSH: Spirituality. | Spirituality–Christianity. | Spirituality. |
Counseling–Religious aspects–Christianity. | Counseling–Religious aspects.
Classification: LCC BV4501.3 .J375 2022 (print) |
LCC BV4501.3 (ebook) | DDC 253.5–dc23/eng/20220605
LC record available at https://lccn.loc.gov/2022015548
LC ebook record available at https://lccn.loc.gov/2022015549

ISBN: 9781032200194 (hbk)
ISBN: 9781032200187 (pbk)
ISBN: 9781003262145 (ebk)

DOI: 10.4324/9781003262145

Typeset in Bembo
by Newgen Publishing UK

To my family, friends, and students.

Contents

Figures

Foreword

David B. Perrin, PhD, DTh

Professor Emeritus, St. Jerome's University at the University of Waterloo, Ontario, Canada

'Human sciences' is an inclusive phrase that describes a wide range of disciplines which study the human component of life. These disciplines include sociology, anthropology, political science, history, and, of course, psychology. With respect to research in any one of these disciplines, the other disciplines are frequently included as integral partners, or at least ought to be, since interdisciplinarity enriches both research and practice. For this reason, *Integrating Spirituality into Counseling: Methods and Practices* does not shy away from this approach.

With its interdisciplinary approach to psychology and counseling, *Integrating Spirituality into Counseling* emphasizes that research in the field of psychology and counseling cannot limit itself to a narrow band of inquiry. Dr. Andrzej Jastrzębski reveals in full force the power of interdisciplinarity both within the research and teaching field of psychology as well as in the practices of counseling that flow from it. The integral inclusion of spirituality into psychological research, teaching, and practice is at the forefront of interdisciplinarity in this volume.

Daniel Helminiak, who possesses earned doctorates in both psychology and theology, points out in *Religion and the Human Sciences: An Approach via Spirituality* (1998) that the assumption for interdisciplinarity is that a 'full account of the human' requires an integrated contribution from a range of bodies of knowledge and ways of looking at the world. Each discipline engaged in psychological and counseling research and practice critically examines the pathway to full human potential within its own point of view – one of many perspectives. He notes that one viewpoint does not necessarily abrogate the findings from another. Truths recognized from within the framework of one research method do not nullify other critical frameworks that may deepen the understanding of what is at stake, not to mention provide corrections and nuances.

As a result, when some topics and disciplines are prejudicially and prematurely excluded in research in psychology and counseling, results can be diminished or even erroneous. Since spirituality and related metaphysical or transcendental concepts have not historically been substantially woven into the research, teaching, and practice of counseling, this book seeks to correct this imbalance. But it begs the question: Why has there been such a hesitancy to include spirituality and other transcendent concepts within the field of psychology, if not outright exclusion? A look back at the origins of the development of psychology as an independent field of study may give some clues.

The scientific method developed in the seventeenth century by Francis Bacon and others posited that authentic knowledge could be obtained only through inductive reasoning by methodical observation of what occurs in nature. It was within this reductionist culture that psychology, with its methods for both research and practice, developed in the mid-nineteenth century. However, these methods stripped the researcher and the practitioner of the possibility of including the transcendent dimension of human life in their work, a movement broadly referred to as secularization.

The philosopher Charles Taylor, in his highly acclaimed volume *A Secular Age* (2007), describes methodically this movement into the secularization of the Western world following the so-called Enlightenment. As a result of this secularization, ideas about the transcendent, reason, nature, and humanity coalesced into a worldview that repositioned reason in the functioning of human intellectual life – and not always in a good way. As subjects of the Cartesian cogito, and awash in the notion of Enlightenment truth, thinkers stripped reason itself of its permission to search for truth outside the narrow confines of the scientific method. The transcendent dimension of human life was relegated to the private and devotional. This is unfortunate, as Taylor explains so well.

The function of human reason – let's call it classical reason – prior to the Enlightenment was far more holistic and inclusive. Classical reason, at the wider service of truth and of the meaning of life, viewed reality as an integral whole and accepted reality as that which encompassed all of life, all of the world, and all human experiences, including those that engaged larger transcendental realities: for example, the phenomena of religion, faith, and spirituality. This was to change with the adoption of a reductionist use of reason developed during the Enlightenment period and the secularization of the West described above. Human beings strive to be in communion with the whole of reality from within whatever perspective we understand that reality to be. Acknowledging this starting point for research and practice in psychology and counseling is a reasonable thing to do.

The irony of the bifurcation of reason – that is, the transition to the dominance of Enlightenment reason from classical reason in the seventeenth and eighteenth centuries – is that the operative approach to life became *rationalistic* but *not reasonable*. A large swath of the anomalies and paradoxes of spiritual human experiences – and potential knowledge, insight, and meaning deriving from them – were not admitted to the rational scrutiny of research in the development of psychology in the nineteenth century and beyond. When it comes to counseling, this exclusion of the spiritual or the transcendent may impede the transformative process longed for in the therapeutic counseling relationship.

For example, compassion and forgiveness are egregiously understudied in the psychoanalytic literature. These words are often filled with religious connotations for the counselor and thus avoided in the therapeutic conversation. This is unfortunate because disregarding these realities concomitantly throws out or diminishes conversations about transcendental notions such as sacrifice, mercy, and care and responsibility for the other: that is, the ethical good that comes with accepting one's mature role in life for oneself, others, and the larger community known as the common good. Furthermore, nonattention to transcendental realities stifles conversations about the sense of a higher goal in the client's life, the very thing that may contribute toward the treatment of what ails.

Donald S. Browning, trained in theology, sociology, and psychology, points out for us the main problem with the exclusion of the transcendental. In *A Fundamental Practical Theology: Descriptive and Strategic Proposals* (1991), he says that it leads researchers and practitioners to distance themselves from their objects of study as well as 'from the cultural and religious traditions that form them.' Surely such an approach diminishes both research and practice in psychology and counseling. In the end, it is the individual before the counselor seeking something more – the client in distress – who suffers from these lacunae.

Integrating Spirituality into Counseling is a step toward reconnecting the psychological and psychotherapeutic literature with the deeper transcendent realities of life. As such, it makes significant concrete proposals to restore human reason to its full depth and breadth of potential. It takes seriously the role of transcendental realities in life, which include the concepts of spirituality, prayer, ritual, spiritual bypass, sacrifice, forgiveness, reconciliation, evil, and sin. In doing so, this important volume takes a step toward diminishing the bifurcation of reason described above.

In *Integrating Spirituality into Counseling*, psychology and counseling are not invited to abandon the usefulness of their quantifying methods but to see the collection of predictably verifiable data as one part of a larger methodological process that includes the commitment to engaging the qualitative phenomenon of transcendence and, in particular, those that appear through faith-based living. Dr. Andrzej Jastrzębski has succeeded admirably in this regard.

Preface

Integrating Spirituality into Counseling: Methods and Practices is the fruit of a number of years spent teaching counseling and spirituality courses at all academic levels (BA, MA, PhD) in the School of Counselling, Psychotherapy and Spirituality at Saint Paul University in Ottawa and has involved numerous years of personal research. It has to be noted that this program started out as a classical pastoral counseling school within the Roman Catholic tradition. Over the years, and with the experience gained through relevant and lively exchanges and discussions with a great diversity of students, it gradually evolved into a more universal approach to integrating spirituality into counseling. The book is meant to illustrate these changes as well as touch on more general societal transformations; although its base is Christian, its content is broad and serves candidates presently enrolled in the program who come from a wide range of religious traditions and cultures, as well as from atheistic backgrounds. Knowing this may be of help in other programs that are undergoing a similar transformation. The content of the book has proven to be interesting and compelling to successive classes of students from a wide variety of backgrounds and has been developed and updated over the years to respond to the needs of this diversity of students while remaining faithful to its roots.

Acknowledgments

I am very thankful to all the students who challenged me for clarifications and thus invited me to develop and fine-tune my knowledge, reflect on my ideas for the future, and correct certain statements. I am grateful for the help and assistance I have received from my colleagues at Saint Paul University in Ottawa, especially to my long-standing teaching assistant, Samoon Tasmim. Together, we could develop a Christian-Muslim interfaith approach to teaching spirituality.

I am extremely thankful to Claudette Gravelle, who supported me over the years as a competent editor and faithful friend. My thanks also go to Marie Danielle De Banné and Suzanne Mary Debanné as well as to Sr. Marie-Pierre Delorme for their work on the manuscript. I would also like to express my gratitude for the invaluable help, pertinent comments, and constant encouragement received from Professor David Perrin during the process of preparing the manuscript for publication.

I am also grateful for the permissions I have received to include certain parts of my previous publications in this book: 'The Challenging Task of Defining Spirituality,' published in *Journal of Spirituality in Mental Health*; 'The Normative Aspect in the Contemporary Understanding of Spirituality,' published in *Wrocław Theological Review*; 'Recent Developments in Understanding Spirituality as Exemplified by the Concept of Self-Transcendence,' published in *Verbum Vitae*, and 'The Neuroscience of Spirituality: An Attempt at Critical Analysis,' published in *Pastoral Psychology*.

Andrzej Jastrzębski, OMI

About the Author

Dr. Andrzej Krzysztof Jastrzębski, OMI, professor at Saint Paul University in Ottawa, holds a postgraduate diploma in Psychotherapy and Pastoral Counseling, a PhD in Metaphysics and Philosophical Anthropology, and a Doctorate (Habilitation) in Spiritual Theology. His passion is research on issues touching spirituality, philosophy, psychology, and neuroscience in order to create a larger and more holistic understanding of the human being in view of the psychotherapeutic process leading to achieving the full human potential. He has authored several books, most recently *Homo theomorphicus et theophoricus: A Receptive-Responsive Theory of Spirituality* (Peeters 2019), has written a number of articles, as well as given many talks and taught many classes on these issues.

Introduction

This book uses the Christian tradition as its point of departure but then develops a more universal framework, mostly based on an existential approach to counseling; it incorporates the objectives of several faith traditions as well as those of spiritual but nonreligious audiences. It attempts to address the diversity, commodification, and fragmentation of contemporary ways of understanding spirituality. The flow of topics is similar to other publications in the field, but has its own specific focus and is divided into the following sections:

- Understanding spirituality,
- Researching spirituality,
- Spiritual processes,
- Helping people in their spiritual quest,
- Evaluating the role of spirituality in one's life,
- Supportive role of spirituality in solving certain life problems,
- Examples of the most common spiritual practices to be integrated into counseling,
- Issues originating in the Roman Catholic tradition and their universal implications.

In light of its interdisciplinary framework, the book explores a wide range of issues pertaining to spirituality, pastoral care, and counseling; it presents the theoretical foundations needed to understand and conceptualize spirituality as well as topics related to it. The reflection follows a path that bridges spirituality, psychology, sociology, philosophy, and theology; it puts an accent, but not exclusively, on Western Christian traditions with the inclusion of dominant Protestant and lesser-known Orthodox theologies. It also presents a meaningful historical and methodological background for each, as has been the approach in the long tradition of pastoral counseling.

The method used in the book includes the historical beginning of the topics presented, their philosophical underpinnings to finally arrive at contemporary and universal proposals of how to conceive these issues for counseling purposes, in an actual pluralistic context. This kind of analytical approach is rather rare in publications of this type. Its practicality also lies

DOI: 10.4324/9781003262145-1

in the concise summarizing of many issues that are usually not presented in mainstream books, enriched by new ideas developed by the author, such as the typology of definitions of spirituality as well as the unconscious dimension of spiritual development. Mainstream textbooks in the field of spirituality and counseling have tended to avoid basic theological/philosophical anthropological issues in favor of more rigidly clinical topics. This book attempts to address this problem as well.

From a practical point of view, the first major issue lies in the positive or negative way spirituality influences our lives. Universal guidelines are proposed to assess this dimension. This section is followed by the presentation of common issues that will most likely surface in spiritually sensitive counseling: spiritual bypassing, struggle, transformation, conversion, and deconversion. Subsequently, prayer and rituals are presented as the possible tools to be used in this therapy. The topics of spiritual discipline and reconciliation are not part of mainstream thought. Although they are certainly very important from the Catholic point of view, including their universal potential for pluralistic counseling, the reasons they are deserving of attention will also be discussed. Many practical examples are presented, but without focusing on lengthy case studies. These are already very well developed in existing publications and the author intends to remain at a more synthetic and general level.

The content of the book proceeds from the theoretical to the more practical, allowing a clear distinction of different topics and attempting to provide a logical flow of them, starting from meta-reflection and finishing with concrete applications. This process is conceived as a creative synthesis of what is happening in the field of counseling and spirituality and is intended to be presented in a user-friendly way. This is not always the case with edited volumes that often end up being more daunting to students. Also, since this book presents more general psychological concepts, it can also be interesting to non-clinically inclined readers. It is written in a way that allows studying one selected topic at a time, providing the reader with an opportunity to assimilate the information contained in each segment separately, in whatever order they prefer; at the end of each chapter is an extensive bibliography recommending other authors and publications that can offer more in-depth knowledge of each topic. It is directed toward students of counseling, pastoral care, spirituality, theology, and chaplaincy. It may also be helpful in a psychospiritual integration class in counseling or chaplaincy.

Readers will learn how to conceptualize the spiritual problems of contemporary people, including their own, from a universal perspective. They will also learn how to work with spiritual issues presented by clients, no matter what their tradition, and know when it is advisable to refer them to religious leaders or ministers; they will deepen their understanding of how spirituality influences a person's life and will become versed in the fundamentals of the counseling process. They will also be given practical tools for integrating spirituality into counseling, and for evaluating its impact on clients' lives.

The expression 'spiritual tradition' rather than 'religion' will be utilized in order to be more inclusive, as certain spiritualities are not necessary religion-based. The social dimension of religion will also be described as 'faith community.' The concept of God or Higher Power will be usually termed 'the divine' or 'the Sacred' in order to include as many conceptualizations as possible.

1 Defining Spirituality

Before reading this material, the students are asked to write their personal definition of spirituality in one or two paragraphs.

Introduction

From the very beginning of scientific endeavors, defining the elements of reality that one is to study has played a crucial role in advancing human knowledge of the world. Despite centuries of scientific development, defining basic concepts such as matter in physics and life in biology still remains a major challenge.

Psychology has also had its share of these difficulties. There still exist many concepts that lack a precise definition, including but not limited to the mind, intelligence, and forgiveness, which are, at this time, often considered challenging by many researchers. Because of this, they are sometimes called 'natural concepts' as they differ from logical concepts, which normally include a list of necessary and sufficient characteristics to describe them with great precision. Researchers prefer to use logical concepts that can be easily operationalized and tend to avoid natural concepts in their investigations since natural concepts require more probabilistic conditions and intuition to be presented (Prager, 1995).

One frequently hears the assertion that spirituality is a 'fuzzy' construct. Because of its multifaceted nature, as it may take many different shapes and forms, both traditional and nontraditional (Pargament, 2007), spirituality has managed to elude a precise definition. When people are asked what spirituality is, they give a wide and sometimes contradictory variety of definitions. In fact, at the beginning of the present century there were at least 40 known definitions of spirituality (Hill et al., 2000).

The lack of clarity regarding spirituality unmistakably reflects the condition of our pluralistic, postmodern society (Reinert & Koenig, 2013). In recent decades, spirituality has gained recognition as an important aspect of psychotherapy and medical care. Professionals in these areas have been eager to learn the best ways for addressing spiritual issues consistent with their professional training (Piedmont & Wilkins, 2020). Despite this fact, there is still a considerable amount of confusion and disagreement about what the term

DOI: 10.4324/9781003262145-2

'spirituality' means. This may be due to the complex and multidimensional nature of this phenomenon (Hill et al., 2000), which includes cognitive, emotional, behavioral, interpersonal, and physiological components (Hill & Pargament, 2003). Moreover, researchers are becoming more inclusive in their definitions of spiritual phenomena and there is growing consensus on what spirituality is. This has particularly useful ramifications in the context of counseling (Perrin, 2007). The true problem arises when they actually have to say what spiritually is not (Piedmont, 2014), which makes researching it quite problematic. Finally, spirituality nowadays involves many disciplines, and its definitions have taken on an interdisciplinary character that requires insights from theology, anthropology, religious studies, semiotics, neurobiology, and quantum physics, among others (Feldmeier, 2015).

Historical Origins

The term 'spirituality' originated in the Christian milieu. Saint Paul, in his first letter to the Corinthians, states that 'This is what we speak, not in words taught us by human wisdom but in words taught by the Spirit, explaining spiritual realities with Spirit-taught words' (1 Corinthians 2:13, NIV). The Christian understanding of spirituality is thus an opening to the Holy Spirit (Wiseman, 2006). 'Those who are spiritual' differ from others, because they act under the influence of the Holy Spirit (Schneiders, 1989).

The meaning of the term 'spiritual' is derived from the Latin word *spiritus*, which means breath, breathing, or respiration and refers to the breath of life. Already the ancient Hebrews and Greeks used the same metaphor of breathing while describing the spirit. These terms were *ruah* for Hebrews and *pneuma* for Greeks (May, 1987). In the Pauline epistles and in the gospels, spirituality was expressed in both the languages of discipleship and that of one's existential response to the call of God's grace. In the monastic tradition, spirituality is defined as an ascetic discipline preparing for the ultimate destination of the human journey, which is communion with God (Sheldrake, 2007).

In the history of philosophy, the concept of spirituality had been primarily understood and defined as immateriality and, only with historical developments did it come to be associated with immortality. For many Greek philosophers, the spiritual and the material were mutually exclusive and they considered immateriality to be the fundamental trait of the human spirit (Špidlik, Gargano, 1983). Spirituality, in this philosophical sense, entailed separateness from matter, pointing to the spiritual element in the human being. In the classic Aristotelian sense, immateriality became a 'form,' a permanent nature. It was not until the sixteenth century, called the Golden Age of mysticism, that the word 'spirituality' began to refer to the inner life, and, more specifically, to prayer (Schneiders, 1989). Originally, in the Christian tradition, spirituality did not refer to the contrast between the spirit (*pneuma*) and the body (*soma*) but rather it referred to the human potential to become a spiritual (*pneumatikos*) person and to be inhabited by the spirit of God. It is only during the later scholastic period that spirituality began to be understood more in contrast to the material world (Sheldrake, 2007).

The noun 'spirituality' became linked to 'the spiritual life' in seventeenth-century France. This term was replaced with 'asceticism' until the end of the nineteenth and the beginning of the twentieth centuries (Sheldrake, 2007). By the eighteenth and the nineteenth century, it tended to be replaced by 'devotion' (Catholic context) or 'piety' (Evangelical) or even 'perfection' (Methodist). Not until the twentieth century, with the publication of the *Dictionnaire de spiritualité* (1932/1937), did the term 'spirituality' return to frequent use. This process was even more visible in the changes pertaining to some periodicals: in 1972 the journal *Revue d'ascétique et de mystique* was renamed *Revue d'histoire de la spiritualité*, and in 1978 *Cross and Crown* became *Spirituality Today* (Feldmeier, 2015).

So far, we have only analyzed the history of the term 'spirituality' and not its content. In order to be precise in describing this aspect of spirituality, one has to underline that that which actually constitutes the reality of spirituality, meaning spiritual paths and destinations, has a much longer history. One has to at least point to the various forms of spiritual traditions such as Hinduism and Buddhism, Sufism within Islam, and Hassidic Judaism, as well as Carmelite and Ignatian schools of spirituality within the Christian tradition (Jastrzębski, 2019). The study of spirituality, in this context, is inspired by a variety of concepts that originate in Eastern, biblical, Hellenistic, Jewish, and Christian traditions such as perfection and transformation, mercy and compassion, knowledge and wisdom, insight and enlightenment, devotion and ascesis, inner life and mysticism (May, 1987; Waaijman, 2002; Mayse, 2019).

The contemporary Christian conceptualizations of spirituality, although in line with the Christian tradition, underline different aspects of this phenomenon such as journeying toward union with the Triune God (Schneiders, 2005) and expressing one's faith and identity through one's values, lifestyle, and spiritual practices (Sheldrake, 2007). In contrast to this Christian view, the contemporary Hasidic religious revival supports spirituality that does not need to be expressed in its typically traditional religious forms such as worshiping God (Ross, 2013).

A Transitional Period

According to Philip Sheldrake (2007), context conditions the various particular understandings of the relationship between God and the world. This is exemplified in twentieth-century developments regarding the understanding of spirituality, which combined a true 'spiritual revolution' with a gradual divorce from institutional religions and a rise of secularism in Western society. The outcome of these changes during the 1960s and 1970s was that spirituality began to be defined separately from religion (Hill et al., 2000). This process was linked to many social and political changes that took place during this period of time: the fight for civil rights, the acceptance of gender diversity and other minority movements, the sexual revolution of the 1960s, the war in Vietnam and the pacifist antiwar movement, and the influence of Billy Graham's nationwide preaching as well as the New Age movement characterized by an explosion of interest regarding the mind-body-spirit relationship and its quest for personal enlightenment (Tacey, 2004; Maxwell & Shields, 2019). During those decades, spirituality took up a new, more universal meaning and its development became a very popular endeavor. This popularization was mainly due to the development of meditation techniques that mostly originated from Eastern spiritual traditions such as Buddhism. Twelve-step programs also played a role in popularizing spirituality (Masters, 2010).

The transformation of our understanding of spirituality has been labeled by Charles Taylor (2003) as a 'subjective turn' (p. 26). For many of our contemporaries, this new understanding of spirituality seems to be more self-serving, oftentimes becoming individualistic, as it has been fueled by a cultural shift that has led to the narcissistic idea of a private spirituality. David Tacey (2004) describes this private spirituality as an illusion, or as 'a transitional stage between a former state of sleep and a future mission of social responsibility and commitment' (p. 148). In contrast, a genuine spiritual awakening leads to a centrifugal movement away from egocentric attitudes toward the willingness to transform the world into a better place for everyone, which is a fruit of spiritual conversion, as noted already by William James (1902/1990). Examples include a growing social awareness and the fight for human rights during this period, as exemplified by the civil rights movement (Maxwell & Shields, 2019). The definition proposed by J. Scott Young and Craig S. Cashwell (2011) clearly reinforces this aspect: 'Spirituality is the universal human capacity to experience self-transcendence and awareness of sacred immanence, with resulting increases in greater self–other compassion and love (p. 7).'

The Contemporary Standpoint

In the contemporary approach, the notion of spirituality is holistic, and is primarily concerned with the sacred, a quest for meaning and a spiritual development in accordance with one's ultimate values. That is to say, spirituality is a multidimensional construct (Elkins et al., 1988). We still develop the traditional understanding of spirituality but, in parallel, we are attentive to the postmodern one. The traditional approach always refers to religion and theism, whereas the postmodern approach is more oriented toward the phenomenological and existential dimensions of spirituality (McSherry, 2007). One can even say that the contemporary person is sometimes obsessed with spirituality. The Western consumer's proclivity tends toward two things: an excessive need for individualistic or private spirituality as opposed to its more communitarian forms, and the compulsive commercialization of all things, including spirituality (Cf. Sheldrake, 2013, pp. 4–5).

Today, compared with traditional understandings, spirituality has taken on a variety of new meanings. For Ralph L. Piedmont (2001), spirituality represents a universal human capacity to view life from a broader, more integrative perspective. It may pertain, for example, to the 'inner life' of someone who, through prayer and ascetic practices, is trying to achieve greater excellence. According to Gillian White (2006), spirituality constitutes an innate potential within all human beings linked to connection, meaning, hope, and other existential values. Spirituality may be viewed as an integral part in defining personal identity and the individual experience of the sacred (Gall, Malette, & Guirguis-Younger, 2011). Spirituality can also be defined in many other different ways: (1) as a fundamental dimension or the essence of our existence, (2) as a deeper union with the universe, (3) as searching for a higher meaning to life, (4) as a balanced and tolerant attitude toward life, or (5) as characteristics of being such as humility, joy, and compassion (Schneiders, 1989). Consequently, when people are asked what spirituality is, they give a variety of definitions. One study (Torskenæs et al., 2015) presents them in eight different groups: theistic, meaning believing in a supreme being; religiously oriented; linguistically oriented, such as using the expression 'inner peace'; politically or culturally oriented; phenomenological, such as learning from a variety of situations and experiences; existential or meaning-oriented; quality-of-life oriented; and mystical.

Understanding spirituality nowadays involves many disciplines, and its definition has taken on an interdisciplinary character. Peter Feldmeier (2015) expresses this as follows:

> Because spirituality incorporates so many aspects of the human condition, it is also interdisciplinary. Since spirituality involves community, it dialogs with sociology. Since it includes issues of justice, spirituality works with moral philosophy. Since it is concerned with human development, spirituality partners with the field of psychology. Indeed, spirituality has become so interdisciplinary that one can even find books in the field focusing on how quantum theory impacts meditation.
>
> (p. 10)

The contemporary understanding of spirituality encompasses a very diverse range of personal phenomena. Sometimes it is related to prayer and similar practices but is no longer confined to the Christian tradition. It may pertain, for example, to the 'inner life' of someone who, through meditation and ascetic practices, is trying to achieve greater excellence. Spirituality also describes the entire experience of faith, or even the fullness of one's personal life, along with its manifold dimensions: somatic, psychic, and sociopolitical (Schneiders, 1989). David Elkins (1998) points out to the following dimensions of spirituality: the desire for something transcendent, the desire to relate our existence to something beyond, the desire for an object that is a separate and higher reality. One may add that normally, spirituality will always be accompanied by appropriate actions expressing it (Rubin, 2006).

General Directions in Defining Spirituality

Generally speaking, the approach to defining spirituality can be divided into a combination of such factors or dimensions as: ontological or pragmatic, and substantive or functional (Oman, 2013). Spirituality can be viewed from either a top-down or a bottom-up perspective (Schneiders, 1989). For the most part, the ontological or substantive approach is a view 'from above.' It is often linked to dogmatic theology and the notion of grace. The pragmatic or functional approach is a view 'from below.' It is connected to the social sciences of anthropology, sociology, and most often of psychology by discovering and accepting spirituality as an integral part of one's everyday life. This first distinction refers to the metaphysical foundation for the study of spirituality, which pertains to issues regarding the nature of reality. This is why ontological definitions are also called real definitions. In the ontological or substantive approach, the question of the existence of God or, more broadly, that of the Sacred, has been addressed (Oman, 2013). This is the traditional approach to the understanding of spirituality as found in St. Paul's writings, where he opposes spirituality to human carnal tendencies and relates it to a life profoundly marked by the presence of the Holy Spirit, as spiritual fruits like peace, joy, or charity become apparent (Jastrzębski, 2019). We can define spirituality ontologically as a connection to the Sacred. On the phenomenological level this connection can be consciously perceived or remain unconscious (Tacey, 2004). Its perception or non-perception does not preclude its existence. The phenomenological version of the definition of spirituality would read as 'a perceived connection to the sacred' or, more broadly as, 'an experienced connection to the Sacred' (Jastrzębski, 2020).

The first is a substantive approach with a relationship to Transcendence. The second is a functional approach (e.g., that of sociology or psychology), which shows the role of spirituality within the dynamism of being human. We can also name the functional approach phenomenological or humanist. On this ground, one can argue that virtually all human life has a spiritual dimension (Culliford, 2002) and that 'spirituality is a human phenomenon and exists, at least potentially, in all persons' (Elkins et al., 1988, p. 8). Some authors (e.g., Puchalski et al., 2009; Oman, 2013) propose to use mixed, substantive-functional definitions of spirituality.

Usually, we say 'spirituality is…,' and the most important word is the first word that comes after 'spirituality,' which is its closest genus. What follows indicates what direction one will take in defining spirituality. There are several ways of doing this. For the ontological group, the genus in the classical definition will be: a relationship, a connection, a dimension, a part of human life. For the functional group, the genus will be: a human phenomenon, a human dynamism, a search, a process (Jastrzębski, 2020). Doug Oman (2013) adds that the definition of spirituality should be neither too narrow nor too broad, and has to include all its essential elements such as its nature, ultimate point of reference, values, concerns, and ways of achieving its full potential.

Ontological or Substantive Definitions

In the ontological definitions, we often refer to a spiritual realm. For the most part, such definitions are found in a religious context. The word 'spirituality' indicates its field of interest: the spirit, which we usually understand as the inner dimension of human reality, a place where human beings are open to the transcendent dimension (Cousins, 1986). David Hufford (2005) defines spirituality simply as a 'personal relationship to the transcendent' (p. 2).

Substantially speaking, defining spirituality is related to the understanding of dynamics, which we call the spirit of this dimension (Waaijman, 2007). But 'spirit' is not the only keyword that defines the field of spirituality. In fact, as mentioned above, the study of spirituality is inspired by a variety of concepts that originate in biblical, Hellenistic, Jewish, and Christian traditions such as: perfection, mercy, knowledge, devotion, inner life, and mysticism (Waaijman, 2002). Further, spirituality may also be related to one's understanding of such processes as birth, love, relationships, awareness, education, dwelling place, and finally death as a way toward the inner core of one's creation and development. Through spirituality, we can come into deeper contact with our createdness (Waaijman, 2010), our fundamental values, and identity, to finally reach a more profound understanding of the divine and of ourselves (Sheldrake, 2013).

Functional Definitions

The functional approach, by defining what purpose spirituality serves, is mainly interested in the spiritual state or spiritual experience. Its impact on the individual's life is considered, but the transcendent component of the relationship is less important. In such an approach to spirituality, a direct description of the subject is more valued than any objective theological argumentation. In the ontological approach, spiritual practices are viewed in their religious or philosophical perspective, as an integral part of the larger system, whereas in the functional/pragmatic approach, spiritual practices are viewed independently and separately from their spiritual source or larger frame of reference (Jastrzębski, 2020).

According to Oman (2013), entirely functional definitions are not sufficient, because they only describe a perfect lifestyle or the highest degree of human well-being and do not mention a connection to a larger transcendental framework. Functional definitions indicate what purpose the defined object serves. For instance, we can say that spirituality provides us with meaning, which helps us to cope with major challenges in life. Oman (2013) boldly states that functional definitions foster conceptual confusion and fragmentation of scholarly energies. On the other hand, substantive (ontological/real) definitions tell us what is distinctive or essential about spirituality. In substantive definitions, spirituality most commonly refers to some form of transcendence and, *per analogiam*, to other realities (Oman, 2013).

Many functional definitions do not explicitly include the relationship to transcendence. For example, Jane E. Myers and Kirk Williard (2003) define spirituality as 'the capacity and tendency present in all human beings to find and construct meaning about life and existence and to move toward personal growth, responsibility, and relationship with others' (p. 149). Another contemporary example of such an understanding of spirituality comes from Daniel Helminiak (2008). He defines spirituality broadly as 'the thoughtful engagement of a human person within the process of full growth in humanity' (p. 162). We can say that in these definitions what distinguishes spirituality from other human phenomena is ambiguous at the least (Jastrzębski, 2020).

Mixed Definitions

Mixtures of substantive and functional definitions also exist. In mixed definitions we will find both elements. We can define spirituality as 'the way individuals seek and express meaning and purpose and the way they experience their connectedness to the moment, to self, to others, to nature, and to the significant or sacred' (Puchalski et al., 2009, p. 887). In this context, Sheldrake (2013) postulates developing an eco-spirituality. An example of this approach can also be Kenneth Pargament 's (2007) definition: 'spirituality is a search for the sacred' (p. 52). From this perspective, Sandra Schneiders (2016) defines Christian spirituality as 'The *lived experience of Christian faith*, which is an ongoing project of life integration in the context of, in response to, and in terms of the revelation of God in Jesus Christ' (p. 425; italics in original).

Among the mixed definitions of spirituality that include both ontological and pragmatical elements, two types stand out as the most common: spirituality understood as an attitude and as a process. Let us look at some examples. Gordon Wakefield (1983) defines spirituality as 'those attitudes, beliefs, and practices, which animate people's lives and help them to reach out towards super-sensible realities' (p. 361). Brian Lancaster and Jason Palframan (2009) define spirituality as the 'feelings, thoughts, experiences, and behaviours that arise from a search for the sacred' (p. 258). And for Robert Wuthnow (1998), spirituality embraces 'all the beliefs and activities by which individuals attempt to relate their lives to God or to a divine being or some other conception of transcendent reality' (p. viii). One of the most common ways of defining spirituality is to present it as a search for something essential to one's life: existential meaning, purpose, the Sacred, and connection. Peter C. Hill et al. (2000) propose a definition that is a combination of attitude and process. For them, spirituality is defined as 'the feelings, thoughts, experiences, and behaviors that arise from a search for the sacred' (p. 66). The first part of this definition describes an attitude (feelings, thoughts, and behaviors) and the second part of it points to a process.

Author's Typology of Definitions

Starting with the most substantive/ontological – one may even say 'conservative' – definitions, we can develop a continuum of intermediary stages of the definitions of spirituality, concluding with the most functional or nominal ones. To illustrate this, I've developed the following typology (Jastrzębski, 2020). It has to be noted that this typology aims to present the actual situation in the field rather than to propose a solution for future research (Figure 1.1).

In the ontological group, we can start with a simple division between theistic and nontheistic definitions. Theistic means oriented toward God conceived as a personal being. Nontheistic would mean related to some kind of Transcendence. A nontheistic (but still ontological) definition could read: 'Spirituality is a connection to the Source of Being.' The theistic subdivision is divided into Christian and non-Christian definitions since, historically speaking, spirituality has its roots there. One could also make a distinction between Abrahamic and non-Abrahamic spiritualities, but in reality, the Christian-informed definitions are in a greater majority so that by using a subdivision of Christian and non-Christian definitions, we can obtain a more faithful picture of the existing situation in the field. A Christian definition would be: 'journeying towards union with the Triune God.' An example of a non-Christian (Islamic) definition would be expressed as: 'that which is related to the world of the Spirit, is in Divine Proximity' (Nasr, 1987, p. vii), whereas a definition coming from the contemporary Hasidic tradition would say: 'spirituality refers to an experience or sense of the sublime' (Ross, 2013, p. 110).

We can divide the nontheistic definition further into two subcategories: transcendent and immanent. The first category is a 'non-divine-like' reality but is still a transcendent one, that is, a supernatural reality like 'Higher

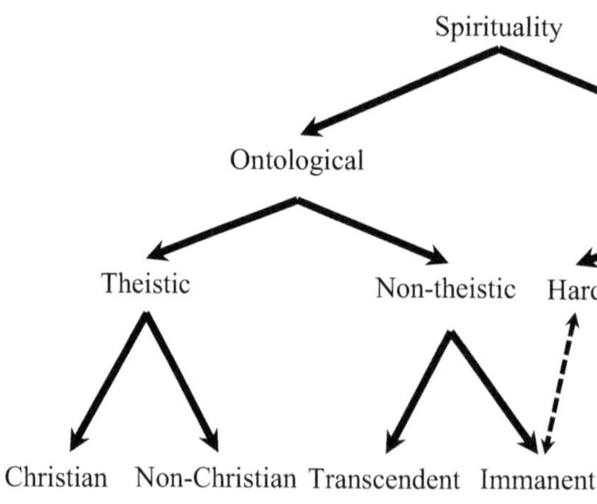

Figure 1.1 Topology of various conceptualizations of spirituality.

Power' or 'the Sacred' (Hill et al., 2000). The transcendent exists outside of the self, but is also experienced within the self (Koenig et al., 2012), or as Hill and colleagues (2000) put it: 'The Sacred is a person, an object, a principle, or a concept that transcends the self. Though the Sacred may be found within the self, it has perceived value independent of the self' (p. 64). This statement brings us to the next category called 'immanent.'

The ontological, immanent definition of spirituality, refers to the most intimate or profound part of being human, the real self, which is also a place of connection to the Universe. We can call this group of definitions self-referential definitions. Indeed, some spiritual traditions, such as Buddhism, do not require that spirituality involve the pursuit of supernatural realities (Feldmeier, 2015). For example, Ewert Cousins (1988) refers spirituality to the spiritual core in the deepest center of the person, where they are open to the ultimate reality, and John Macquarrie (1972) says that spirituality 'has to do with becoming a person in the fullest sense' (p. 40). In this group we can also find ecologically oriented definitions where spirituality is an internal energy associated with the environment (Torskenæs et al., 2015).

The functional group of definitions can also be divided into more specific categories. I would propose to name them hard and soft versions respectively. Hard functional definitions retain certain dimensions from the ontological group of definitions in terms of actions oriented toward an ontological goal (a prescriptive dimension). In Oman's (2013) terms, they would be mixed definitions such as: 'spirituality is a search of the Ultimate Reality.' The soft functional definitions would remain only descriptive or purely phenomenological in nature: 'spirituality is being at peace with oneself.' This category describes a nonsacred dimension of our own life (human values), or an ideology or a lifestyle (Hill et al. 2000) such as: social connectedness, inner peace or strength, harmony, well-being, hope, meaning and purpose in life, contentment, gratefulness, the capacity to forgive, and self-discipline, existential well-being and life satisfaction, fulfillment, happiness, and low levels of conflict in life (Janse van Rensburg et al., 2014, p. 1840). Usually, they are either very difficult to distinguish from the description of the mental well-being of a person (Koenig, 2008) or are rejected as not being adequate definitions of spirituality at all (Hill et al., 2000).

Historically speaking, the first point of reference for spirituality was immateriality and, subsequently, immortality. These can again be two different ways of defining spirituality 'the immaterial part of being human' and 'the immortal dimension of the human being.' These two are ontological, nontheistic definitions (Jastrzębski, 2020).

Harold G. Koenig (2008) believes that in order to have an effective definition of spirituality, we have to go back to its origins in religion. In fact, as we explained at the beginning of this chapter, spirituality has historically been associated with the supernatural realm. Koenig (2008) argues that, 'to call something spiritual, it must have some connection to religion' (p. 17), and Hill and colleagues (2000) add: 'Given the significant sociological and psychological overlap among religion and spirituality, attempts to measure spirituality as a separate construct from religion are difficult' (p. 71). Thus, they favor ontological theistic definitions, which are probably the easiest to be operationalized and measured.

According to Hill et al. (2000) and Koenig (2008), religion, like spirituality, includes searching for the Sacred or Transcendence. When there is no connection with the supernatural, we should use the term 'humanistic' rather than spiritual. Humanism is a broader category that affirms the dignity and worth of all people, appealing to universal human qualities such as rationalism and freedom. It includes the search for truth but only through self-determined human means, while also rejecting any transcendental justifications (Koenig, 2008). This distinction will be developed further in Chapter 2.

Existential Interpretation of the Typology Based on the Concept of Self-Transcendence

Contemporary research in humanities and social sciences shows that people who see themselves related to something greater than the self often feel happier and have a deeper sense of purpose in their lives. Some contemporary psychologists turned to the concept of self-transcendence to explain new tendencies in today's society related to virtue, happiness, hope, and the meaning of life (Frey & Vogler, 2019). Generally speaking, we can say that the human spirit is the underlying dynamism of human self-transcendence, which intentionally directs itself naturally to what can be known and loved. This spirit is not designed to be enclosed in itself, but to go out into the world and to reach out to other persons through noble actions such as self-giving sacrificial love (Helminiak, 2008).

One can distinguish two different dimensions of self-transcendence: horizontal and vertical. Vertical self-transcendence means confronting one's own existence with a point of reference that is to be found beyond one's personal human limitations such as an entirely free and intentionally chosen self-dependence on the truth or, for Christians, on God. Horizontal self-transcendence is an intentional act such as directing ourselves toward other persons or objects (Wojtyła, 1979; Hood & Chen, 2013).

Combining both forms of self-transcendence allows us to define spirituality in a very interesting way, helping us to understand the shift in the notion of spirituality that has taken place recently. What is proposed is to name the vertical self-transcendence 'ontological' and the horizontal 'moral' or 'ethical' transcendence. When we conceive spirituality as reaching out to something beyond the human person, it becomes a very useful, two-dimensional concept. From a religious perspective, ontological self-transcendence means reaching out to the divine and searching to enter into and to sustain a relationship with the Sacred or, in more Christian terms, with the Holy Spirit. The secularization of spirituality in modern social sciences has gradually caused the disappearance of this dimension. Ontological self-transcendence or, more precisely, the ontological dimension of self-transcendence, refers to the understanding of a spirituality that is sometimes called 'substantive,' meaning that it acknowledges the existence of a supernatural reality (Jastrzebski, 2021).

The ethical dimension of self-transcendence refers to the human capacity of reaching beyond oneself, through selflessness and intentional sacrifice, thus overcoming one's weakness and egoistic tendencies. For example, human beings can transcend their physiological limitations by continuing to work despite chronic pain. In a similar fashion, we are also capable of dealing with mental constraints such as depression, thus overcoming both our material and immaterial functioning (Frankl, 1988). This can be exemplified by acts of love, protection of human dignity, and respect for human rights and freedom. To some extent, this dimension of self-transcendence can be related to the concept of 'functional' spirituality, indicating the purpose that spirituality serves rather than its nature. Certainly, both dimensions of self-transcendence are essential from a faith-based perspective. From a secular perspective, spirituality is seen from a more pragmatic vantage point where the horizontal/ethical aspect is more valued than any ontological motivation (Jastrzębski, 2021).

In contemporary society, there is a strong tendency to reflect on self-realization or self-actualization. This opens the door to an entirely subjective understanding of spirituality without any reference to the concept of self-transcendence, not even to its horizontal dimension. Although highly praised nowadays, an exclusive focus on self-awareness, albeit an important element of being human, may impair our capacity for developing self-transcendence, which is crucial for one's self-fulfillment (Wojtyła, 1993). For Frankl (1988), self-actualization is a by-product of self-transcendence. It is obvious that in our contemporary culture there is a tension between the secular and religious dimensions of human life, which is clearly demonstrated in various notions of spirituality. Analyzing the concept of self-transcendence helps us to understand it more systematically. The common point of interest for both secular humanism and religion can be ethical self-transcendence. It can be a platform of dialogue for both (Jastrzębski, 2021).

Conclusions

At every level of contemporary society, including in a counseling relationship, people can live their spirituality in a number of ways, for example, through their religious engagement, through their individual experience of the Sacred, and through their connection to nature, sports, or art. Thus, in a secular society, people can experience their spirituality either within religious traditions and their institutions, or outside of religion. This experience of spirituality may come in one of these four categories: (1) a religious orientation expressed in prayer and belief in a Divine Being, (2) a search for insight or wisdom, (3) a conscious interaction rooted in compassion and generosity, and (4) a conviction of transcendence linked to the concepts of rebirth and a higher dimension of life (Zwingman et al., 2011).

Defining spirituality is challenging and will remain so for the foreseeable future. However, we at least know what the possible directions of defining spirituality are: ontological, functional, academic, or clinical as well as their respective subdivisions. Even though it is very unlikely that scholars will soon agree on one common definition of spirituality, by deliberately matching the kind of definition with the purpose for which it will be used, we will already bring significantly more clarity to this field of research and analysis. This is a work in progress (Jastrzębski, 2020).

Discussion questions

1. Based on your personal definition of spirituality, try to situate it in the frame of the above-presented typology. Is your definition more ontological or functional?
2. What is your personal opinion on the relationship between religion/religiosity and spirituality? Please explain.
3. Do you think that we hold onto one definition of spirituality throughout life, or there are substantial changes in this process? If yes, would you explain why?
4. How would you apply this knowledge about defining spirituality into your counseling practice?

References

Cousins, E. (1986). Preface. In E. Cousins (Ed.), *World spirituality: An encyclopedic history of the religious quest* (pp. i–xii). Crossroad.

Cousins, E. (1988). Preface. In B. McGinn, J. Meyendorff, & J. Leclercq (Eds.), *Christian spirituality* (pp. i–xiii). Continuum.

Culliford, L. (2002). Spiritual care and psychiatric treatment: An introduction. *Advances in Psychiatric Treatment, 8*, 249–261.

Elkins, D. N. (1998). *Beyond religion: A personal program for building a spiritual life outside the walls of traditional religion*. Quest Books.

Elkins, D. N., Hedstrom, L. J., Hughes, L. L., Leaf, J. A., & Saunders, C. (1988). Toward phenomenological spirituality: Definition, description, and measurement. *Journal of Humanistic Psychology, 28*(4), 5–18.

Feldmeier, P. (2015). *Christian spirituality: Lived expressions in the life of the church*. Anselm Academic.

Frankl, V. E. (1988). *The will to meaning: Foundations and applications of logotherapy*. Meridian.

Frey, J., & Vogler, C. (Eds.). (2019). *Self-transcendence and virtue*. Routledge.

Gall, T., Malette, J., & Guirguis-Younger, M. (2011). Spirituality and religiousness: A diversity of definitions. *Journal of Spirituality in Mental Health, 13*(3), 158–181.

Helminiak, D. A. (2008). Confounding the divine and the spiritual: Challenges to a psychology of spirituality. *Pastoral Psychology, 57*, 161–182.

Hill, P. C., & Pargament, K. I. (2003). Advances in the conceptualization and measurement of religion and spirituality: Implications for physical and mental health research. *American Psychologist, 58*, 64–74.

Hill, P. C., Pargament, K. I., Hood, R. W., Jr., McCullough, M. E., Swyers, J. P., Larson, D. B., & Zinnbauer, B. J. (2000). Conceptualizing religion and spirituality: Points of commonality, points of departure. *Journal for the Theory of Social Behaviour, 30*, 51–77.

Hood, R. W. Jr., & Chen, Z. (2013). Mystical, spiritual, and religious experiences. In R. F. Paloutzian & C. L. Park (Eds.), *Handbook of the psychology of religion and spirituality* (pp. 422–440). Guilford Press.

Hufford, D. J. (2005). An analysis of the field of spirituality, religion, and health (S/Rh). *Metanexus Online*. Accessed on 3 March 2020.

James, W. (1902/1990). *The varieties of religious experience*. Penguin.

Janse van Rensburg, B., Poggenpoel, M., Myburgh, C., & Szabo, C. (2014). Defining and measuring spirituality in South African specialist psychiatry. *Journal of Religion and Health, 54*, 1839–1855.

Jastrzębski, A. (2019). Concepts of spirituality at universities of today. *Roczniki Teologiczne, 66*(5), 99–113.

Jastrzębski, A. K. (2020). The challenging task of defining spirituality. *Journal of Spirituality in Mental Health, 24*(2). https://doi.org/10.1080/19349637.2020.1858734

Jastrzębski, A. K. (2021). Recent developments in understanding spirituality as exemplified by the concept of self-transcendence. *Verbum Vitae, 39*(2), 513–523.

Koenig, H. G. (2008). *Medicine, religion and health: Where science and spirituality meet*. Templeton Press.

Koenig H. G., King, D., & Carson V. (2012). *Handbook of religion and health*. Oxford University Press.

Lancaster, B. L., & Palframan, J. T. (2009). Coping with major life events: The role of spirituality and self-transformation. *Mental Health, Religion & Culture, 4*(3), 257–276.

Macquarrie, J. (1972). *Paths in spirituality*. Harper & Row.

Masters, R. A. (2010). *Spiritual bypassing: When spirituality disconnects us from what really matters*. North Atlantic Books.

Maxwell, S., & Shields, T. (2019). *The long southern strategy: How chasing white voters in the South changed American politics*. Oxford University Press. https://doi.org/10.1093/oso/9780190265960.001.0001

May, G. G. (1987). *Will and spirit: A contemplative psychology*. Harper One.

Mayse, A. (2019). Expanding the boundaries of the holy: Hasidic devotion, sacred speech, and early modern Jewish thought. *Jewish Social Studies, 25*(1), 45–101. https://doi.org/10.2979/jewisocistud.25.1.03

McSherry, W. (2007). *The meaning of spirituality and spiritual care within nursing and health care practice*. Quay Books.

Myers, J. E., & Williard, K. (2003). Integrating spirituality into counselor preparation: A developmental wellness approach. *Counseling and Values, 47*, 142–155.

Nasr, S. (1987). *Islamic spirituality*. Routledge.

Oman, D. (2013). Defining religion and spirituality. In R. F. Paloutzian & C. L. Park (Eds.), *Handbook of the psychology of religion and spirituality* (pp. 23–47). Guilford Press.

Pargament, K. I. (2007). *Spiritually integrated psychotherapy: Understanding and addressing the sacred*. Guilford Press.

Perrin, D. B. (2007). *Studying Christian spirituality*. Routledge.

Piedmont, R. L. (2001). Spiritual transcendence and the scientific study of spirituality. *Journal of Rehabilitation, 67*, 4–14.

Piedmont, R. L. (2014). Looking back and finding our way forward: An editorial call to action. *Psychology of Religion and Spirituality, 6*(4), 265–267.

Piedmont, R., & Wilkins, T. (2020). *Understanding the psychological soul of spirituality*. Routledge.

Prager, K. J. (1995). *The psychology of intimacy*. Guilford Press.

Puchalski, C., Ferrell, B., Virani, R., Otis-Green, S., Baird, P., Bull, J., Chochinov, H., Handzo, G., Nelson-Becker, H., Prince-Paul, M., Pugliese, K., & Sulmasy, D. C. (2009). Improving the quality of spiritual care as a dimension of palliative care: the report of the Consensus Conference. *Journal of Palliative Medicine, 12*(10), 885–904.

Reinert, K. G., & Koenig, H. G. (2013). Re-examining definitions of spirituality in nursing research. *Journal of Advanced Nursing, 69*(12), 2622–2634.

Ross, N. (2013). Can secular spirituality be religiously inspired? The Hasidic legacy in the eyes of skeptics. *AJS Review, 37*(1), 93–113. https://doi.org/10.1017/S0364009413000056

Rubin, J. B. (2006). Psychoanalysis and spirituality. In D. M. Black (Ed.), *Psychoanalysis and religion in the 21st century: Competitors or collaborators* (pp. 132–153). Routledge.

Schneiders, S. M. (1989). Spirituality in the academy. *Theological Studies, 50*, 676–697.

Schneiders, S. M. (2005). Christian spirituality: Definition, methods and types. In P. Sheldrake (Ed.), *The new Westminster dictionary of Christian spirituality* (pp. 1–6). Westminster John Knox.

Schneiders, S. M. (2016). Biblical spirituality. *Interpretation: A Journal of Bible and Theology, 70*(4), 417–430.

Sheldrake, P. (2007). *A brief history of spirituality*. Blackwell.

Sheldrake, P. (2013). *Spirituality: A brief history* (2nd ed.). Wiley-Blackwell.

Špidlik, T., & Gargano, I. (1983). *La spiritualità dei padri greci e orientali, 'Storia della spiritualità, 3/A.'* Borla.

Tacey, D. (2004). *The spirituality revolution: The emergence of contemporary spirituality*. Routledge.

Taylor, C. (2003). *The ethics of authenticity*. Harvard University Press.

Torskenæs, K., Baldacchino, D., Kalfoss, M., Baldacchino, T., Borg, J., Falzon, M., & Grima, K. (2015). Nurses' and caregivers' definition of spirituality from the Christian perspective: A comparative study between Malta and Norway. *Journal of Nursing Management, 23*(1), 39–53.

Viller, Baumgartner, C., & Rayez, A. (1932/1937). *Dictionnaire de spiritualité ascétique et mystique : doctrine et histoire*. G. Beauchesne et ses fils.

Waaijman, K. (2002). *Spirituality: Forms, foundations, methods*. Peeters.

Waaijman, K. (2007). Spirituality – a multifaceted phenomenon: Interdisciplinary explorations. *Studies in Spirituality, 17*, 1–113.

Waaijman, K. (2010). Primordial spirituality. *Hervormde Teologiese Studies, 66*(1), 1–5.

Wakefield, G. S. (1983). Spirituality. In G. S. Wakefield (Ed.), *Westminster dictionary of Christian spirituality* (pp. 361–363). Westminster Press.

White, G. (2006) *Talking about spirituality in health care practice*. Jessica Kingsley.

Wiseman, J. O. (2006). *Spirituality and mysticism: A global view*. (Theology in Global Perspective Series). Orbis Books.

Wojtyła, K. (1979). *The acting person*, trans. A. Potocki, *Analacta Husserliana* (Vol. 10). D. Reidel.

Wojtyła, K. (1993). *Person and community: Selected essays*. Peter Lang.

Wuthnow, R. (1998). *After heaven: Spirituality in America since the 1950s*. University of California Press.

Young, J. S., & Cashwell, C. S. (2011). Integrating spirituality and religion into counseling: An introduction. In C. S. Cashwell & J. S. Young (Eds.), *Integrating spirituality and religion into counseling: A guide to competent practice* (pp. 1–24). American Counseling Association.

Zwingmann, C., Klein, C., & Büssing, A. (2011). Measuring religiosity/spirituality: Theoretical differentiations and categorization of instruments. *Religions (Basel, Switzerland)*, *2*(3), 345–357.

2 Researching and Measuring Spirituality

Challenges and Opportunities

General Problems in Researching Human Phenomena

Over the course of its short history, psychotherapy has undergone many changes (Perrin, 2007b). At the beginning of the twentieth century, research in the realm of psychiatry led to the development of psychoanalysis. In the 1930s, behaviorism made its appearance and focused on maintaining maximum scientificity, as it is part of the study of natural sciences. However, with time, the understanding of the human person and their inner world of experiences, the discovery of what is individual and unique to them, made its way into psychological methodology, fostering a dispute over the questions 'what?' and 'how?,' within the realm of psychology. Should cognitive processes, emotions, self-awareness, the whole person or only their parts be considered?

The aim of science is to discover the laws that govern all reality rather than address questions about the meaning of existence. The main goal of scientific activity is to obtain a description of how things function under various conditions. This description is achieved through observation and experimentation (Brysbaert & Rastle, 2009). Applying such a method to the human person is rather challenging. It is very difficult to predict human behavior since we do not have sufficient knowledge about all the stimuli that affect it (Perrin, 2007a; Jastrzębski, 2011). And yet, the group of scientists called The Vienna Circle (Carnap, Neurath, Schlick), postulated that all theorems of psychology could be expressed in theorems of physics. In this vision, psychology was to become a part of physics (Eacker, 1983).

Reacting to this trend, scientists like Wilhelm Dilthey, Wilhelm Windelband, and Heinrich Rickert, and more recently Hans-Georg Gadamer and Jürgen Habermas, demonstrated that the humanities possess a separate subject of interest, which is what is individual and unique to the human being. Also Henri Bergson, Edmund Husserl, and Martin Heidegger spoke out against determinism, mechanicism, and reductionism in an attempt to defend human free will. This created a certain dichotomy. Whereas the exact sciences dealt with the body, or more precisely with the human brain (physical methods), psychology and philosophy dealt with mental processes

DOI: 10.4324/9781003262145-3

(broadly understood as the soul, psyche or mind), which included intuition as part of their scientific method (Valentine, 1992).

Humanistic methods, as they were called, enabled the scientific study of the human subject, focusing on understanding phenomena rather than explaining them through laws (e.g., history). Dilthey was the founder of 'descriptive' psychology, in contrast to classical experimental psychology based on the neopositivist paradigm of science (as developed by Gustav Fechner and Wilhelm Wundt). Its aim was to research human freedom and creativity (Jastrzębski, 2012).

Reductionism

For centuries we have been presented with an astounding variety of clearly defined studies and viewpoints on the world, and these have always galvanized researchers into developing a variety of metaphysical and theological views. We encounter materialistically oriented scientists who, through their biased views, regress to an ideology of scientific materialism. Their research becomes contaminated by the metaphysical principles of monism, universalism, reductionism, physicalism, and in general the principle of a complete, closed system (Wallace, 2000). According to Viktor Frankl (1988), reductionism ignores the human dimension of phenomena, reducing them to the rank of subhuman phenomena. Reductionism presents all phenomena as being reducible to their smallest workings, their atomic features, but ignores what makes us human (Frankl, 1988).

Generally speaking, scientific reduction allows one to deduce the laws of one particular theory from other more basic ones, keeping the cornerstone of explanation at the lower level. A good example of this is the attempt to reduce the whole of psychology to neurobiology. Nonetheless, it would be more fruitful to use an interdisciplinary approach that relies on simultaneous input from different scientific theories rather than on reduction. This is because there is far more to be discovered by including laws of sociology, biology, and psychology than by simply reducing them to the lowest levels of scientific explanation (McCauley, 2007).

There is always the temptation to interpret all processes, especially mental ones, as we do with certain physical processes and to reductively explain away everything else. In fact, '[many] neuroscientists hold a materialist view of the world, believing that the physical world is the only reality and that everything is explainable in terms of matter and physical phenomena, including thoughts, feelings, mind, and will' (Dixon & Wilcox, 2016, p. 93). For instance, Michael Persinger (1987, 2010, criticized by Pehr Granqvist et al., 2005, and Craig Aaen-Stockdale, 2012) declared that the experience of God is nothing more than the activation of certain areas of the brain (particularly the parietal lobes), and concluded that all spiritual experiences are ultimately nothing more than physical processes, specifically those that cause certain forms of epilepsy. To the contrary, the neurologist John Hughes (2005) underlined the fact that hallucinations are actually very uncommon in epilepsy and said that epileptic phenomena are nearly always brief and primitive, which is far from anything like the ecstatic and elaborate visions reported by the fifteenth-century heroine Joan of Arc, for example.

The crucial problem that distinguishes the interpretation of results, as presented by the worldview of biased researchers in neuroscience, is whether scientific research into the neurobiology of a spiritual experience can explain the experience away. Andrew Newberg (2010) is very much aware of this issue:

> One has to be very careful interpreting neurotheology as being able to comment on whether or not God does exist and whether the brain creates God or God creates the brain. [...] The perspective that is most appropriate from a neurotheological perspective is to carefully evaluate all ways of understanding God, including an absence of God, in order to best determine what the brain can know about reality.
>
> (p. 542)

Complexity of Mental Phenomena

As we know, mental phenomena, including the spiritual, are very complex. Neuroscientists try to find their basic components, for example, reward, linguistic, semantic or episodic, visuospatial, somatosensory, and so on. Research so far confirms that spiritual experience is a complex phenomenon that involves many brain regions and processes (e.g., Beauregard & O'Leary, 2007; Schjoedt, 2009). We know for instance that daily contemplative practice, such as mindfulness-based prayer and meditation, lowers the neuronal activity in the amygdala and, subsequently, deactivates the stress region of the brain (Bingaman, 2013). This should not come as a surprise. By virtue of their functioning, our bodies as well as our brains are instruments for interacting with the world. If we accept its existence, the otherworldly is also capable of being attained (Transcendence). Some would therefore suggest the hypothesis of a special brain structure responsible for interacting with the Sacred. But obviously various psychic experiences will involve brain activity in one way or another. Finding the neural correlates of a given experience is not, in the final analysis, to deny its source (Jastrzębski, 2018). Whatever phenomenon we want to measure, it has to be effectively operationalized. Unfortunately, in the process, researchers often oversimplify these phenomena and lose sight of their complexity (Stewart-Sicking et al., 2020).

Subjective Experience

Without a degree of subjective value, spiritual experiences would certainly have no meaning. In the neuroscience of spirituality, the 'subjective' and 'objective' components are both considered. First, there is a biological fingerprint that identifies a phenomenon's occurrence; second, there is the meaning attributed to the particular spiritual experience. The most perplexing question is, which comes first? – the neurobiological phenomenon (e.g., epilepsy leading to the experience of transcendence), or the meaning of it? Or do both happen simultaneously (Jastrzębski, 2018)?

Knowing the neurobiological correlates of spiritual experience is one thing, but without other fields such as anthropology, metaphysics, philosophy, and theology we cannot fully capture what it means to have a spiritual experience. To defenders of transcendent reality, this has nothing to do with reducing God to mere brain activation, but rather the activated area of the brain shows God interacting with a person and bringing them to experience God's presence concretely. Spiritual experiences correlated with brain states are, it must be emphasized, the experiences of a particular individual and not religion itself (Weissenbacher, 2015). Regardless of how we look at it, only the person having such an experience is capable of assigning meaning to it and reporting it as spiritual (Feit, 2004).

We are living at a time when people have a strong aversion to studying subjective states of consciousness; this has led to a discrediting of any possible new empirical facts. These are discarded even before they have had a chance to be heard. There seems to be a blockage or ideological taboo in neuroscience against the empirical study of consciousness as subjective experience (Wallace, 2000). The denial of mental states has been part of behaviorists' way of thinking for almost half a century. Behaviorists have come and gone, but the reality of mental states is still part of our research, study, and reality. Moreover, in activating relevant parts of the brain, artificial perceptual experience can be set in motion; however, this cannot be termed a false functioning of the brain. It is only the perceptions that may be termed false. Again, pleasure centers of the brain may be stimulated, but this will never create authentic joy, which is always linked to the real world. Meaning and truth can thus be attributed to mental states, but not to neuronal ones (Jastrzębski, 2018).

Non-representative Samples

For the sake of convenience, most psychological research uses participants who are easily accessible, such as white, middle-class individuals (Graham, 1992). As a consequence, the majority of studies use cohorts of college students who are mostly of Caucasian origin, male, with English as their first language, and who come from Judeo-Christian backgrounds (Kvale, 1992; Sieber & Saks, 1989, Hill, 2013). This is a well-known issue that goes under the acronym WEIRD (Western, Educated, Industrial, Rich, Democratic), and is used as a cultural identifier of psychology test subjects in order to detect sampling bias in research on human persons. Yet, in order to really understand topics related to spirituality, one would need to broaden the number of researched samples so that the vast differences between various cultures are recognized and included (Nielsen et al., 2017).

Problematic Relationship between Religion and Spirituality

One of the important questions regarding the study of spirituality pertains to its relationship to religion. There is a widespread conviction that they are related rather than independent constructs (Hill et al., 2000; Pargament, 2007; Sheldrake, 2007; Koenig, 2008). Although they both are characterized by a search for the Sacred, the nature of this search is different in regard to their respective context and function. Religiously based definitions of spirituality commonly include such elements as faith in a Divine Being or practices such as prayer, church attendance, and meditation (substantive approach). On the opposite end, when spirituality is defined from a purely psychological point of view, it is understood as an independent, motivational personality trait (Piedmont, 1999). From this functional perspective, spirituality has been defined as one's perceived connection with a transcendent reality. It is also related to how people create ultimate meaning for their lives. Some even see spirituality as the central organizing aspect of one's personality (Piedmont & Friedman, 2012). In the religion-related approach, importance is placed on the degree to which an individual practices prayer and sacred rituals in order to communicate with the divine, whereas in the psychological or in a functional approach, the emphasis is put on the degree to which one seeks to effect positive change in the world through acts of kindness and charity (Cramer et al., 2008).

But maybe a more important question pertains to the relationship of spirituality to religiosity or religiousness. Note is made that researchers tend to use the terms 'religiosity' and 'religiousness' interchangeably (e.g., King & Williamson, 2005), sometimes even within the same publication (e.g., Fox et al., 2020). Their relationship may take many forms such as 'spiritual and religious, spiritual but not religious, more spiritual than religious, neither spiritual nor religious, and the occasional religious but not spiritual' (Stewart-Sicking et al., 2020, p. 188). Gerald May (1987) develops this last option in the following way:

> What is spiritual is not necessarily religious, and vice versa. Religion can exist without spirituality if it consists only of standards of conduct, nonexperiential theology and rituals that are practiced for no felt reason. Insofar as I know, all major religions were born in a distinctively spiritual atmosphere, but many modern forms and expressions of these religions have lost much of their spiritual essence. They are still religions in the formal sense, but they have forgotten their spiritual core. Similarly, a spiritual quest becomes decidedly religious only when one begins to identify a relationship with the Ultimate Spirit or Mystery of life and when that relationship begins to manifest itself in specific behaviors such as worship.
>
> (p. 32–33)

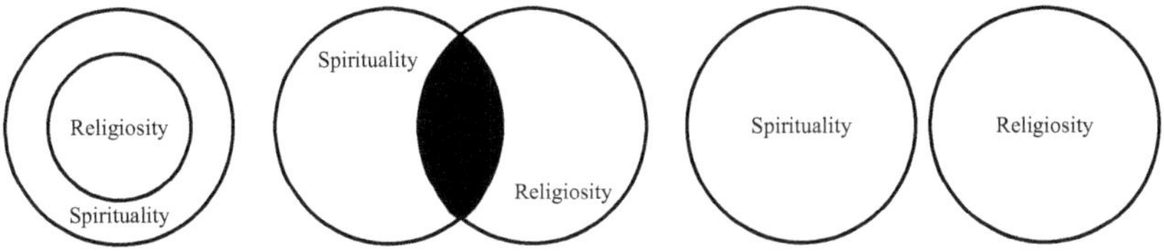

Figure 2.1 Various relationships of spirituality and religiosity.

To shed more light on this issue, at least three models (Figure 2.1) can be used to illustrate the relationships between spirituality and religiosity (Jastrzębski, 2020). Also, a very interesting comparison between religion and spirituality has been presented by J. Scott Young and Craig S. Cashwell (2011) in the introduction to their edited textbook.

Religiosity as a Subcategory of Spirituality

Oftentimes, we can find concepts that amalgamate religiosity and spirituality for research purposes. They come down to acronyms such as R-S or R/S, meaning 'religious-spiritual' or even more broadly 'religion and spirituality' (e.g., Wilt et al., 2019; Fox & Piedmont, 2020). Studies show that both religion and spirituality are defined very similarly by respondents (nominal definitions) so that their definitions overlap (Oman, 2013). In research studies involving 838 persons, participants were asked to categorize themselves as either religious, spiritual, both, or neither. As a result, close to 90% indicated that they were both religious and spiritual (Koenig, 2008).

According to Kenneth Pargament (2007) both spirituality and religiosity can be understood as a search for the Sacred. Although in the case of religiosity, this search takes place in a religious context (Hill et al., 2000), what distinguishes both religiosity and spirituality from other phenomena is the Sacred (Hill & Pargament, 2003). Religiosity is one's spirituality lived within a more institutional frame (Kahle & Robbins, 2004; Zwingman et al., 2011). In this case religiosity would be simply a subcategory of spirituality. This is the approach taken in this book in order critically analyze the broadest range of phenomena labeled 'spiritual.'

Religiosity as Partly Similar to and Partly Different from Spirituality

Many authors see spirituality and religiosity as sharing much in common (e.g., Hill & Pargament, 2003) and some interpret them as being quite the same (e.g., Zinnbauer et al., 1999). In order to differentiate the study of religion from other phenomena, it is crucial to include the spiritual core of religion as it nurtures people's relationship with whatever they hold sacred. Although some scholars suggest divorcing spirituality from religion, Kenneth

Pargament and Annette Mahoney (2002) view spirituality as the most central function of religion that facilitates the search for the Sacred in one's life. There are also attempts at distinguishing between empirical measures of religiosity and spirituality (Fox et al., 2020). For example, spirituality can be considered as a personal or collective search for the Sacred, whereas religiosity also involves a traditional religious context (Zinnbauer, 2013).

Religiosity as Different from Spirituality

Despite the fact that both are strongly correlated, there is also some empirical evidence to view religiosity and spirituality as distinctive realities. Indeed, some scholars emphasize the distinctiveness between these two constructs (e.g., Piedmont, 2001; Piedmont et al. 2009; Casey, 2013), underlining the fact that equating them with each other can lead to a misunderstanding of their respective roles. When conceptualized distinctively, spirituality is viewed as the characteristic of a person, similar to a personality trait, and is related to one's personal relationships to larger, transcendent realities. Religiosity is related more to the beliefs, rituals, and practices within an institutional context, a community, or a social organization.

Making a distinction between the personal orientation of spirituality and the social orientation of religiosity can be helpful in both semantic and research contexts, but remains problematic in view of the general population's opinion, as demonstrated above. It is true that both religion and spirituality have a social dimension. Even people who label themselves 'spiritual, nonreligious' desire to meet with other like-minded persons and, subsequently, to formalize their gatherings. It is also acknowledged that institutional religion can provide individuals with ways of developing their spirituality (Oman, 2013).

The same diagram (Figure 2.1) can be applied to understanding the relationship of spirituality and religiosity in a client's life. Some clients may identify with both religiosity and spirituality, some see a difference between the two but understand religiosity as a subcategory of spirituality, some see only part of spirituality and religiosity as having certain characteristics in common, and, finally, some are simply spiritual and nonreligious or only culturally religious. Moving between these various possibilities may also mark the spiritual development of a given person.

Specific Challenges to Measuring Spirituality

How to measure spirituality? That is, how can we see and know it with some measure of objectivity and consistency? Over the last decades, many instruments to measure it have been developed. They are both a curse and a blessing for the field as the great interest and diversity of ideas that characterize research on spirituality are brought to the forefront. Unfortunately, many of these instruments have not been compared so that we do not really know how these different scales all relate to one another. Without a close examination of the overlap between these instruments, little can be gained from them because it is almost impossible to combine findings from studies that use different scales. Because of this, the field's ability to develop a cumulative body of knowledge remains relatively limited.

Intermingling with Other Concepts

Critics maintain that spirituality cannot be classified as a unique, independent concept, but should rather be considered as a 'religification' of existing psychological variables. In order to avoid this, researchers attempt to demonstrate that the spiritual variables included in a given measurement tool 'show predictive power over and above other established constructs, such as social support and personality' (Stewart-Sicking et al., 2020, p. 191). The lack of well-developed theories that could supply researchers with necessary conceptual clarity is problematic (Hill, 2013).

A Lack of Contextual Understanding

Although recent research supplies us with a number of historical and contemporary factors shaping the nature of spirituality, we have used simplified and generic understandings of spirituality and religion without taking into account history, tradition, and geographical and ethnical specificity. Even if it is not necessary to be well versed in theology, spiritual writings originating from the world's major spiritual traditions do suggest ways of understanding spirituality that should be seriously considered (Dein et al., 2012). In fact, the most research in the field of spirituality has involved Judeo-Christian mainline Protestant concepts of religion in white, North American populations (Koenig, 2008; Hill, 2013). In the United States, most samples were composed of older white Christian adults, so that any generalization of such findings remains questionable (Park et al., 2015). The specificity of such research makes it relevant only to particular population groups and communities and does not develop a general understanding of the psychological dynamics that are at work (Piedmont & Wilkins, 2020). For instance, a tool measuring conversion that has been developed based on an experience common to Protestant Christianity would not be of much use for studying the spiritual experiences of Buddhists (Stewart-Sicking et al., 2020).

Artificial Positivity

When answering a questionnaire in a research study, it has been observed that respondents have a tendency to answer 'true' or 'yes' to a question. This can become a real source of error in testing because affirmative responses artificially inflate scores on a scale, which in turn has a negative impact on the validity of the measuring tool. One hopes that a particular scale would indicate the extent to which some quality is present in a person. For instance, if one has a tendency to answer 'true' or 'yes' in an ill-considered way, the results will indicate higher scores even though this does not represent the degree to which they possess this quality. This error in measurement leads to errors in interpretation such as false associations with other measured items. Unfortunately, a large number of instruments used to study spirituality have no control over acquiescent responding, thus posing serious questions regarding the quality of this research (Piedmont & Wilkins, 2020).

A Limited Usefulness of Correlational Designs

Correlational designs are useful in identifying potentially meaningful relationships between different variables. Beyond this, their usefulness is limited, because they are insufficient for assessing the empirical distinctiveness of the constructs they measure and leave research open to a variety of interpretations (Hood & Belzen, 2013). The measurement of spiritual items is associated with a wide variety of outcomes and is influenced by a number of other characteristics, such as age, culture, and religious denomination. One would need to control for these other variables if one wants to have a clear view of the impact of the spiritual dimension and prevent falsely elevated associations as well as erroneous interpretations. Multivariate tests and related analyses can be helpful in identifying and controlling data for the presence of other influential factors or potential mediators (Piedmont & Wilkins, 2020).

The way spirituality is measured in research becomes problematic when well-being is included as one of the measured components. Also, measuring spirituality has rarely addressed spiritual beliefs unconnected with religious practice (King et al., 2013). Relating spirituality to inner peace, connection with the universe, purpose and meaning, values, feelings of wonder, awe, or love, brings about a risk of confusing spirituality with its fruits (Koenig, 2008).

A Constrained Choice of Research Methods

Generally, psychological tests measuring spirituality rely on closed-ended, self-report questionnaires (Hill, 2013). In order to better understand this situation from a psychological vantage point, we need to develop other types of research methods; doing this has proven to be a sound research technique when applied to other scientific disciplines. It is no wonder that any two closed-ended questionnaires will correlate with each other to some degree as they both share a common research methodology. Only the use of a variety of research methods can help prevent any spurious associations. Moreover, using only similar types of measurement tools misses the larger issue if all of them remain self-reporting in nature, and the person's unique patterns of responding will be perceivable in all their test outcomes, regardless of their format. This is termed 'common error variance' and is due to the reliance on a single source of information (Piedmont & Wilkins, 2020; Truijens et al., 2021).

It is improbable that researchers would agree to use a unified method of researching spirituality when the points of view are too heterogeneous, and one should most likely talk about different spiritualities (conceptualizations) measured by different tools (operationalizations). This approach is surely more attractive but also less precise. Apart from research instruments, we also need plausible practical frames of reference to be used in various settings. Certainly, there is no one perfect instrument to measure spirituality as a multifaceted concept. Several instruments exist to cover different facets of spirituality: the easiest to measure being the behavioral components of spirituality, the more challenging to measure the attitudinal components of spirituality, and finally, the 'background' or numinous dimensions of spirituality, which are the most difficult to operationalize and to measure (Büssing, 2017).

Exclusiveness of Spiritual and Nonreligious Dimensions

From the research point of view, religiosity seems to be an easier object of study because there is a long tradition of well-developed measurement tools. A direct and simple assessment method for researching religiosity has been to correlate the frequency of religious participation such as church attendance, or practices such as prayer and reading religious literature, with a variety of outcomes, such as higher levels of well-being. Spirituality, interpreted as an internal process of the person such as an inner search for something transcendent or sacred, presents a bigger challenge in terms of conceptualization and operationalization. P. C. Hill et al. (2000) add: 'Given the significant sociological and psychological overlap among religion and spirituality, attempts to measure spirituality as a separate construct from religion are difficult' (p. 71).

Some instruments used to study spirituality, although already well established and conceptually very clear, are rather 'exclusive' because they specifically target distinct groups and religious orientations. Their strength is clear conceptualizations and operationalizations, but their weakness is that they are not inclusive enough to be used for persons with more secular perspectives. To address this issue, multidimensional tools were developed covering existential, prosocial, religious, and nonreligious forms of spirituality for culturally and spiritually diverse populations. The disadvantage of these more inclusive instruments is that they are conceptually unspecific and potentially too similar to personality traits as well as to dimensions of mental health and well-being. Using these instruments can give 'false positive' results since they do not measure specific aspects of spirituality (Büssing, 2017). Inclusive definitions embrace secular concepts of spirituality but are less specific. Conversely, these more 'exclusive' definitions are specific to circumscribed religious groups and thus, not suited for spiritual but nonreligious persons (Büssing, 2019).

As identified above, in the so-called Western world, a growing number of individuals identify themselves as 'spiritual, but not religious' and to survey this group one needs a more inclusive concept of spirituality encompassing nonreligious beliefs and practices. This inclusive approach is very similar to other secular concepts such as humanism, existentialism, and to some esoteric views (Zwingman et al., 2011). Using the term 'religiosity' for an exclusive approach and 'spirituality' for an inclusive one (spiritual, nonreligious) could be an option, but would require some reconstruction of research projects. Logically speaking, it would create a very clear dichotomy, and this would need to be broadly accepted in the academic community.

Research-Based versus Clinical Approach

Researching spirituality has yet another context, which is the scientific purpose of research (Figure 2.2). For scientific research, a rigorous definition of spirituality is needed. But in a clinical setting, the spiritual assessment of a client needs to be more inclusive in order to give them an opportunity to openly express their spirituality. Susan Tinley and Anita Kinney (2007) propose to name two approaches, one research-based and the other clinically based. The first approach, which is more theory driven, aims at measuring different elements of spirituality, and reworks them within a statistical frame, while the clinical approach is focused on gathering and analyzing observations or information shared by the client (Hall et al., 2008). Some (e.g., Johnson, 2013) suggest that clients should be given the opportunity to present their own definition of spirituality in a counseling session, especially when they are spiritual, nonreligious. In this situation, although they might not consider themselves to be religious, they could nonetheless be on a quest for greater meaning in their lives or may be struggling with multiple existential concerns (Koenig, 2008).

This kind of approach is based on a qualitative rather than a quantitative methodology such as using open-ended questions that are usually applied to case studies. Also, the clinical material that is obtained can be a starting point for many future research projects and should not be neglected. Only with time can it become a useful approach that is more measurable. Many operationalizations of certain dimensions of spirituality started with soft data coming from clinical practice, anecdotal stories, and subsequent case studies. The second stage was phenomenological/qualitative research, and only in the last stage was an attempt made to operationalize and measure

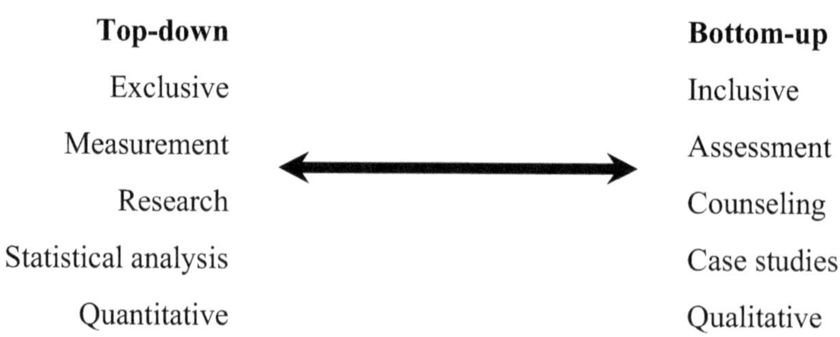

Figure 2.2 Research-based versus clinical approach to spirituality.

these dimensions. One should also be aware that a continuous feedback loop between psychological research and clinical practice is a necessary condition for fine-tuning our understanding of spirituality (Jastrzębski, 2020).

Neuroscientific Study of Spirituality

Thanks to neuroimaging technology, neuroscientists are attempting to explore the neurological foundations of spiritual experiences. Newberg (2010) advocates calling this field of neuroscience 'neurotheology,' a term that was first popularized by James Ashbrook (1984). According to Newberg (2010), the neuroscience of spirituality should include both the philosophical and theological analyses of various emotional, rational, and perceptual concepts used in elaborating theological arguments as well as theoretical aspects of the human psyche and mind such as questions regarding consciousness, spirit, mind, and brain (Newberg, 2010).

An analysis of the methodological obstacles in neuroscientific experimentation shows that the task of overcoming the challenges defies whatever means are currently available to the researcher. We are faced with the need for ongoing discussion between the human and the social sciences to help develop a deeper understanding and interpretation of individual subjective experiences, which I once described as the dialectics of explanation and interpretation. Many researchers seem to have come to similar conclusions (Jastrzębski, 2012, 2021).

Challenges of Neuroscientific Research of Spirituality

As in the case of any developing field, the neuroscience of spirituality has some major weaknesses. Some of these challenges are parallel to those found in psychology.

Subjective States

The individual's subjective states present a major challenge for neuroscience. After all, we never precisely know what a research subject is thinking at the moment that brain scan is being performed. In reality, brain images may differ from subject to subject, and we must control for background noise in order to dissect the input signal from baseline brain activity. Otherwise, there is the possibility of an erroneous interpretation (Jastrzębski, 2018).

Small Samples

In this type of research, the number of enrolled subjects is also often very small, which makes any results difficult to interpret. Many of those who participate in this research are university students, so there is no guarantee that this limited research can be extrapolated to the entire population. Even if significant findings are reported, the limited sample size usually casts doubt on the findings because it is difficult to generate adequate statistics. And because brain-scan results are a statistical average, it is very risky to state that the final results reveal the precise nature of any given spiritual experience. It would be necessary to combine and coordinate efforts from a variety of neuroscientific research centers so that the statistical outcomes may be more representative (larger and diversified study groups). Optimally, it would be ideal to include subjects from all over the world (Jastrzębski, 2018).

Test Bias

To measure spiritual states empirically without influencing such states is almost impossible – in accordance with twentieth-century physicist Werner Heisenberg and his principle of uncertainty. Several factors related to the scanning procedure itself can potentially compromise the authenticity of results. There is no doubt that for some people, merely being in a hospital is enough to make them exceedingly anxious. An even more important problem is claustrophobia. For many subjects, having their heads immobilized in the tube of the scanner will alter their experiences. The injection used in PET (positron emission tomography) studies to generate brain scans can be associated with discomfort, and the actual noise from the MRI (magnetic resonance imaging) scanner may alter subjects' concentration. Also, when overly vague instructions are given to the subjects, this can cause the task at hand to be executed in ways that are not compatible with the researcher's expectations (Schjoedt, 2009).

Level of Significance

Yet another source of error comes from the researcher's decision regarding what constitutes a significant level for brain activation. PET scan technology uses a standardized color map to facilitate the visual identification of areas of interest in the brain on the computer screen. Warm colors such as yellow and red indicate areas of increased activity in the brain whereas blue and green are used for areas of lower activity. Obviously, it is up to the experimenter to set the lower and upper limits for each color interval and to decide what level of activation is significant. If the experimenter is too conservative, important brain activity could be missed, and if they are not conservative enough, unimportant brain activation might be misinterpreted as significant. If the experimenter does not respect the activity thresholds that were initially chosen, they can conclude whatever they wish (Weissenbacher, 2015; see also Schjoedt, 2009). It is also noteworthy than any unexpected emotional excitation during the procedure can produce false results. Similarly, even something as seemingly trivial as the movement of a finger or the clenching of teeth can introduce error (Reiman et al., 2000).

As in the case of small sample sizes, the smaller numbers of subjects may increase the chance of misinterpreting the implications of the dynamism of brain activation. To avoid major mistakes in this regard, comparative studies with a larger number of subjects would be necessary to obtain more fine-tuned activation thresholds. This would provide a more realistic picture of what happens in the human brain during a subject's spiritual experiences (Jastrzębski, 2018).

Lack of Controls

With regard to spiritual experiences, there is also a significant need to compare the correlates of brain states in a diversity of subjects – 'any conclusions implying that a neural system or pattern of neural activation is specific to a religious state or behavior needs to be supported by the incorporation of many similar but nonreligious control conditions' (Brown, 2006, p. 242). Without such controls it is unwarranted to conclude that any particular brain activation is somehow specific to spiritual experience. What if a brain area associated with spiritual experiences were not activated even though the subject reported a sincere spiritual experience? Or what if the locus were activated without any spiritual experience being reported (Feit, 2004)?

To address this issue, a broader collaboration and a more consolidated approach in the field of neuroscience is desirable. Ideally, we could start with what we know best about the human brain and, subsequently, venture into regions that are less known. In this way, a feedback loop will be in place that will enable the corrections necessary for the development and the interpretation of research in more poorly understood areas of brain function. An example of this is to be found in the emotional component of almost every human experience. Assuredly, it also appears in spiritual experiences. Our understanding of the neuronal underpinnings of emotional experiences can shed light on our understanding of the spiritual experiences themselves (Jastrzębski, 2018).

Remaining Challenges

The limitation of the methodology used in neuroscientific research on spiritual phenomena is that data taken from micro-levels of human functioning are used to explain experiences that take place on a social, that is, macro-level. For example, despite the development of advanced technological methods enabling research into the brain structure, we still do not know much about how brain activity translates into specific behavior. Warren Brown (2006) uses this terminology (micro- and macro-levels) to describe how neuroscientists engaged in research on the spiritual quest skip over many levels of explanation, thus reducing the complexity of spiritual phenomena (Doehring, 2010).

The neuroscience of spirituality could become a helpful tool to examine controversial or doubtful issues studied by psychology or even by theology rather than simply trying to dismiss the findings of those fields of research. If the neuroscience of spirituality is to be developed and used properly, it will be necessary to utilize well-established theories of brain function for the interpretation of experiments instead of developing new controversial hypotheses that introduce mechanisms supposedly unique to religious experience. Spiritual experiences involve various forms of already well-known cognitive processing such as those involved in the emotions. The only 'new' feature should be to recognize that spiritual experiences have a link to the Sacred. One of the major challenges of the neuroscience of spirituality should be to investigate how specific spiritual traditions change cognitive processes of the brain. This may lead to less exciting theories, but it will contribute to more precise research on spiritual experiences (Schjoedt, 2009; Newberg, 2014).

Another development needed for an adequate neuroscience of spirituality must be that of taking 'a person-centered approach' (Bulkeley, 2002). The responsibility for assessing the reality of spiritual experience could be transferred from the researcher to the subject of study. In the final analysis, only the subject is truly qualified to declare that a genuine spiritual experience has taken place and could thus become an object of study (Feit, 2004; Newberg, 2014).

Conclusions

In summary, all research methods have both strengths and limitations, and each can enlighten the researchers in its own way. For instance, quantitative research brings to the forefront the correlates and predictors demonstrating how spirituality influences mental health. On the other hand, qualitative research gives researchers access to the content and meaning embedded in spiritual phenomena (Stewart-Sicking et al., 2020). Academics who want to operationalize spirituality for their research have to demonstrate empirically that their understanding of spirituality has unique properties that cannot otherwise be explained by other positive character traits or positive mental health indicators (Koenig, 2009). Otherwise, only the expected outcomes will be achieved. Without more methodological attention, the results pertaining to spirituality will never be conclusive nor will it determine exactly what is affecting what.

Discussion questions

1. Is it possible to research spirituality, something that is so unique and personal to each of us?
2. What do we lose in the psychological research of spirituality?
3. What do you think of the idea of studying spirituality using brain scans?
4. Do you think one can actually measure spirituality? Explain.

References

Aaen-Stockdale, C. (2012). Neuroscience for the soul. *Psychologist, 25*(7), 520–523.

Albright, C., & Ashbrook, J. (2001). *Where God lives in the human brain.* Sourcebooks.

Ashbrook, J. (1984). Neurotheology: The working brain and the work of theology. *Zygon, 19*(3), 331–350.

Beauregard, M., & O'Leary, D. (2007). *The spiritual brain: A neuroscientist's case for the existence of the soul*. Harper Collins.

Bingaman, K. A. (2013). The promise of neuroplasticity for pastoral care and counseling. *Pastoral Psychology, 62*, 549–560.

Brown, W. S. (2006). The brain, religion, and baseball: neurology of religion and religious experience. In P. McNamara (Ed.), *Where God and science meet: How brain and evolutionary studies alter our understanding of religion* (Vol. 2, pp. 229–244). Praeger.

Brysbaert, M., & Rastle, K. (2009). *Historical and conceptual issues in psychology*. Pearson Education.

Bulkeley, K. (2002). The evolution of wonder: Religious and neuroscientific perspectives. Paper delivered at the Annual Meeting of the American Academy of Religion, Toronto, Canada, 23–26 November.

Büssing, A. (2017). Measures of spirituality/religiosity—description of concepts and validation of instruments. *Religions (Basel, Switzerland), 8*(1), 11.

Büssing, A. (2019). Introduction to the Special Issue 'Measures of Spirituality/Religiosity (2018).' *Religions (Basel, Switzerland), 10*(3), 214.

Casey, P. R. (2013). I'm spiritual but not religious: Implications for research and practice. In C. C. H. Cook (Ed.), *Spirituality, theology and mental health: Interdisciplinary perspectives* (pp. 20–39). SCM Press.

Cramer, R. J., Griffin, M. P., & Powers, D.V. (2008). A five-factor analysis of spirituality in young adults: Preliminary evidence. In R. Piedmont (Ed.), *Research in the social scientific study of religion* (Vol. 19, pp. 43–57). Leiden, The Netherlands: Brill.

D'Aquili, E., & Newberg, A. B. (1999). *The mystical mind: Probing the biology of religious experience*. Fortress Press.

Dein, S., Cook, C., & Koenig, H. (2012). Religion, spirituality, and mental health: Current controversies and future directions. *Journal of Nervous & Mental Disease, 200*, 852–855. https://doi.org/10.1097/NMD.0b013e31826b6dle

Dixon, S., & Wilcox, G. (2016). The counseling implications of neurotheology: a critical review. *Journal of Spirituality in Mental Health, 18*(2), 91–107.

Doehring, C. (2010). Minding the gap when cognitive neuroscience is a cognate discipline in pastoral theology: Lessons from neurotheology. *Journal of Pastoral Theology, 20*(2), 93–108.

Eacker, J. N. (1983). *Problems of metaphysics and psychology*. Nelson-Hall.

Feit, J. S. (2004). Probing neurotheology's brain, or critiquing an emerging quasi-science. *Council of Societies for the Study of Religion Bulletin, 33*(1), 3–9.

Fox, J., & Piedmont, R. (2020). Religious crisis as an independent causal predictor of psychological distress: Understanding the unique role of the numinous for intrapsychic functioning. *Religions (Basel, Switzerland), 11*(7), 329.

Fox, J., Picciotto, G., Cashwell, C. S., Worthington, E. L., Jr., Basso, M. J., Brow Corrigan, S., & Zeligman, M. (2020). Religious commitment, spirituality, and attitudes toward god as related to psychological and medical help-seeking: The role of spiritual bypass. *Spirituality in Clinical Practice*, 7(3), 178–196. https://doi.org/10.1037/scp0000216

Frankl, V. E. (1988). *The Will to Meaning. Foundations and Applications of Logotherapy*. Meridian.

Graham, S. (1992). 'Most of the subjects were white and middle class': Trends in published research on African Americans in selected APA journals, 1970–1989. *The American Psychologist, 47*(5), 629–639. https://doi.org/10.1037/0003-066X.47.5.629

Granqvist, P., Fredrikson, M., Unge, P. et al. (2005). Sensed presence and mystical experiences are predicted by suggestibility, not by the application of transcranial weak complex magnetic fields. *Neuroscience Letters, 379*(1), 1–6.
Hall, D. E., Meador, G. M., & Koenig, H. G. (2008). Measuring religiousness in health research: Review and critique. *Journal of Religion and Health, 47*, 134–163.
Hill, P. C. (2013). Measurement assessment and issues in the psychology of religion and spirituality. In R. F. Paloutzian & C. L. Park (Eds.), *Handbook of the psychology of religion and spirituality* (pp. 48–74). Guilford Press.
Hill, P. C., & Pargament, K. I. (2003). Advances in the conceptualization and measurement of religion and spirituality: Implications for physical and mental health research. *American Psychologist, 58*, 64–74.
Hill, P. C., Pargament, K. I., Hood, R. W., Jr., McCullough, M. E., Swyers, J. P., Larson, D. B., & Zinnbauer, B. J. (2000). Conceptualizing religion and spirituality: Points of commonality, points of departure. *Journal for the Theory of Social Behaviour*, 30, 51–77.
Hood, R. W. Jr., & Belzen, J. A. (2013). Research methods in the psychology of religion and spirituality. In R. F. Paloutzian & C. L. Park (Eds.), *Handbook of the psychology of religion and spirituality* (pp. 75–93). Guilford Press.
Hughes, J. R. (2005). Did all those famous people really have epilepsy? *Epilepsy & Behavior, 6*(2), 115–139.
Jastrzębski, A. (2011). *W obronie integralności człowieka. Próba adekwatnego ujęcia filozofii psychologii*. Eneteia.
Jastrzębski, A. (2012). Towards a better understanding of the Philosophy of Psychology. *History & Philosophy of Psychology, 14*(1), 13–33.
Jastrzębski, A. (2018). The neuroscience of spirituality: An attempt at critical analysis. *Pastoral Psychology, 67*(5), 515–524. https://doi.org/10.1007/s11089-018-0840-2
Jastrzębski, A. K. (2020). The challenging task of defining spirituality. *Journal of Spirituality in Mental Health, 24*(2), 113–131. https://doi.org/10.1080/19349637.2020.1858734
Johnson, R. (2013). *Spirituality in counseling and psychotherapy: An integrative approach that empowers clients*. John Wiley.
Kahle, P., & Robbins, J. (2004). *The power of spirituality in therapy*. Haworth Press.
King, J. E., & Williamson, I. O. (2005). Workplace religious expression, religiosity and job satisfaction: Clarifying a relationship. *Journal of Management, Spirituality & Religion, 2*(2), 173–198.
King, M., Marston, L., McManus, S., Brugha, T., Meltzer, H., & Bebbington, P. (2013). Religion, spirituality and mental health: Results from a national study of English households. *British Journal of Psychiatry, 202*(1), 68–73. https://doi.org/10.1192/bjp.bp.112.112003
Koenig, H. G. (2008). *Medicine, religion and health: Where science and spirituality meet*. Templeton Press.
Koenig, H. G. (2009). Research on religion, spirituality, and mental health: A review. *Canadian Journal of Psychiatry, 54*, 283–291.
Kvale, S. (1992). Postmodern psychology: A contradiction in terms? In S. Kvale (Ed.), *Psychology and postmodernism* (pp. 31–57). SAGE.
May, G. G. (1987). *Will and spirit: A contemplative psychology*. Harper One.
McCauley, R. N. (2007). Reduction: Models of cross-scientific relations and their implications for the psychology-neuroscience interface. In P. Thagard (Ed.), *Philosophy of psychology and cognitive science* (pp. 105–158). Elsevier B.V. https://doi.org/10.1016/B978-044451540-7/50021-9

McIlhenny, R. (2015). A revolution in mind: Andrew Newberg's principles of neurotheology. *American Theological Inquiry*, *8*(1), 81–84.

Newberg, A. (2010). Methodological principles for research in neurotheology. *NeuroQuantology*, *8*(4), 531–545.

Newberg, A. (2014). The neuroscientific study of spiritual practices. *Frontiers in Psychology, 5*(215), 1–6.

Newberg, A., & Waldman, M. R. (2010). *How God changes your brain: Breakthrough findings from a leading neuroscientist*. Ballantine Books.

Nielsen, M., Haun, D., Kärtner, J., & Legare, C. H. (2017). The persistent sampling bias in developmental psychology: A call to action. *Journal of Experimental Child Psychology*, *162*, 31–38. https://doi.org/10.1016/j.jecp.2017.04.017

Oman, D. (2013). Defining religion and spirituality. In R. F. Paloutzian & C. L. Park (Eds.), *Handbook of the psychology of religion and spirituality* (pp. 23–47). Guilford Press.

Pargament, K. I. (2007). *Spiritually integrated psychotherapy: Understanding and addressing the sacred*. Guilford Press.

Pargament, K. I., & Mahoney, A. (2002). Spirituality: Discovering and conserving the sacred. In C. R. Snyder (Ed.), *Handbook of positive psychology* (pp. 646– 675). American Psychological Association.

Park, C. L., Sherman, A. C., Jim, H. S. L., & Salsman, J. M. (2015). Religion/spirituality and health in the context of cancer: Cross-domain integration, unresolved issues, and future directions. *Cancer*, *121*(21), 3789–3794. https://doi.org/10.1002/cncr.29351

Perrin, D. B. (2007a). *Studying Christian spirituality*. Routledge. https://doi.org/10.4324/9780203944776

Perrin, D. B. (2007b). The uneasy relationship between Christian spirituality and the human sciences: Psychology as a test case. *Spiritus: A Journal of Christian Spirituality*, Johns Hopkins University Press, Fall edition, 169–192.

Persinger, M., Corradini, P., Clement, A., Keaney, C., MacDonald, M., Meltz, L., Murugan, N., Poirier, M., Punkkinen, K., Rossini, M. & Thompson, S. (2010). Neurotheology and its convergence with neuroquantology. *NeuroQuantology*, *8*, 432–443. https://doi.org/10.14704/nq.2010.8.4.372

Persinger, M. A. (1987). *Neurobiological bases of God beliefs*. Praeger.

Piedmont, R., & Friedman, P. (2012). Spirituality, religiosity, and subjective quality of life. In K. Land, A. Michalos, & M. Sirgy (Eds.), *Handbook of social indicators and quality of life research* (pp. 313–329). Springer.

Piedmont, R., & Wilkins, T. (2020). *Understanding the psychological soul of spirituality*. Routledge.

Piedmont, R. L. (1999). Does spirituality represent the sixth factor of personality? Spiritual transcendence and the five-factor model. *Journal of Personality*, *67*, 985–1013.

Piedmont, R. L. (2001). Spiritual transcendence and the scientific study of spirituality. *Journal of Rehabilitation*, *67*, 4–14.

Piedmont, R. L., Ciarrocchi, J. W., Dy-Liacco, G., & Williams, J. E. G. (2009). The empirical and conceptual value of the spiritual transcendence and religious involvement scales for personality research. *Psychology of Religion and Spirituality*, *1*, 162–179.

Reiman, E., Lane, R. D., Van Petten, C., & Bandettini, P. A. (2000). Positron emission tomography and functional magnetic resonance imaging. In G. Berntson, J. T. Cacioppo, & L. G. Tassinary (Eds.), *Handbook of psychophysiology* (pp. 85–118). Cambridge University Press.

Schjoedt, U. (2009). The religious brain: A general introduction to the experimental neuroscience of religion. *Method and Theory in the Study of Religion, 21*, 310–339.

Sheldrake, P. (2007). *A brief history of spirituality*. Blackwell.

Sieber, J. E., & Saks, M. J. (1989). A census of subject pool characteristics and policies. *The American Psychologist, 44*(7), 1053–1061. https://doi.org/10.1037/0003-066X.44.7.1053

Stewart-Sicking, J., Fox, J., & Deal, P. (2020). *Bringing religion and spirituality into therapy: A process-based model for pluralistic practice*. Routledge.

Tinley, S. T., & Kinney, A. Y. (2007). Three philosophical approaches to the study of spirituality. *Advances in Nursing Science, 30*(1), 71–80.

Truijens, F., De Smet, M. M., Desmet, M., & Meganck, R. (2021). Validity of data as precondition for evidence: A methodological analysis of what is taken to count as evidence in psychotherapy research. *Philosophy, Psychiatry, & Psychology, 28*(2), 115–128. https://doi.org/10.1353/ppp.2021.0018

Valentine, E. R. (1992). *Conceptual issues in psychology* (2nd ed.). Routledge.

Wallace, A. (2000). *The taboo of subjectivity: Toward a new science of consciousness*. Oxford University Press.

Weissenbacher, A. C. (2015). Ten principles for interpreting neuroscientific pronouncements regarding human nature. *Dialog: A Journal of Theology, 54*(1), 40–50.

Wilt, J. A., Stauner, N., Harriott, V. A., Exline, J. J., & Pargament, K. I. (2019). Partnering with God: Religious coping and perceptions of divine intervention predict spiritual transformation in response to religious–spiritual struggle. *Psychology of Religion and Spirituality, 11*(3), 278–290. https://doi.org/10.1037/rel0000221

Young, J. S., & Cashwell, C. S. (2011). *Integrating spirituality and religion into counseling: An introduction*. In C. S. Cashwell & J. S. Young (Eds.), *Integrating spirituality and religion into counseling: A guide to competent practice* (pp. 1–24). American Counseling Association.

Zinnbauer, B. J. (2013). Models of healthy and unhealthy religion and spirituality. In K. Pargament (Ed.), *APA handbook of psychology, religion, and spirituality* (Vol. 2: *An applied psychology of religion and spirituality*, pp. 71–89). American Psychological Association.

Zinnbauer, B. J., Pargament, K. I., & Scott, A. B. (1999). The emerging meanings of religiousness and spirituality: Problems and prospects. *Journal of Personality, 67*, 889–920.

Zwingmann, C., Klein, C., & Büssing, A. (2011). Measuring religiosity/spirituality: Theoretical differentiations and categorization of instruments. *Religions (Basel, Switzerland), 2*(3), 345–357.

3 What Is a Spiritual Experience?

Introduction

One may say that our life is full of spiritual experiences. Of course, the scope and spectrum of these experiences will depend on how one understands spirituality. We have already studied this issue at length. Nonetheless, literally any phenomenon of everyday life may become a unique experience that takes our breath away. Holding your newborn for the first time, a sunrise or sunset, meeting an old friend, running a marathon, walking barefoot, jogging, hiking, gardening, cooking, listening to a piece of music, as well as a simple moment of silence: these can become spiritual moments, sometimes even without our recognizing them as being spiritual or being able to name them as such.

Academics want to understand more. For over a century, beginning with William James in the field of psychology as well as in the wisdom of various traditions for many centuries, there have been ways of conceptualizing and structuring what we call a spiritual experience. There are also many names given to it: mystical experience, unifying experience, transcendental experience, religious experience, and others. Some argue (e.g., Hood et al., 2018) that mystical experiences should be treated separately. There is also an attempt to make a sharper distinction between spiritual and mystical experiences, where mystical experiences are understood as sudden, subjective experiences, whereas spiritual experiences are more ordinary, even seen as gradual changes such as spiritual struggles and transformation, conversion and deconversion (Taves, 2020).

It is quite difficult to do justice to the long history of studying spiritual experiences in theology, philosophy, and psychology (Hood & Chen, 2013), and, since this book attempts to develop a universal and practical approach, we will focus on some select models that can become effective tools to understand clients in counseling without attempting to cover all present day theories pertaining to this theme. We will continue to use the expression 'spiritual experiences' to include all of them and consider mystical and religious experiences as subcategories of spiritual experiences. And finally,

DOI: 10.4324/9781003262145-4

although mystical experiences are presented separately in this chapter, the main focus will be on spiritual experiences as a universal category.

Major spiritual traditions cherish their founder's spiritual experiences. This is the case with the stories of Abraham, Isaac, Jacob, and Moses in Judaism; Jesus in Christianity; the experience of Allah by Mohammed for Islam; as well as the enlightenment experience of Shakyamuni Buddha for his followers. Spiritual traditions underline the importance of having a personal experience of the Sacred, whether it is called 'being born again' or enlightenment. Such direct personal spiritual experiences may be at the origin of many perceived blessings such as a clearer purpose for living, a shift away from egocentrism toward altruism and compassion, a new sense of time, and a growing sense of personal freedom (Gunn, 2020).

Spiritual experiences in many mystical traditions focus on the immanence of the Sacred within the human heart or soul. Although the divine is normally perceived as distant and transcendent, in mystical experience, for example in Christianity, 'the wholly other God' becomes very intimately present to the human self (Komarovski, 2015). In Buddhism, there is a long tradition of reflecting on mystical experiences, even though this is not done through a theistic framework. Their essence is an experience of enlightenment, which reveals that there is no duality in the universe (e.g., matter versus spirit). And since language always operates within dualistic concepts, this enlightenment cannot be expressed linguistically. Its fruit should be the eradication of one's suffering as well as the end of one's cycle of rebirths (Burton, 2020). In Jewish and Muslim traditions, there is a special place for mystical experiences (Idel & McGinn, 1996). Within Islam, Sufism is a spiritual tradition focused on the way of encountering God (Chittick, 2020). In Christianity, mystical experiences are rooted in the firsthand encounter with the person of Jesus Christ. The goal of Christian mysticism is not so much any particular moment of encounter with the divine, but rather living within the mystery of the Sacred, with all the creative acts that flow from Christian belief, hope, and love. Thus mystics are able to give witness to the profound yet hidden presence of the Sacred actively transforming the lives of otherwise ordinary people (Perrin, 2007). Spiritual experiences can also be seen as self-transcendent experiences (STEs) that range from something as simple as losing oneself in a book to the intense and potentially transformative experiences of unity with the whole universe. They are usually accompanied by the dissolution of one's bodily sense, reduced self-boundaries, and self-salience (Yaden et al., 2017).

It seems that major world spiritual traditions share a number of elements pertaining to the understanding of spiritual experiences. And whereas some researchers in the tradition of perennial philosophy (e.g., Huxley, 2004) or others (e.g., Chen et al., 2011) attempt to establish universal core elements or a set of beliefs valid for all spiritual traditions, others criticize this idea (Katz, 2020; Jones, 2021). We will now present select psychological and phenomenological characteristics of spiritual experiences that can be applied universally.

The Nature of Spiritual Experiences

William James and Evelyn Underhill

William James is one of the pioneers in the psychological study of spirituality. His phenomenological and pragmatic approach to religious experiences influenced generations of academics and thinkers. James defines spiritual experiences by the subjective acts, feelings, and attitudes of an individual toward something they consider sacred (James & Marty, 2015). James's definition of a sacred or divine object included any idea, figure, or situation that enhanced one's trust and security in the universe. For James, communitarian and cognitive dimensions of this experience were secondary to the distinctive factor of spiritual emotions, or feelings (Roy, 2001).

Spiritual experiences, or 'religious experiences' in James's terms, are distinguished by a qualitative difference in the intensity of emotions, as well as by the connectedness to an infinite reality. James (1902/1990) indicates four characteristics of these experiences: (1) *Ineffability*, or the inability to find accurate words to describe or convey the experience. This usually implies that a high level of openness is required to understand these accounts. (2) *Noetic quality*, meaning insights that do not appear in the regular state of consciousness. Louis Roy (2001) states that such experiences are about perception rather than conception since these are emotional and spiritual insights and not cognitive understandings. (3) *Transiency*. These experiences are temporary, lasting from a few seconds to a few minutes or hours. Nevertheless, they leave lasting effects, and often become a point of departure for a spiritual journey. (4) *Passivity*. One is invited to surrender to the experience, as if held by a divine presence (James, 1902/1990).

To these four characteristics Evelyn Underhill (1911/2009) adds her own four rules. (1) Mystical experiences are active and personal, lived in inner encounters, not in passive, theoretical, or abstract terms. (2) Their aim is purely spiritual and transcendent: reaching union with God. (3) They are pursued as a personal love for the eternal One, which transcends dialectic and reason. (4) They change the entire orientation of life as they lead to major life decisions fueled by the desire of sanctity. In addition, she concludes that mysticism is not a self-seeking endeavor. Nor is it a search for spiritual joys and knowledge. It is all about love for love's sake. She also refers to the classical stages of spiritual development: the awakening of the self, the purification of the self, and finally the illumination of the self.

While James underlines the emotional as well as the authoritative aspects of spiritual experiences, it is also important to reflect on their content. The benefits of the insights gained from such experiences are the results of an emotional, cognitive, and behavioral process of integration. One is invited to make sense of these events and integrate them meaningfully into one's life. There is empirical evidence supporting James's conviction that such experiences have lasting, positive, and transformative consequences for one's life (Miller & Bacag, 2001).

Louis Roy

Louis Roy (2001) proposes that we pay attention to the numerous ways of describing mystical-type experiences such as cosmic consciousness, religious and transcendent experience, the numinous, peak experience, and other similar experiences. Their common characteristic seems to be an emotional and intuitive discovery of reality in an unrestricted and open way. This kind of experience stretches beyond the limits of daily life and surpasses one's understanding. Roy (2001) calls it 'transcendent experience.' Nonetheless, he differentiates transcendent experiences from religious experiences, the latter including specific religious acts, while not necessarily involving the experience of a transcendent reality. Transcendent experiences can be lived in both a religious as well as a secular context regardless of religious affiliation (Roy, 2001).

Roy (2001) also differentiates four types of transcendent experience, linking them to the occasion that triggered them. While they are distinct, these experiences can overlap. (1) Aesthetic experiences, including a feeling of connection with nature or the universe. (2) Ontological experiences, characterized by feelings of security and of being outside of time and space. They are often accompanied by intellectual questions and can bring about insights regarding questions of meaning. (3) Ethical experiences, such as grasping the meaning of a certain value as well as its truthfulness. It can be facilitated by moral questioning and result in increased identification with this value. (4) Interpersonal experience characterized by a sense of presence and felt connection (Roy, 2001).

Gerald May

As we know, there exist a variety of spiritual experiences. These include conversions: a dramatic change in one's faith or acceptance of divine love, charismatic healings or visions, private revelations, extrasensory perceptions, and experiences of being possessed by evil spirits. Apart from these, there are *intuitive* experiences, where one obtains an inner understanding of what is necessary in a given situation. But the most profound of all spiritual experiences is the unitive experience when one loses one's sensed self and experiences being absorbed into some other entity. This is the most paradigmatic and mysterious experience of human consciousness and contains true intuition as well as radical spontaneity. These experiences occur, for instance, when in the middle of everyday life, one is caught up in awe, and time in its familiar duration ceases to exist, while one's awareness becomes radically broadened, transparent, and seemingly boundless (May, 1987).

Unitive experiences are quite transient and mostly happen in association with nature or other aesthetic settings, while listening to a beautiful piece of music, watching a sunset, or contemplating a breathtaking piece of art. They may occur through intimacy with another person. Paradoxically, they can even be associated with such things as a close encounter with death, a major life crisis, suffering, or living through other extremely stressful situations such as combat during a war. Because these experiences alter one's state of consciousness, it can be tempting to try and recreate them at will through meditation, psychedelic drugs, and biofeedback, but these do not produce the same results. Essentially, one cannot make unitive experiences happen. Any attempt of this kind proves self-defeating. One can only prepare oneself, through certain spiritual disciplines, to be more open and ready to recognize and accept these experiences when they appear, but there is no cause-and-effect relationship (May, 1987).

Among the elements characteristic of unitive experiences, the first is the being-at-one ontological state without any self-defining activities.

> The cessation of self-defining activities includes many things that we generally take for granted. In full realization of union there is, for example, no idea of controlling, accomplishing, or even of *doing* anything. Time seems to stop – and actually does, for time is a way of defining and locating oneself in terms of past, present, and future. Thus, in looking back upon unitive experiences, people are given to say that they were suspended in the 'eternal present,' immersed in immediacy.
>
> (May, 1987, p. 60; italics in original)

During unitive experiences, people do not lose their body sensations and are able to safely walk and get from one place to another. They can even perform certain actions and speak, but without any consideration of self (May, 1987).

The second characteristic of unitive experiences is the change in awareness as it becomes alert, sharp, awake, and radically open. In this state of consciousness all senses are acute, but they are not directed to any object as there is no particular attention given to any 'outside reality' (May, 1987).

The third characteristic is related to the feelings that may appear directly after such experiences. Among these are awe, beauty, wonder, and truthfulness. Sometimes there is a sense of fulfillment and love, but when a person tries to prolong the experience, they may become anxious and frustrated (May, 1987).

Although unitive experiences are very powerful, they tend to be easily forgotten and do not always bring any particular change to one's life. Only rarely does this superior experience get meaningfully integrated into one's attitudes because it menaces one's self-identity and the sense of security of one's ego. Normally, the fruit of a unitive experience is not a sense of grandiosity but a humble awareness of being human and fragile (May, 1987).

If the impact of any spiritual experience is to increase humility and cause one to become more other-concerned and compassionate, it can probably be assumed that the integration of the experience is moving in a creative direction. But if the impact is to increase self-concern and self-importance; if it makes one feel distanced from rather than closer to other people; and if it stifles rather than encourages humble compassion, one should be suspicious. In such a case it may be assumed that either the experience itself was contrived to meet some narcissistic need or that if it was legitimate, it proved so threatening to the individual's self-image that a compensatory overreacting has occurred (May, 1987, p. 63).

One needs to underline that the impact of unitive experiences can be constructive, destructive, or neutral, depending on certain factors. One of these is the presence or absence of the quality of loving. Another is the strength of one's self-image or self-identity; unitive experiences can be repressed by a threatened or weak ego. Finally, the situation and context in which the experience takes place play a significant role. For example, many unitive experiences are so brief that they remain unnoticed. At other times, the individual is left only with some kind of unidentified longing. The longer the experience, the more noticeable the traces left in one's life (May, 1987).

Forms of Spiritual Experience

Human life is characterized by a variety of experiences in which mind, spirit, and heart all play a role and interact with each other. There are psychological reactions to spiritual experiences. There are spiritual experiences that are mistaken for primary psychological changes and psychological phenomena that masquerade as spiritual experiences. Through all of these phenomena, one may also detect classical God-given consolations and desolations as described in Christian spiritual literature. In times of consolation the Christian God is felt as deeply present, loving, guiding, and sustaining. In times of desolation, one feels only the absence and silence of that God. At other times, one can be in a state that seems devoid of all experience (May, 1992).

Spirituality can be experienced from the point of view of the experience itself or from the point of view of its interpretation. At one extreme is affective or emotional spirituality. This form of spirituality is marked by visions, emotions, or sensations as well as an attraction to dramatic experiences during spiritual practices. One of the most dangerous mistakes to which one can fall prey is to evaluate spiritual experiences according to their intensity. In fact, because a state of intense emotions cannot be sustained for a long period of time, people tend to burn out, and consequently, abandon the spiritual path completely. At the other extreme, the experience of spirituality is more intellectual and relies on the interpretation one gives to the content of such experiences. It is based on ideas about spirituality and the intellectual inspiration one can draw from spiritual experiences. An intellectual approach is more stable but also drier since this kind of spirituality does not really touch one's heart (May, 1987).

However, in order to identify and more fully understand a client's spiritual reality, one must remember that the core of spirituality can only be found beyond words and beliefs. The psychological meaning of an individual's spiritual life can only become clear by the client's spiritual practice or day-to-day activities, which are the proving ground of spiritual experiences. By observing and taking into consideration the interoperability of beliefs, practices, and experiences present in a client's life, the psychological meaning of an individual's spiritual life comes more clearly into focus. In making these observations, one must also include the purposes of religion and spirituality and distinguish between their translative and transformative purposes (Wilber, 2008).

> The translative aim of spirituality is to assist with the meaning-making and purpose-seeking aspects of life. Thus, the translative aspect of religion is frequently connected to the formation of beliefs. Conversely, the transformative aspects of spirituality entail those practices and experiences that enable a person to develop transpersonally, or toward 'humanity's highest potential, and with the recognition, understanding, and realization of unitive, spiritual, and transcendent states of consciousness.'
>
> (Young & Cashwell, 2011, p. 9)

According to May (1992), human consciousness represents one of the essential ways the divine reveals itself to us. Each spiritual experience occurs within the boundaries of our awareness, which is part of a larger field of consciousness. It is in our awareness that we encounter thoughts, images, visions, and other similar phenomena. This is the fabric of human experience that can be the subject of both psychological examination and spiritual discernment. In his classic theological approach, Augustin Poulain (1950) identifies three forms of vision: exterior, imaginative, and intellectual. Exterior visions can also be termed 'corporal' or 'ocular' because they are perceived externally by one's eyes. Underhill (1911/2009) proposes a trifold division regarding the phenomenon of voices: (1) immediate or inarticulate voices like an infusion of new knowledge, (2) interior and distinct voices where the individual collaborates in creating them, and (3) exterior words perceived clearly by one's ears.

May (1992) goes on to say that there is an even more subtle level where one can experience hints, intuitions, formless qualities, and perceptions of good or evil auras. For example, experiences attached to visions may vary from intentional imagination or visualization (imagery) to spontaneous visions that seem to originate from without. Between these two extremes, there is a whole continuum of possibilities. Sometimes one can begin with meditative imagination and finish with more spontaneous visions. Some people hear an interior voice that conveys a message, or they experience certain intuitive interior insights. Still others see light or feel temperature changes, tremors, or profound relaxation. Moreover, there are experiences of an intellectual nature like the sudden illumination about or clear understanding of certain truths. Sometimes spiritual experiences include extrasensory sensations such as described in parapsychology: telepathy, precognition, out-of-body experiences, seeing auras, and telekinetic influences on matter. One can also add to these experiences originating in Christian charismatic prayer groups: miraculous healing, speaking in tongues, and prophecy, as well as more dramatic, dissociative or trancelike states termed 'being slain in the Spirit.' For the most part, spiritual experiences are pleasant, but can sometimes be marked by darkness and fear. One should distinguish the fear of God as a natural response to an encounter with the divine from experiences of encountering evil (May, 1992).

It turns out that extrasensory experiences such as prophetic dreams and subtle telepathic senses are quite common in the general population. Usually, such experiences are more distressing than exciting for the person who lives through them because they do not provide any guidance as to what should be done with the new information. For instance, what do we do with a prophetic dream that foretells trouble for a person that we know? Precognition can be more of a curse than a blessing! Dreams are another example of this type of experience. The danger with dream analysis is that it can become so mesmerizing that it leaves no time and energy for other spiritual work. Some currents in contemporary psychology support dream analysis, which can certainly be quite interesting and stimulating, but people who are especially curious about their inner psychic experiences run the risk of exaggerated self-absorption in their dream exploration. When confronted with an excess of unconscious symbolism, individuals with excessively weak ego defenses may experience psychological decompensation. Still others, who are mostly 'out of touch' with their inner life, may actually benefit from dream exploration. In conclusion, one may say that, although dreams may or may not be useful tools for spiritual growth, it is important to discern how, when, and how much to rely on them (May, 1992).

The interpretation of spiritual experiences will always present a major challenge. According to Underhill (1911/2002), regardless of the way in which an experience manifests itself, be it through visions, voices, or other extraordinary phenomena, its interpretation will always be subjected to larger context of debates regarding the understanding of such matters. There will always be believers and skeptics, holists and reductionists, or supernaturalists and rationalists, as well as philosophers and ideologists with a very clear agenda on how to approach issues such as the existence of God, faith, the supernatural, and finally the relationship between spirituality and psychology (Klimek, 2018).

> The question for their critics must really be this: do these automatisms, which appear so persistently as a part of the contemplative life, represent merely the dreams and fancies, the old digested percepts of the visionary, objectivized and presented to his surface-mind in a concrete form; or, are they ever representations – symbolic, if you like – of some fact, force, or personality, some 'triumphing spiritual power,' external to himself? Is the vision only a pictured thought, an activity of the dream imagination; or, is it the violent effort of the self to translate something impressed upon its deeper being, some message received from without, which projects this sharp image and places it before the consciousness.
>
> (Underhill, 1911/2009, p. 157)

In this context, there is an ongoing debate between constructivism and receptivity. Are such extraordinary experiences only a human construction, either natural or pathological, or are they an authentic connection to an external, spiritual, and supernatural agent? Underhill (1911/2009) argues that such authentic experiences have to come from a higher spiritual source but, at the same time, they are also filtered through the human psyche and its preexistent cultural concepts and the ideas with which it interprets, understands, and frames each of these experiences. Certainly, such spiritual experiences are subjective, and for that reason, they always produce an interplay between what the human mind and the spiritual source bring about in such experiences (Klimek, 2019).

Roy's Stages of Spiritual Experience

Beyond extracting structural elements and characteristic of spiritual experiences, there are also attempts to explain the chronological elements of such experiences. A very illustrative example of that is the proposal of Roy (2001), discussed previously. He identified six chronological elements of transcendent or spiritual experiences.

The preparation includes one's lifestyle, concerns, problems, and questions as well as the cognitive and affective characteristics of one's personality. Before the experience takes place, there is also some anticipation or basic predisposition linked to one's openness, meaning an 'ability to receive a certain revelation about one's existence' (Roy, 2001, p. 5).

The preparation has both long- and short-range elements. It may take years, weeks, or only a few days, during which time something has been fermenting, making the person more receptive to such an experience. Another part of the preparation context is the psychological and existential situation in which one has to face the uneasiness, tension, or even struggle that often exists immediately before the experience happens (Roy, 2001).

The occasion or context is the factor that triggers the experience. This context can be an action, a person, a painting, a musical piece, a dream, a vision, a phrase heard or recalled, or good or bad news. Other triggers can be sensory deprivation, exhaustion, fasting, the use of a special diet, and other ascetic practices. All these factors can bring about a sudden release of tension and, consequently, the emergence of a novel feeling. The context of spiritual experiences belongs in our everyday life where we discover signals of transcendence within the mundaneness of our existence, signals that nonetheless point to something beyond it (Roy, 2001).

The feeling constitutes the core of the transcendent experience as it goes much further than a simple presence to the object of the experience, and touches the very intimacy of the object. The object does not really belong to the person that encounters it. One has to 'yield to it with generosity, trust, fervor, and indeed love' (Roy, 2001, p. 6). Feeling is one of the ways of getting to know reality, especially when we cannot find words to describe it intellectually (Perrin, 2018).

Discovery or disclosure is an insight regarding something essential to one's life whose significance suddenly takes on extraordinary depth. One becomes aware of something confronting, engaging, or challenging. The presence of an unlimited reality is disclosed. It can be seen as life, light, love, or goodness. Regular religious and aesthetic experiences do not include such a sense of the infinite. The difference between them is not a matter of intensity but rather one of being opened up to the infinite, not necessarily overwhelming in nature, but certainly not unnoticed. Although people do not often find the fitting words to describe it, they indicate that 'they are aware of having been touched, moved, and grasped in a unique way, and of having discovered something highly significant' (Roy, 2001, p. 7).

The interpretation or awareness of the experience. People often struggle to find words to name their feelings and insights. Still, they want to understand what has happened and integrate this new content into the rest of their life experiences.

> Intuition yields to wonder, even questioning the truth or validity of what has taken place, and eventually assessing and even ratifying it. As time goes on and circumstances change, we may slowly modify our interpretation and see our transcendent experience in a new light.
>
> (Roy, 2001, p. 8)

The interpretation remains conditioned by the mental framework that people had before the experience. Naturally, to communicate experience, a person uses images, concepts, and words that are already known and thus they insert new experiences into their already existing worldview or spiritual tradition (Katz, 2020). Yet, they can also use an old mental frame in a creative fashion and even invent new expressions in order to account for their experience. The interpretation of spiritual experience can be conveyed by novel combinations of partly known and partly new symbols. It can include such expressions as prose, poetry, drama, painting, sculpture, architecture, ballet, music, oratorio, liturgical ritual, and many more. All of these help people to discover anew how the mystery that lies beyond their psychic life penetrates human consciousness as well as the collective unconscious (Roy, 2001; Perrin, 2018).

The fruits of the experience. New discoveries originating in spiritual experiences have the potential to bring about concrete changes in people's lives. The resulting fruit can be understood as the benefits obtained from the experience in terms of knowledge, wisdom, attitude, and motivation. It may even cause a profound transformation, a conversion, or a major shift in one's perception of the world. When regarded from the perspective of time, one can distinguish between a fruit that comes right after the experience, and a fruit that requires time to ripen (Roy, 2001).

Unconscious Dimension of Spiritual Experiences

The idea of unconscious spiritual experiences in psychological research is not new. James (1902/1990), followed by Carl Jung (1934/1981) and then by Frankl (1943/2000), brought this theme to academic attention. For Jung, the unconscious dimension of spirituality is experienced as something numinously powerful in the core of the human soul. This experience can only be mediated through archetypal figures (Tacey, 2013). For Frankl, we are always related to something that can be called the 'transcendental unconscious,' meaning that every human person is constantly in relationship with the Sacred (Jones, 2019). Not surprisingly, this relationship can remain unconscious. In this context, Frankl even proposes a concept of the 'unconscious God' (Frankl, 1943/2000), by which he means a God who stays permanently in intimate relationship with every human person no matter whether they are conscious of this fact or not. God remains 'unconscious' only from the human point of view (Okan & Ekşi, 2017).

> I do not argue with people who say they aren't spiritual, and I feel no need to convince anyone to think of themselves that way. What would be the point of that? But I do believe that, conscious of it or not, everyone is spiritual. People don't have to be conscious of oxygen to breathe, or believe in the unconscious to dream. [...] We're all free to regard or disregard the spiritual dimension of our lives. We're free to identify as spiritual or not. But, in my view, we have no choice about whether we are spiritual beings, any more than we do about whether we are physical, psychological, or social beings.
>
> (Jones, 2019, p. 38)

The psychoanalytic heritage embedded in contemporary psychodynamic therapy schools continues to develop ideas related to the unconscious aspect of spirituality (e.g., Loewald, 1978; Corbett, 2005; Rizutto, 2005), which shows that the concept can shed even more light on the nature of spiritual experiences. In fact, certain spiritual processes are unconscious, and it is possible to become aware of them. Clients who are naturally more introspective are usually more aware of spiritual processes that take place within them (Jastrzębski, 2021). We will return to this topic in Chapter 4.

Conclusions

It is almost impossible to talk about spirituality without mentioning spiritual experiences. And yet this remains a major challenge since there is a variety of ways in which world spiritual traditions but also particular individuals describe their spiritual experiences. It seems that we can find some common elements in all of these attempts to grapple with the unknown divine. Increasingly, our contemporaries seem to see the subtle spiritual dimension of simple moments in their everyday life and they highly cherish them. Only privileged friends can hear the stories of encountering the Sacred in their lives. Often, these stories are full of light and hope. Being able to acknowledge the possibility of such sacred encounters may be very beneficial for a counselor and the counseling process.

Discussion questions

1. What was surprising or new for you in this chapter?
2. Would you consider yourself to be a mystic in the broader sense?
3. Do you know someone who has been transformed by a kind of spiritual experience?
4. Do you think that you would be able to recognize that your client has just had an important spiritual experience in their life?

References

Burton, D. (2020). Religious experience in Buddhism. In P. Moser & C. Meister (Eds.), *The Cambridge companion to religious experience* (pp. 187–207). Cambridge University Press. https://doi.org/10.1017/9781108575119.013

Chen, Z., Hood, J., Yang, L., & Watson, P. J. (2011). Mystical experience among Tibetan Buddhists: The common core thesis revisited. *Journal for the Scientific Study of Religion, 50*(2), 328–338. https://doi.org/10.1111/j.1468-5906.2011.01570.x

Chittick, W. (2020). Religious experience in traditional Islam. In P. Moser & C. Meister (Eds.), *The Cambridge companion to religious experience* (pp. 134–156). Cambridge University Press. https://doi.org/10.1017/9781108575119.010

Corbett, L., & Stein, M. (2005). Contemporary Jungian approaches to spiritually oriented psychotherapy. In L. Sperry & E. P. Shafranske, (Eds.), *Spiritually oriented psychotherapy* (pp. 51–73). American Psychological Association.

Frankl, V. E. (1943/2000). *Man's search for ultimate meaning*. Basic Books.

Gunn R. K. (2020) Religious experience. In D.A. Leeming (Ed.), *Encyclopedia of psychology and religion*. Springer. https://doi.org/10.1007/978-3-030-24348-7_580

Hood, R. W., Hill, P. C., & Spilka, B. (2018). *The psychology of religion: An empirical approach* (5th ed.) Guilford Press.

Hood, R. W. Jr., & Chen, Z. (2013). Mystical, spiritual, and religious experiences. In R. F. Paloutzian & C. L. Park (Eds.), *Handbook of the psychology of religion and spirituality* (pp. 422–440). Guilford Press.

Huxley, A. (2004). *The perennial philosophy* (1st Perennial Classics ed.). Perennial Classics.

Idel, M., & McGinn, B. (1996). *Mystical union in Judaism, Christianity, and Islam: An ecumenical dialogue*. Continuum.

James, W. (1902/1990). *The varieties of religious experience*. Penguin.

James, W., & Marty, M. E. (2015). *The varieties of religious experience: A study in human nature*. Penguin Books.

Jastrzębski, A. K. (2021). Unconscious spirituality: Toward a contemporary conceptualization. *Journal of Religion and Health*. https://doi.org/10.1007/s10943-021-01320-8

Jones, R. H. (2021). Perennial philosophy and the history of mysticism. *Sophia*. https://doi.org/10.1007/s11841-021-00847-3

Jones, R. S. (2019). *Spirit in session: Working with your client's spirituality (and your own) in psychotherapy*. Templeton Press.

Jung, C. G. (1934/1981). The archetypes and the collective unconscious. In *Collected Works* (Vol. 9). Bollingen.

Katz, S. (2020). Exploring the nature of mystical experience. In P. Moser & C. Meister (Eds.), *The Cambridge companion to religious experience* (pp. 239–260). Cambridge University Press. https://doi.org/10.1017/9781108575119.016

Klimek, D. (2018). *Medjugorje and the supernatural: Science, mysticism, and extraordinary religious experience*. Oxford University Press. https://doi.org/10.1093/oso/9780190679200.001.0001

Komarovski, Y. (2015). *Tibetan Buddhism and mystical experience*. Oxford University Press.

Loewald, H. (1978). *Psychoanalysis and the history of the individual*. Yale University Press.

May, G. G. (1987). *Will and spirit: A contemplative psychology*. HarperCollins.

May, G. G. (1992). *Care of mind-care of spirit: Psychiatric Dimensions of Spiritual Direction*. Harper & Row.

Miller, W. R., & Bacag, C. J. (2001). *Quantum change: When epiphanies and sudden insight transform ordinary lives*. Guilford Press.

Okan, N., & Ekşi, H. (2017). Spirituality in logotherapy. *Spiritual Psychology and Counseling*, *2*, 143–164.

Perrin, D. B. (2007). *Studying Christian spirituality*. Routledge. https://doi.org/10.4324/9780203944776

Poulain, A. (1950). *The graces of interior prayer*. Routledge and Kegan Paul.

Rizzuto, A.-M. (2005). Psychoanalytic considerations about spiritually oriented psychotherapy. In L. Sperry & E. P. Shafranske (Eds.), *Spiritually oriented psychotherapy* (pp. 31–50). American Psychological Association.

Roy, L. (2001). *Transcendent experiences: Phenomenology and critique*. University of Toronto Press.

Tacey, D. (2013). *The darkening spirit: Jung, spirituality, religion*. Routledge.

Taves, A. (2020). Psychology of religion approaches to the study of religious experience. In P. Moser & C. Meister (Eds.), *The Cambridge companion to religious experience* (pp. 25–54). Cambridge University Press. https://doi.org/10.1017/9781108575119.004

Underhill, E. (1911/2009). *Mysticism: A study of the nature and development of man's spiritual consciousness*. Evinity.

Wilber, K. (2008). *The pocket Ken Wilber*. Shambhala.

Yaden, D. B., Haidt, J., Hood, R. W., Vago, D. R., & Newberg, A. B. (2017). The varieties of self-transcendent experience. *Review of General Psychology*, *21*(2), 143–160. https://doi.org/10.1037/gpr0000102

Young, J. S., & Cashwell, C. S. (2011). *Integrating spirituality and religion into counseling: An introduction*. In C. S. Cashwell & J. S. Young (Eds.), *Integrating spirituality and religion into counseling: A guide to competent practice* (pp. 1–24). American Counseling Association.

4 How to Understand Spiritual Development and Growth

Introduction

Human spiritual existence is characterized by continual change, continuous streams of consciousness, and all states of consciousness are combined within it. The present moment is the consequence of all the previous ones, but it is capable of acquiring a whole new quality. For a conscious being, existence means change, change as becoming, and becoming as evolving oneself. Nonetheless, it must be remembered that the human being is not endowed with the capacity for absolute self-creation. In a theistic perspective, spiritual development is to be carried out in cooperation with divine grace (Jastrzębski, 2019). From a psychological perspective we know that any growth is limited by genetic, social, and personality factors.

Spiritual and human growth do not occur in a linear way and we clearly perceive their interruptions. In some spontaneous and naive visions of human development, they are seen as a continuous progression without setbacks, pitfalls, or dead ends. In reality, spiritual growth is more complex. People have both fruitful and adverse times in their lives. They proceed forward nicely for a while, but then sometimes have to return to a point where they had already been. This movement can be linear, as evoked by the expression 'One step forward, two steps back,' and sometimes it seems that we are 'going around in circles.' But we believe that our growth continues and even though we seem to return to the same places, knowingly or not, transformation is taking place. Thus, the most appropriate geometric picture of spiritual development is probably a spiral (e.g., Nelson, 2009). Although we revisit some places and have to face similar problems or challenges, they are not exactly the same, because we are now further along the path of growth.

The journey of counseling often initiates some form of spiritual development. In the context of spiritually oriented counseling, this should not come as surprise. Although it is not the counselor's role to guide their clients on the path of spiritual development, they can still create conditions to make this area of growth possible, and encourage their clients to proceed with this journey. From the very beginning, one has to be aware that spiritual

DOI: 10.4324/9781003262145-5

development is not always pleasant. All spiritual traditions advise people to find a proper guide for this journey. Taking this into account, it would be good for counselors to have proven referral resources for those clients who want to focus specifically on their spiritual journey (Stewart-Sicking et al., 2020).

When it comes to spiritual experiences, 'staging' can describe rather accurately different dimensions or styles of growth, faith, or love; however, because of its hierarchical approach, it may, contrary to the realities of life and love, imply a steady progression. For example, the most narcissistic child can experience moments of filial or agapic love, and the most saintly and wise old sage can be derailed by sudden erotic passion or selfish indulgence. Although some extensively researched models of psychological maturation, such as those of Erik Erikson and Sigmund Freud, which precisely describe the experience of some people, they are not sufficient to deal with those individuals who do not fit into their models. However carefully we apply staging to love and spiritual growth, this approach has important limitations and the end result is far from accurate. It is vital to recognize that these stages are simply illustrative aspects of spirituality and not phases that one must live through in sequence (May, 1987).

Many psychoanalysts prefer the development of a personal form of spirituality, something like an individually defined mysticism devoid of rite, structure, and religious authority, while strongly criticizing all forms of fundamentalism, dogmatism, or primitivism present in religion (Blass, 2006). Among psychoanalysts, there is a prevailing conviction that religious ways of thinking provide a way to escape the conflicts of life. This argument is that specific states of consciousness (e.g., prayer) are used as a way of circumventing conflicts and that this can result in serious negative consequences for the person, including a psychic breakdown in early adulthood. This mechanism often applies to people who unilaterally try to work through successive stages of spiritual development (Black, 2006).

Frankl (1976) divides spiritual development into two phases using a metaphor. The first is a psychophysical maturing aimed at preparing the instrument (the piano) that will then be used by the spiritual person (the pianist). Frankl does not specify exactly when the process is deemed to be complete. The second step is the development of a personality, that is, becoming oneself. One's development is based on one's potentialities and happens through spiritual growth. This process is never-ending and is only interrupted by death, for the human person never just 'is,' but lives as always 'becoming.' Frankl (1976) also emphasizes our moral development. We cannot ever say that the person simply 'is not,' because from the standpoint of metaphysics, Frankl (1976) holds that spiritual existence is the consistent and durable basis of our development. We can only say that a spiritual person is increasingly revealed through the psyche and the body, and healthy human development requires a harmonious balance between self-preservation and the ability to self-transcend by giving and receiving (Jastrzębski, 2019).

Spiritual Development in Western Theology and Mysticism

From the Christian point of view, spiritual development leads to a greater love of self, of others, and of God. The fruits of spiritual growth are also seen in one's ability to manage difficult emotions as well as to live with passion and purpose (Cloud & Townsend, 2001; Benner, 2015). There has been a long tradition of conceptualizing human and spiritual development in Christianity. These conceptualizations are not so much academic theories as they are a recording of life experiences of men and women who have succeeded on their journeys toward holiness. This process is not solely dependent on their personal merits, but is woven into the collective journey of other individuals who are also transformed by God. The understanding of spiritual development in the Christian tradition must also be linked with the tradition of mysticism and the practice of asceticism. In fact, mysticism has often been viewed as an advanced state of spiritual growth marked by a greater degree of human development as well as holiness or perfection. It is often accompanied by ecstatic or extraordinary experiences. Yet many people have had such experiences in their everyday lives while struggling with the ordinary hardships of life. Even children have been reported having mystical experiences (Perrin, 2007).

The traditional model of spiritual development in the Christian life comprises three elements: the purgative way, the illuminative way, and the unitive way. Although they are often presented in a linear fashion, they can also be conceptualized as the cyclical movements of God's grace in human life so that even those considered advanced on the spiritual journey may experience the purgative stage at different moments in life. The first purgative step can begin when people come to a realization that there is something more to be achieved by moving beyond the current state of their lives. Entering into the illuminative stage is characterized by a passage from discursive prayer and active self-discipline or self-preoccupation into contemplation and self-control sustained by an active love of others, the world, and God. This spontaneous, self-giving love is characteristic of the illuminative way. The unitive stage completes the process of spiritual transformation. At this stage, all aspects of one's life have been directed toward the love of God (Perrin, 2007).

In the context of spiritual development, the concept of the dark night of the senses and of the soul needs to be mentioned (Coe, 2000). It stems from the writings of John of the Cross (2005, 2008), a Spanish poet, Roman Catholic mystic, and a Carmelite priest in the sixteenth century. He maintained that the dark night was a necessary part of the purification process for anyone desiring to grow closer to God. He described this purification as drawing our spirit away from non-important things in order to make way for a new contemplative sensibility. During the dark night, the person experiences suffering because of their fully emerging longing for

God (Madden, 2020), as well as a fundamental reorientation of their personality structure (Perrin, 2007). This first dark night, the night of the senses, has two stages: active and passive. The active stage should purify the person from the lowest forms of pleasure, attachments, and unhealthy desires. The passive stage means being deprived of all sensual consolations. Both are part of the purification process. The dark night of the soul, in both its active and passive forms, leads directly to spiritual transformation (Saint John of the Cross, 2008). We will return to this topic in Chapter 8 when we discuss the healthy signs of spirituality. Another model of spiritual development using the depiction of seven spiritual mansions was developed by Saint Teresa of Avila (Ashbrook, 2019).

Psychological Models of Spiritual Development

Fowler's Faith Stages

James W. Fowler (1981) developed a theory that describes seven developmental stages related to an individual's relationship with the Sacred. His theory originates in Erikson's epigenetic principle, Lawrence Kohlberg's theory of moral development, as well as Piagetian structuralism, indicating that faith is organized as a dynamic system that undergoes development. Since development implies an increase in complexity on the one hand and simplification on the other, the progression of faith stages builds on prior foundations, leading to qualitative changes as these stages progress. Far from being a linear path, faith development is the product of a constant interaction between an individual and society, from birth until the end of life, and its stages should be understood as guides, rather than fixed entities (Seel, 2012; Streib & Keller, 2018; Hart, 2020).

Fowler (1981) proposes the following stages: (0) *Primal/Undifferentiated* faith, from birth to two years. This stage relates to an undifferentiated relationship with the primary caregiver and a trusting attachment to this person. (1) *Intuitive-Projective* faith, from three to seven years, characterized by an incapacity to distinguish between subjectivity and objectivity. At this stage imaginations and reality remain intermingled. (2) *Mythic-Literal* faith, from seven to twelve years, where myths and stories are understood literally. Moral judgment based on a system of divine reward and punishment is common at this stage. (3) *Synthetic-Conventional* faith, which usually develops during adolescence. Here, a deeper value is put on authentic friendships that give individuals their identity. The individual conforms to the group. (4) *Individuative-Reflective* faith appears from the mid-20s to the late 30s. At this stage the focus is put on the independence of self. Contrary to the previous stage, individuation and self-definition are valued. (5) *Conjunctive* faith, midlife. At this stage, people tend to pay more attention to their subjective experiences and their capacity for individual choice, especially in the face of life transitions and uncertainty. (6) *Universal* faith, a rare phase equal to spiritual enlightenment, characterized by the experience of being one with the universe.

Fowler's model demonstrates how spiritual development goes from simple-mindedness to final simplicity, although through intermediate stages of complexity (Levenson et al., 2013). This model was originally formulated to explain how people find meaning in daily experience in relation to their personal beliefs (Streib & Keller, 2018). It was supposed to be as inclusive as possible. One study measured stages of faith development that compared different cultures using the Faith Development Scale. This scale gives the highest score to personal spirituality as opposed to a spirituality based on the religious conformity required by very orthodox communities. (This study did not report differences between countries.) The conclusion is that cultural ideology may greatly influence a person's faith style, resulting in either a personal spirituality or one that ensues from collectivism (Ashdown & Gibbons, 2012).

Genia's Model of Spiritual Growth

Vicky Genia (1990) proposed a spiritual development model built on both psychoanalytic developmental psychology and object relations theory, combining hers with existing models of moral, cognitive, and psychosocial development. It is a more theoretical than empirical model (Foster & Holden, 2011).

According to Genia (1990), there are five stages of spiritual development. The first stage is equivalent to an egocentric faith based on need, satisfaction, and dichotomist thinking opting for either 'all good' or 'all bad.' People who are stuck at this stage mistrust themselves, others, and the divine. They also tend to reexperience past interpersonal wounds within the dynamics of their spirituality (Genia, 1990, 1995).

The second stage is dogmatic faith, which produces a fixation on the rules and laws of behavior and on our relationship with the divine. Here, people are looking for absolute right and wrong in their respective spiritual texts. They never question any spiritual authority and are very sensitive to external judgments. The third stage represents a transitional time of faith when people begin to question their preexisting belief systems and to actively analyze their cultural or spiritual identity. This can also be a time of spiritual experimentation with new beliefs and practices. The fourth stage is a time of reconstructed faith, meaning a commitment to a chosen spiritual tradition; this occurs once people have processed and integrated the spiritual experiences from the third stage. At this point, it is possible to find personal meaning and purpose. As well, people become capable of contextualizing the spiritual commandments of their traditions (Genia, 1990).

Finally, the fifth stage leads to a transcendent faith, when people are able to adjust to different and new situations. They demonstrate a mature spiritual outlook and behave in a way that is consistent with their spiritual convictions. This stage is also characterized by a deep concern about universal human struggles and by actions taken to make this world a better place for everyone. Unfortunately, most individuals do not reach transcendent faith (Genia, 1990).

Mabry's Faith Styles

Another model pertaining to how people believe has been proposed by John Mabry (2006), a spiritual director who examined the different ways people relate to the Sacred across religions. His model is composed of six poles, none of which have a privileged position (Figure 4.1). These are simply the ways people believe. One can start at any pole of the model. We begin with *Traditional Believers*, who identify themselves as members of a concrete religious tradition. Going clockwise, we have *Liberal Believers*, who are marked by authenticity and generosity, followed by *Spiritual Eclectics*, who choose elements from various spiritual traditions. *Religious Agnostics* cherish their personal experience and wisdom; *Ethical Humanists* regard life itself as a sacred domain that requires compassionate action; and finally *Jack Believers* are estranged from religion and have a negative view of faith. According to the author of this model, people change their faith styles according to the rule of proximity. For instance, *Liberal Believers*, because they are placed between *Traditional Believers* and *Spiritual Eclectics*, can take either direction in their spiritual development, becoming more traditional or eclectic in

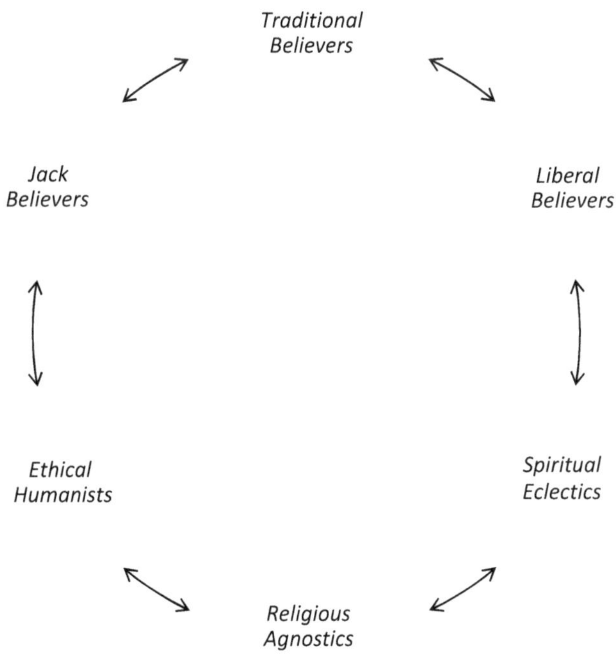

Figure 4.1 Mabry's faith styles.

their faith. It is very unlikely that people skip over either of the stages that are closest to them on the above diagram (Mabry, 2006). The same author has also presented another interesting theory regarding the characteristics of spirituality and beliefs in various generations of peoples such as builders, baby boomers, millennials, and others (Mabry, 2013).

While this theory describes the different ways people believe depending on their culture and includes dimensions of agnosticism and atheism, it does not have a clear operationalization. Its nature is circular and does not privilege any position in particular. This conceptualization can potentially help understand clients in the psychotherapeutic setting, but, unfortunately, has not yet been adapted into a method for psychological research. Nonetheless, in both of his models, Mabry (2006, 2013) analyzes possible outcomes and challenges for the work of the therapist and client representing a given faith style or generation, as well as imagining their work together. This can be of great practical benefit to counselors wanting to integrate spirituality into counseling.

Spiritual Grounding

At some point, all spiritual exploration encounters need to become grounded in a particular tradition. May (1987) calls it the need of location (p. 320) and differentiates it from the need of identification, which may cause a blind allegiance to that tradition. Spiritual location has the potential to help people grow in a more secure and historically tested way. In the course of spiritual development, there also comes a time when we need external support in order to venture further into our spiritual quest for the Source of Being and to venture further into our spiritual quest. In order to achieve this, we need certain valid means to help us move forward, as well as kind, constructive criticism to keep us grounded in reality. This sometimes involves joining an established tradition after years of an autonomous, personal struggle. It can also mean returning to the client's own spiritual tradition after years of wandering and searching. Although it is possible to yearn for the Source of Being in their own heart, going about this without adequate support makes it easier to overlook or ignore certain traits of its essence. For example, in Christianity, the person is called to *koinōnia*: shared spiritual communion, fellowship, and service. These are key aspects of the Christian life, as well as a reminder that our journey benefits from being shared with others. In this context, all spiritual traditions can be helpful as they propose certain spiritual paths that have stood the test of time (May, 1987).

In many spiritual traditions, genuine spiritual wisdom is often obscured by distortions or oversimplifications. Joining a spiritual tradition or confession simply out of the felt need to belong somewhere, or to attain some form of personal identification may cause one to form a blind allegiance to that tradition. Rather than self-surrender, this can serve self-definition and result in increased separation from others. On the contrary, accepting the mysterious divine is part of true surrender. Any pathway undertaken with the aim of relating to God, however genuine and sincere, will always remain incomplete. These paths are only momentary windows giving us partial access to the divine mystery. Paradoxically, accepting this tenet provides us with the most pertinent insights into divine reality, which can never be objectified or limited (May, 1987).

The Search for the Sacred: Pargament's Model

Kenneth Pargament (2007) developed a very useful model for counselors who want to integrate spirituality into their clinical work. The advantage of this model is that it illustrates not only 'eternal progress' but also the kinds of traps and setbacks that can occur during an individual's spiritual quest. According to Pargament (2007), the beginning of a spiritual journey is the discovery of something sacred. The possibility of discovering the Sacred in our life is based on the assumption that we are striving beings. We shall return to this concept shortly. After discovering the sacred domain of their lives, people usually begin to look for more information or formation regarding what they have just discovered and placed in the center of their being. This stage Pargament (2007) calls 'holding onto the sacred' (p. 77) or conservation. This is usually a period of calm in which a person is content to develop new spiritual practices and to gain new knowledge.

But life is not easy, and after the period of conservation there comes what Pargament (2007) calls 'violation, threat, and loss of the sacred' (p. 94). The many challenges of life lead to important questions about the meaning of suffering, injustice, and tragedies, to name but a few examples. These demand satisfactory answers. When people are able to find these answers in their spiritual traditions, we say that successful spiritual coping has taken place and they are back to the conservational stage. But when this coping is unsuccessful, we talk about spiritual loss that leads to a stage of spiritual struggle. The fruit of spiritual struggle can be either deep spiritual transformation or spiritual disengagement. In the latter case, the individual abandons the spiritual path that they had initially chosen. However, after spiritual disengagement people can begin their spiritual search anew (Pargament, 2007).

The strength of Pargament's model lies in its dynamism, which illustrates many possible scenarios of spiritual development and helps to conceptualize clients' most challenging moments and thus to assist them in their most difficult situations.

Author's Addition to Pargament's model

At the beginning of his proposal, Pargament (2007) mentions that humans are striving beings. In this context we can talk about an unconscious spirituality (Jastrzębski, 2021). From a theological or ontological perspective, we can say that every human is a created being that remains in constant relationship with the Creator (*homo capax Dei*) whether or not they are aware. From the existential or phenomenological perspective, every human being is intrinsically capable of becoming aware of this relationship. Paraphrasing St. Augustine,[1] we can say that we will always lack something because we were created in such a way that we cannot be fulfilled apart from the divine. The question now is what happens in a person before they reach the phase of discovery in the Pargament's model?

Some spiritual processes are preconscious. At times, one can recall them. Other spiritual processes are unconscious and accessing them is far more difficult. Naturally, more introspective individuals usually become spontaneously aware of spiritual processes as they occur. Similarly to other psychic content, spirituality can be repressed or stifled. Unfortunately, denying spirituality can prevent one from discovering meaning to life (May, 1987). So how would spiritual processes find their way into consciousness?

William James states that this unconscious spirituality may either be well developed and 'habitually ripen in silence' (1902/1990, p. 184) or barely present. When there is a shift from an unconscious to a preconscious spiritual experience, this is always accompanied by a sense of marvel. We can link this with Abraham Maslow's peak experiences or Karl Jaspers's limit situations. Whatever the case, preconscious experiences seldom leave the individual without a major mental energy shift (James, 1902/1990).

Frankl (2000) is convinced that the human being has both an instinctual unconscious and a spiritual one and that the true spiritual–existential personality is always unconscious in its depths. He states: 'Thus the center of the human person in his very depth is unconscious. In its origin, the human spirit is unconscious spirit' (p. 37).

We can easily imagine that people only get as far as a preconscious spiritual awakening that soon returns into oblivion, leaving only an undefined spiritual thirst in its wake. When spiritual energy reveals itself fully to the conscious mind, we can talk about a discovery. Sometimes spiritual disengagement may result in a return to the unconscious spiritual stage, which allows a new discovery to emerge. Unconscious does not mean that the person is disconnected from their sacred core, but that they do not perceive this connection. This is a dynamic process that can be presented in a graphic way (Figure 4.2). The last stage mentioned by many authors is a full

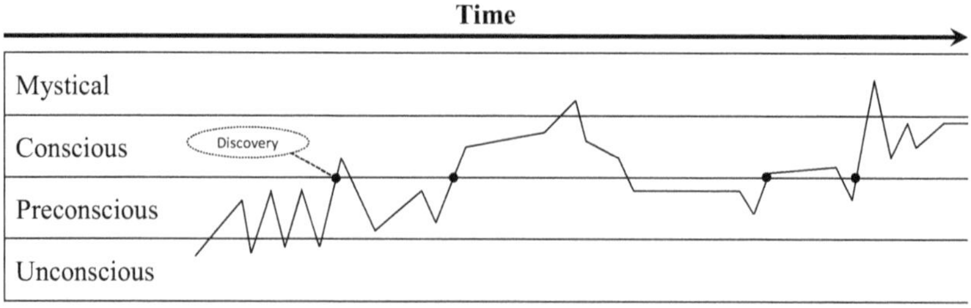

Figure 4.2 Unconscious part of spiritual development.

awakening or the emergence of deep-seated spiritual consciousness (mystical experience).

Development of Spiritual Identity

Joseph Stewart-Sicking and colleagues (2020) present a four-stage process of achieving one's spiritual identity: diffusion, foreclosure, moratorium, and achievement. In the first stage, diffusion, we find individuals who have not been educated in any specific spiritual tradition or faith community. They are simply not interested in spiritual issues, although they may be sensitive to a certain spiritual dimension of their lives. The second stage, foreclosed identity, denotes people who are happy with their spirituality and their faith community and do not want to be challenged to change anything in their status quo. In Pargament's (2007) terms, they prefer to conserve their status. In Mabry's (2006) terms, they are traditional believers and in Fowler's (1981) this represents synthetic-conventional faith. Unfortunately, the extreme form of the foreclosed identity can lead to fundamentalism and stigmatization of outsiders. Foreclosed counselors should be very attentive not to impose preconceived orthodox structures upon their clients when they belong to the same faith community (Stewart-Sicking et al., 2020).

The third stage, identity moratorium, is a moment of crisis when one allows one's spiritual identity to be challenged. Pargament (2007) calls it a threat and possible loss of the Sacred; for Mabry (2006) this stage is characteristic of religious agnostics, and for Fowler (1981) it is called individuative-reflective faith. At this stage, there is much confusion and searching for answers as the person courageously embraces doubt, and explores different possibilities. No final decision is taken regarding one's spiritual commitment. The last stage, achievement, is the fruit of a long and honest process of questioning oneself that concludes with a newly achieved identity, in which one affirms certain elements of one's spirituality but rejects others. The authors of this model add that there is also the possibility of multiple identities emerging. Mabry (2006) calls these individuals spiritual eclectics. This happens for instance in the case of children of interfaith marriages, whose primary identity is rooted in one spiritual tradition, but who are enriched by the second one (Stewart-Sicking et al., 2020).

Spirituality of Different Age Groups

Research on spiritual development has also focused on specific age groups: children, adolescents, adults, and seniors.

The research regarding the spirituality of children focuses on their cognitive–developmental framework, family dynamics, parent–child interactions, and children's well-being (Roehlkepartain et al., 2006), as well as children's styles of attachment in view of their relationships with religious figures (Richert & Granqvist, 2013). Among them, the most studied topic is the child's concept of God within Western monotheistic cultures. Research shows that their images of God are anthropomorphic. Another studied topic is the child's understanding of prayer and death. In this context one presumes that parents shape their children's values and beliefs (Boyatzis, 2013).

Research regarding the spirituality of adolescents focuses on their growing sense of self and on an ongoing search to find their place in the world. Spiritual traditions can help youth to discover their identity by offering them appropriate resources in their quest for ultimate meaning. Apart from that, spirituality can serve as a protection, potentially buffering young people against health-compromising behaviors or practices. Normally, emerging adults explore their spiritual traditions and identities through a process of questioning previously undisputable worldviews and self-concepts, as described earlier in the model of spiritual identities (Stewart-Sicking et al., 2020). This period of sharp critical thinking is an essential marker of the emerging adult's spiritual development. In this context, it is crucial that these young adults find a supportive spiritual milieu that can effectively foster their quest for a noble purpose in life as well as a sense of belonging (King et al., 2013). During this period of time, many adolescents shift from being traditionally religious toward more universal expressions of spirituality (Levenson et al., 2013).

It is commonly assumed that because elderly people are closer to death, they should have greater feelings of death anxiety and therefore look for more spiritual consolation. Studies using retrospective data show that the narratives of older participants demonstrate increasing religiosity over time. This does not necessary correlate with an increasing participation in a faith community (Dein et al., 2012). Moreover, research suggests that both problems in their faith community as well as their personal spiritual struggles may influence the health and well-being of elderly persons. It is still not empirically proven that people turn to spirituality as they grow older. Therefore, studies will need to be oriented toward discovering all the variables that contribute to this question (Krause, 2013). Faith-inspired resilience is also another popular research topic in this age group (McFadden, 2013).

Spiritual Breaking Free

Normally, spiritual development is accompanied by a gradual lessening of our attachment to various desires and addictions. Before gaining a degree of spiritual maturity, we may perceive that nearly all our motivations come from some form of attachment, or that we are simply led by the desire to gain pleasure and avoid pain, to ensure security and success, and, finally, by a concerted effort to avoid loss of control. One of the earliest indications of spiritual growth is that these sources of motivation begin to lose their attractiveness, and this can cause real consternation. Often, the first manifestation of this process is the appearance of a mild form of sadness, which begins to color one's overall attitude. Usually, it does not develop to such a degree as to be called depression, since one continues to function relatively well. During this period, laughter may not come as easily and quiet self-reflection as well as feelings of uncertainty may appear. This is caused by a subtle, underlying grief process. One becomes aware that certain things that used to be vitally important such as financial success or accomplishment become less meaningful than before. Also, favorite hobbies and recreational activities may lose their usual attractiveness. This is not to say that such activities totally disappear, but they just become less important and take up less and less time and energy (May, 1992).

All of this represents a certain loss. We do not lose the things themselves, but our investment in them is significantly diminished. Nonetheless, our feeling of loss is very real, and at some level has to be mourned. Furthermore, this mourning is not typically mitigated by the positive changes that have taken place, for example newfound freedom and a liberating capacity to love. This is often a short-lived period since attachments keep recurring as the journey continues. Moreover, certain previously unconscious attachments come more clearly into awareness as the more superficial ones are dealt with. These deeper and more serious attachments are often so troublesome that they leave only a limited time to mourn the loss of the others (May, 1992).

Models of Linking Psychological and Spiritual Development

Several possibilities exist that relate human development at the psychological and spiritual levels. Benito Goya (2001), working from the Christian perspective, divides them into three categories.

(1) ***Parallelism*** assumes a fundamental correlation between the processes of mental development and spiritual progress, making the second a form of the first. Human maturity would be a necessary condition for the development of holiness.
(2) ***Contrast*** implies that an overabundance of mental well-being may result in the conviction of our own self-sufficiency and lead to spiritual pride. However, God finds delight in the poor of heart and the powerless, God's power shining most brightly through the strength and courage of the martyrs. At times, God's wonders can more easily be seen through more fragile personalities, the weakened, the ailing, and the humble. Here, the emphasis is put on the exceptional manifestations of God's grace.
(3) ***Coexistence*** assumes that God's grace and human freedom have to encounter each other and work together. Some moments of conflict cannot be avoided; certain shortcomings in mental maturity may coexist with a sincere commitment to spiritual growth and the effort of opening our self up to the actions of the Holy Spirit.

Religious development is accompanied by a choice of moral attitudes. In the beginning, these choices are dictated by the fear of God's punishment. Over time, this is replaced by a desire to please God and, finally, to choose God as the ultimate value, around whom our whole life begins to revolve (Goya, 2001; Pisón, 2018).

Conclusions

To be human is to grow. For many, human and spiritual growth should go hand in hand. And yet at times spiritual growth seems to thrive on psychological challenges. The diagnosis of a psychological problem does not necessarily mean that it must be resolved before progress in the spiritual life is possible. There always will be numerous questions and phenomena in our psyche that require attention and psychological work. But for the most part their importance for spiritual growth is relative. We risk wasting time if we focus too much on our personal psychology in order to prepare ourselves for a better life. Unfortunately, such endeavors can end up taking the place of spiritual life. In fact, an exaggerated self-preoccupation makes our spiritual search and growth almost impossible as it encourages a never-ending journey of self-perfection (May, 1992).

Discussion Questions

1. Do you think that people are always concerned with their human and spiritual development?
2. What model of spiritual growth do you find the most helpful? Explain why.
3. Which moments of spiritual development are most crucial for the counseling process?
4. Are you personally comfortable in engaging in a client's exploration of their self-identified spiritual experiences? Why or why not?

Note

1 *Confessiones*, I 1: 'You have made us for yourself, O Lord, and our hearts are restless until they rest in you.'

References

Ashbrook, R. T. (2019). *Mansions of the heart: Exploring the seven stages of spiritual growth*. Fortress Press.

Ashdown, B. K., & Gibbons, J. L. (2012). Faith development and collectivism among emerging adults in Guatemala and the United States. *Advances in Psychology Study*, *1*, 22–28.

Benner, D. G. (2015). *The gift of being yourself: The sacred call to self-discovery*. InterVarsity Press.

Black, D. M. (2006). The case for a contemplative position. In D. M. Black (Ed.), *Psychoanalysis and religion in the 21st century: Competitors or collaborators* (pp. 63–79). Routledge.

Blass, R. B. (2006). Beyond illusion: Psychoanalysis and the question of religious truth. In D. M. Black (Ed.), *Psychoanalysis and religion in the 21st century: Competitors or collaborators* (pp. 23–43). Routledge.

Boyatzis, C. J. (2013). The nature and functions of religion and spirituality in children. In K. I. Pargament & J. W. Jones (Eds.), *APA handbook of psychology, religion, and spirituality* (Vol. 1: *Context, theory, and research*, pp. 497–512). American Psychological Association. https://doi.org/10.1037/14045-027

Cloud, H., & Townsend, J. (2001). *How people grow: What the Bible reveals about personal growth*. Zondervan.

Coe, J. H. (2000). Musings on the dark night of the soul: Insights from St. John of the Cross on a developmental spirituality. *Journal of Psychology and Theology, 28*(4), 293–307. https://doi.org/10.1177/009164710002800408

Dein, S., Cook, C., & Koenig, H. (2012). Religion, spirituality, and mental health: Current controversies and future directions. *Journal of Nervous & Mental Disease, 200*, 852–855. https://doi.org/10.1097/NMD.0b013e31826b6dle

Foster, R. D., & Holden, J. M. (2011). Human and spiritual development and transformation. In C. S. Cashwell & J. S. Young (Eds.), *Integrating spirituality and religion into counseling: A guide to competent practice* (pp. 97–118). American Counseling Association.

Fowler, J. W. (1981). *Stages of faith. The psychology of human development and the quest for meaning*. Harper & Row.

Frankl, V. E. (1976). *Homo patiens*. PAX.

Frankl, V. E. (2000). *Man's search for ultimate meaning*. Basic Books.

Genia, V. (1990). Religious development: A synthesis and reformulation. *Journal of Religion and Health, 29*, 85–99.

Genia, V. (1995). *Counseling and psychotherapy of religious clients*. Praeger.

Goya, B. (2001). *Psicologia e vita spirituale. Sinfonia a due mani*, Edizioni Dehoniane.

Hart, C. W. (2020) Faith development theory. In D. A. Leeming (Ed.), *Encyclopedia of Psychology and Religion*. Springer. https://doi.org/10.1007/978-3-030-24348-7_229

James, W. (1902/1990). *The varieties of religious experience*. Penguin.

Jastrzębski, A. (2019). *Homo Theomorphicus et Theophoricus: A receptive-responsive theory of spirituality*. Peeters.

Jastrzębski, A. K. (2021). Unconscious spirituality: Toward a contemporary conceptualization. *Journal of Religion and Health*. https://doi.org/10.1007/s10943-021-01320-8

King, P. E., Ramos, J. S., & Clardy, C. E. (2013) Searching for the sacred: Religion, spirituality, and adolescent development. In K. I. Pargament, J. J. Exline, & J. W. Jones (Eds.), *APA handbook of psychology, religion, and spirituality* (Vol. 1: *Context, theory, and research*, pp. 513–528). American Psychological Association. https://doi.org/10.1037/14045-028

Krause, N. (2013). Religious involvement in the later years of life. In K. I. Pargament, J. J. Exline, & J. W. Jones (Eds.), *APA handbook of psychology, religion, and spirituality* (Vol. 1: *Context, theory, and research*, pp. 529–545). American Psychological Association. https://doi.org/10.1037/14045-029

Levenson, M. R., Aldwin, C. M., & Igarashi, H. (2013). Religious development from adolescence to middle adulthood. In R. F. Paloutzian & C. L. Park (Eds.), *Handbook of the psychology of religion and spirituality* (pp. 183–197). Guilford Press.

Mabry, J. R. (2006). *Faith styles: The way people believe*. Morehouse Publications.

Mabry, J. R. (2013). *Faithful generations: Effective ministry across generational lines*. Morehouse.

Madden K. (2020). Dark night of the soul. In D. A. Leeming (Ed.), *Encyclopedia of Psychology and Religion*. Springer. https://doi.org/10.1007/978-3-030-24348-7_153
May, G. G. (1987). *Will and spirit. A contemplative psychology*. HarperCollins.
May, G. G. (1992). *Care of mind/care of spirit: Psychiatric dimensions of spiritual direction*. Harper & Row.
McFadden, S. H. (2013). Old persons, old age, aging, and religion. In R. F. Paloutzian & C. L. Park (Eds.), *Handbook of the psychology of religion and spirituality* (pp. 198–214). Guilford Press.
Nelson, J. M. (2009). *Psychology, religion, and spirituality*. Springer Science + Business Media. https://doi.org/10.1007/978-0-387-87573-6
Pargament, K. I. (2007). *Spiritually integrated psychotherapy: Understanding and addressing the sacred*. Guilford Press.
Perrin, D. B. (2007). *Studying Christian spirituality*. Routledge. https://doi.org/10.4324/9780203944776
Pisón, R. (2018). Stages of moral (human) development and images of God. *Roczniki Teologiczne, 65*, 157–172. https://doi.org/10.18290/rt.2018.65.5-11.
Richert, R. A., & Granqvist, P. (2013). Religious and spiritual development in childhood. In R. F. Paloutzian & C. L. Park (Eds.), *Handbook of the psychology of religion and spirituality* (pp. 165–182). Guilford Press.
Roehlkepartain, E. C., Benson, P. L., King, P. E., & Wagener, L. (2006). Spiritual development in childhood and adolescence: Moving to the scientific mainstream. In E. C. Roehlkepartain, P. E. King, L. Wagener, & P. L. Benson (Eds.), *The handbook of spiritual development in childhood and adolescence* (pp. 1–15). SAGE.
Saint John of the Cross. (2005). *The dark night of the soul* (E. A. Peers, Ed.). Doubleday-Image Books.
Saint John of the Cross. (2008). *Ascent of Mount Carmel* (E. A. Peers, Trans.). Wilder.
Seel, N. M. (2012) Fowler faith stages. In N. M. Seel (Ed.), *Encyclopedia of the sciences of learning*. Springer.
Stewart-Sicking, J., Fox, J., & Deal, P. (2020). *Bringing religion and spirituality into therapy: A process-based model for pluralistic practice*. Routledge.
Streib, H., & Keller, B. (2018). *Manual for the Assessment of Religious Styles in Faith Development Interviews* (Fourth, rev. ed. *of the Manual for Faith Development Research*). Center for Biographical Studies in Contemporary Religion. https://doi.org/10.4119/UNIBI/2920987

5 From Spiritual Direction to Spiritually Integrated Therapy

The History

Addressing spiritual issues in psychotherapy is relatively new, but without naming it as such, many spiritual teachers and leaders have been doing it for ages. For centuries, religious ministers provided pastoral care to believers interested in spiritual growth and who may have been searching for support to face personal problems. Some of these had been diagnosed with psychological issues while others lived with mental illness. Nowadays, pastoral care provided by members of the clergy is rooted in contemporary clinical and pastoral education (Stone, 1999).

In recent years, we have observed an increased need for individual spiritual guidance, especially in the Western world, where more and more people commit themselves to spiritual pilgrimages as well as to the pursuit of other spiritual paths, and reach out to the wisdom of an ancient spiritual master. At the beginning of the spiritual journey, many people need some form of concrete guidance. With this perspective in mind, we can easily see the role of a Buddhist master, a Hindu guru, a Hasidic rebbe, spiritual mothers and fathers of Eastern Orthodoxy, and spiritual directors of the Catholic tradition. A pastoral counselor is someone who is also on a spiritual journey themselves, without necessarily having completed it. It should also be noted that without being a 'master,' a friend, through compassion and honesty, can also help us move forward spiritually (May, 1987). Presently, there are multiple ways in which spirituality is being integrated into clinical work (Captari et al., 2021). Pastoral integration is a term that is used to describe the bringing together of both the psychological and the spiritual dimension of the client's life in order to provide them with a possibility of deeper insight and growth. Generally speaking, pastoral counseling refers to the attempt to facilitate this integration. In fact, this field is very broad and contains a wide array of perspectives and modalities (Piedmont & Wilkins, 2020).

Spiritually integrated/oriented psychotherapy is the newest of the three approaches, and originated in psychological theory and research, its primary goal being psychological change, while spiritual change or growth is seen as secondary (Pargament, 2007). In this context, clinical situations have been identified where spirituality becomes an important resource for coping with

DOI: 10.4324/9781003262145-6

serious problems and traumatic situations such as a crisis of faith as well as searching for a deeper meaning in life or simply pursuing an increase of well-being and spiritual growth (Sperry & Shafranske, 2005). Interestingly, more and more people prefer psychotherapists to religious ministers when they seek to foster their spiritual growth and development. An important distinction should be made between spiritually integrated/oriented psychotherapy and spiritual direction. In the first case, the emphasis is put on psychological growth and the resulting increase in autonomy and independence. Spiritual direction, on the other hand, encourages spiritual growth and acknowledges how much it is dependent on divine grace as received through other people (May, 1987).

Spiritually integrated/oriented therapy leads people to increase their awareness of how their beliefs and spiritual practices can provide opportunities to become more grounded, providing an avenue of healing. More concretely, prayer or meditation, church services, hiking in nature, and creative arts whether they be visual arts, literature, or performing arts, develop a person's connection with emotions and thoughts. Boosted by an awareness of the present moment and by the felt sense of their body, they gain access to their inner experiences and intuitions. Spiritual practices are also helpful in clarifying our values and lead to a more profound personal integrity as expressed in a value-driven life, which lead us to follow our inner-generated beliefs and moral compass. Spiritually integrated/oriented therapy helps people take greater ownership of their values and life choices, leading to a sense of congruence and integrity (Johnson, 2013).

People who desire therapy typically have similar concerns: they need to make sense out of their struggles or suffering. Although various approaches can address these issues, they differ in what they each emphasize. Pastoral counseling and spiritual direction primarily work toward spiritual change. Whereas spiritually integrated/oriented psychotherapy leans toward psychological change where people are helped to draw on spiritual resources in order to address psychological and relational problems, pastoral counselors and spiritual directors usually encourage people to draw directly from spiritual resources rooted in a particular spiritual tradition. Psychotherapists who do not venture into the area of spiritually integrated/oriented psychotherapy usually remain neutral toward any particular religious solution (Sperry, 2013).

Enlisting the help of a member of the clergy can be very beneficial in many given situations. They can provide an appropriate cultural background to help promote healing while introducing rituals specific to their faith community. Spiritual direction and counseling are similar in that they both are concerned with the process of human transformation. The big difference lies in their focal points, with the emphasis of spiritual direction being moral and spiritual development. Spiritual direction is more interested in the growth in holiness, whereas psychotherapy's goal is promoting health, meaning emotional well-being and resilience (Stewart-Sicking et al., 2020).

Spiritual Direction

Spiritual direction, also known as spiritual guidance or companionship, and sometimes soul friendship, finds its roots in the third century when it was practiced primarily by Christian monks and priests. Later, it thrived in all Christian traditions and was reflected in the writings of many well-known spiritual teachers. Among them, Ignatius of Loyola and Teresa of Avila are undoubtedly the most familiar (Perrin, 2007). Spiritual direction has been rediscovered in our times and has evolved so that it is now practiced in various spiritual traditions while still being primarily associated with the Catholic tradition. The primary goal of spiritual direction is to facilitate spiritual growth, though psychological change is also desirable (Jastrzębski, 2021).

Christian spiritual direction can be seen as the art of listening while keeping our focus on the interior movements produced by the work of the Holy Spirit within the client's life story (Perrin, 1998). It involves a director who accompanies persons called directees. It can sometimes take place in a group, but occurs most commonly within the context of an individual relationship. Its central theme is the spiritual discernment of the ultimate meaning of events and circumstances in our life in connection with God. The relationship in spiritual direction is based on the assumption that both are walking the same spiritual journey. Some say a moderate degree of psychological health and the relative absence of psychopathology are prerequisites for requesting and undertaking spiritual direction (Sperry, 2002, 2013; Moon, 2002).

The meetings with a spiritual director are scheduled on a regular basis, usually weekly or monthly, and continue for a year or longer. Throughout this process, a commitment to actively engage in a life of prayer is made by the directee. What distinguishes them, especially from crisis interventions, is that they are planned. The role of the spiritual director is to be an objective point of reference for person's spiritual experiences, offering their perspective on what the directee shares. This process takes time and for this reason continuity and regularity of these encounters are essential (Perrin, 2007).

All mainstream religious faiths are concerned with the spiritual growth of their members. Spiritual direction is intended to help people live a fulfilling and meaningful life within the context of their religious values while examining the role of the divine within their lives. Spiritual direction is characterized by the utilization of techniques and rituals identified by a particular tradition engaged in fostering spiritual growth. What distinguishes spiritual direction from a more integrative, psychotherapeutic approach is its goal. Whereas in spiritually integrated/oriented therapy, the goal is to help clients better respond to the psychosocial demands of their lives, in spiritual direction the goal is to define the directee's objective within their faith journey. It is understood that this entire process relies on the classical concept of grace since the directee is being led by God (Piedmont & Wilkins, 2020).

Sometimes spiritual directors may choose to refer directees with certain psychological problems to psychotherapists and will put the spiritual direction on hold until this alternative therapy is successfully completed (May, 1992). Mixing these two approaches can become confusing for the client (Piedmont & Wilkins, 2020) and, even for well-trained professionals, it remains a disputable course of action (May, 1992).

Pastoral Care and Pastoral Counseling

In the past, the terms 'pastoral care' and 'pastoral counseling' were often used interchangeably. Today, pastoral care refers to pastoral communication exercised through interpersonal relationships such as visiting the sick. It may involve the use of natural counseling skills by the caring person, but it does not involve full-fledged therapy as in pastoral counseling. It can be seen as a form of pre-counseling that takes place outside a formal counseling context. Pastoral counseling is a complex form of pastoral communication that must be requested by the individual seeking help. Formal sessions, times, and fees are involved as in the case of traditional psychotherapy, and for the most part, pastoral counseling is exercised by religious ministers with formal supervised training in the psychotherapeutic context. In pastoral counseling, a therapist's personal orientation toward the God of their understanding influences the process of engaging clients in a collaborative spiritual journey (Snodgrass, McCreight, & McFee, 2014). Compared to counselors who are not familiar with this kind of personal orientation, they are therefore less likely to pathologize some unusual spiritual experiences, such as hearing the voice of God (Maynard, 2017). Pastoral counseling may include a scriptural-based approach using sacred texts, for example, the Koran, Hebrew Bible, Christian Scriptures, or the Vedas and the Upanishads, where the therapist encourages believers to reexamine their religious beliefs as well as to involve themselves in particular rituals and activities (Piedmont & Wilkins, 2020).

Pastoral counselors should maintain a professional identity distinct from that of other therapists. Since the goal of pastoral counseling is spiritual growth, the counselor will focus on the client's spirituality, yet without neglecting the client's immediate psychological concerns. Generally speaking, pastoral counseling is an extension of the Judeo-Christian practice of soul care, which also promotes the emotional and spiritual well-being of the client (Maynard, 2017).

In the 1970s, the role of the clergy as pastoral counselors began to open up to include female counselors as well as people of many ethnicities and spiritual traditions, and laypersons, especially mental health professionals such as social workers and psychologists (Doehring, 2006). Although up to now the majority of pastoral counselors have come from a Christian background, their ranks have expanded to include a growing number of Jewish, Buddhist, and Muslim persons, as well as representatives of other spiritual traditions (Maynard, 2017). There are three forms of pastoral counseling: (a) brief situational single session counseling; (b) problem-solving counseling of two to five sessions; and (c) long-term counseling, called *pastoral psychotherapy*, often psychoanalytically oriented and focused on personality change (Montgomery, 2010).

Even if a therapist has expertise in both pastoral care and psychotherapy, there may be concerns about the development of a dual relationship, both pastoral as well as therapeutic. It is of crucial importance that therapists provide clear information regarding the proposed treatment and its nature including the procedures, obligations, and expectations regarding outcomes. Even if clients engage in a religion-based belief system, they may want to consult a therapist for psychosocial issues and address these specifically from a psychological perspective. Sometimes they may wish to include their beliefs in the therapeutic process, but at other times not. Clients also have the right to be assured that there will be no hidden religious agenda (Piedmont & Wilkins, 2020).

Spiritually Integrated/Oriented Psychotherapy

Spiritually integrated/oriented psychotherapy is a term that describes a variety of psychotherapeutic approaches which are sensitive to the spiritual dimension in human life. Michelle Pearce and colleagues (2019) propose to name it 'spiritually competent mental health care.' It is distinct from pastoral counseling and spiritual direction as it focuses treatment on psychological problems; although it draws from spiritual resources, it does so without restricting itself to any particular spiritual tradition. Here, spiritual interventions such as prayer and meditation are also practiced, and collaboration with or referral to clergy or a chaplain is encouraged (Sperry, 2001).

Spiritually integrated therapy intends to help people develop a coherent narrative of their spiritual journey, by way of gaining a deeper understanding of the events that have shaped their spiritual beliefs, values, practices, and identity. Our beliefs reflect themes that are part of our relational past. For instance, having an abusive parent will cause difficulty in developing a trusting relationship with the divine. Experiencing any kind of spiritual struggle results in the creation of spiritual templates that are marked by restricted views mixed with a longing for connection and healing. By increasing our understanding of the genesis of our spiritual beliefs and patterns, we can stimulate the healing process. Therapy can make people more aware of the etiology of their relational and spiritual ways of reacting, help heal from spiritual injury, and enable them to take greater ownership of their spiritual journey (Johnson, 2013).

Many times, psychotherapy offers the means to initiate a client's spiritual quest, because in certain contexts it addresses fundamental existential issues such as a sense of meaninglessness, feelings of dissatisfaction and emptiness, as well as matters of faith, such as a desire for a more intentional spiritual practice (Sperry & Shafranske, 2005). At times people search for guidance from an expert in spiritual discernment to sort out their spiritual issues by reaching out to a pastor, rabbi, imam, spiritual director, or even to a spiritually oriented therapist. The majority seek help with personal difficulties that are sometimes linked to spiritual longings or fears. At other times, the catalyst may be conscious or unconscious unhealthy religious or spiritual convictions when these interfere with life's goals or with spiritual commitments. People may turn to a therapist or spiritual guide to obtain relief from suffering and to seek orientation in moments of confusion, but also on their journey toward spiritual self-transformation (Rizzuto, 2005).

May (1987) says that psychology is unable to include and adequately address our deepest spiritual longings nor can it respond to the questions dealing with the ultimate meaning of our life. Paradoxically, spirituality has to incorporate psychology into its foundations since the psychological dimension is a part of every human endeavor. Every spiritual act has some psychological dimension to it, but not every psychological act is deeply spiritual. Psychology has attempted to explain spiritual experiences on its own terms but usually has not succeeded (May, 1987).

Select Universal Models of Spiritually Integrated/ Oriented Psychotherapy

Logotherapy

Logotherapy is an existential psychotherapy that focuses on the search for meaning in our life (Frankl, 2006; Dawbarn & McQuillan, 2020). It was developed before World War II by the Viennese psychiatrist Viktor Frankl, who recognized the need for this kind of spiritually integrated psychotherapy (Lukas & Hirsch, 2002). The preliminary concept of logotherapy was solidified through Frankl's experience in Nazi concentration camps (Frankl, 2006). He believed that the human experience relates to a combination of three parts: the physical domain, the mental domain, and the meaning or spiritual domain (Schulenberg et al., 2008). Frankl called this meaning domain the 'noological dimension' and related it to the spiritual domain of human experience, which did not pertain to any particular spiritual tradition, but could be individualized according to the patient's values (Frankl, 2014). With his understanding of the human person as soma, psyche, and spirit, Frankl attached the will to meaning to the spiritual dimension of being human (Marshall & Marshall, 2017).

Spiritually Integrated Psychotherapy as the Search for the Sacred

According to Pargament (2007), spiritually integrated psychotherapy assumes that clients regularly bring spiritual issues into counseling; it welcomes this fact, and even encourages a free expression of such issues. As a result, spiritually integrated psychotherapy can make the implicit explicit, identifying clearly, what the client holds sacred, thus making better use of spirituality in view of a successful psychotherapy. Spiritually integrated psychotherapy is based on a systematic way of thinking about spirituality, both in terms of theory and research. This approach should be explicit, psychospiritual, pluralistic (welcoming diverse religious and nonreligious backgrounds), integrative (and not in opposition to other approaches), and value oriented (Pargament, 2007). It includes both theistic and nontheistic expressions, offers a developmental model of the search for the Sacred as well as differentiates between healthy and unhealthy spiritual practices (Stewart-Sicking et al., 2020). We will come back to Pargament's approach in the next chapters.

Integrative Spiritually Oriented Psychotherapy

In this approach, the clinician functions as both psychotherapist and spiritual guide. As an integrative approach, it is based on an integrated model of development and pathology that includes biological, psychological, social, and spiritual dimensions. It focuses on the comprehensive assessment of a person's overall health status, including psychological strengths and defenses, as well as moral and spiritual development as exemplified by their relationship with God, their image of God, and their spiritual practices in a spiritually supportive community. Through the use of various psychotherapeutic and spiritual tools, the therapist is able to promote the cure of their client's symptoms as well as their self-transformation, and tries to be sensitive to both the psychological and the spiritual aspects of the client's life situation (Sperry, 2005).

Clinical Paradigm of Integrating the Numinous into the Counseling Process

Ralph Piedmont and Teresa Wilkins (2020) present a counseling model that focuses on including the numinous in counseling. The numinous includes elements of transcendence, spirituality, religiousness, and mysticism, but at the same time does not pretend to have any theological characteristics (Fox & Piedmont, 2020). Conceptualized in this way, the numinous has the potential for including spirituality in clinical paradigms for assessment, diagnosis, and treatment, resulting in a more holistic understanding of our psychological functioning. The strength of this approach is that it does not require any formal theological preparation and that it is applicable to people from different cultures and backgrounds (Piedmont & Wilkins, 2020).

The Ways Paradigm

Stewart-Sicking and colleagues (2017) underline that spirituality is always present within the foundation of counseling because spiritual issues such as hope, meaning, and suffering are central to every human being. The Ways Paradigm proposed by Joseph A. Stewart-Sicking, Jesse Fox, and Paul J. Deal (2017) consists of three dimensions – a way of understanding, a way of being, and a way of intervening, and is based on Cheston's (2000) previous research. The authors state that these dimensions should be applied to the integration of spirituality and religion into the counseling process. The 'way of understanding' applies to science in general and to psychology in particular. The 'way of being' means the way of encountering another human being, and the 'way of intervening,' in the context of counseling, denotes the therapeutic work whose focus is to integrate spirituality. The process model based on the Ways Paradigm can serve as a framework that enables counselors to understand and to integrate spirituality into counseling. The authors intend to develop a model that is universal and applicable to any spiritual tradition, but at the same time remains independent of any particular school of psychotherapy. The counselor does not need to be affiliated to any spiritual tradition but must be open to developing the understanding and skills required to work comfortably with the spiritual issues of their clients. The above-mentioned three dimensions do not provide immediate transformative blueprints but rather support the therapist with a framework to help understand the origin of spiritual practices and their potential for counseling, especially in terms of the motivational force that leads to a desired therapeutic change (Stewart-Sicking et al., 2020).

Some Examples of Spiritually Integrated/Oriented Therapy by Approaches

Apart from general models of integrating spirituality into the counseling process, there are also models that address this issue from the perspective of a particular psychotherapeutic approach. Let us illustrate this with selected examples.

A Psychoanalytic Approach to Spiritually Oriented Psychotherapy

Working with the spiritual dimension in the context of psychoanalysis is a high-risk venture into the unknown (Corbett & Stein, 2005). A spiritually oriented psychoanalytic approach examines developmental factors of human beliefs in particular, but without negating the divine dimension. This allows the exploration of both psychological and spiritual trajectories as related, but also as fundamentally distinct realities. In practice, it means taking a non-reductionist, hermeneutic, and open stance that allows listening to spiritual experiences with an empathic ear and avoiding any potential misunderstandings (Shafranske, 2005).

Spiritually Oriented Cognitive-Behavioral Therapy

The spiritually oriented cognitive-behavioral therapy (SO-CBT) perspective offers another way of working with religious clients. It uses certain therapeutic interventions such as cognitive disputation that are supported by religion's sacred scripture. The aim is to argue against irrational and self-defeating beliefs that, for the most part, are simply not in line with a sound religious doctrine. SO-CBT encourages spiritual imagery to decrease anxiety, scripture reading or prayer during the sessions, as well as cognitive homework. The cognitive disputation of problematic beliefs may be exercised at either a general or a specialized level. At the general level one's beliefs are challenged without addressing any particular religious views. The specialized level requires that the therapist possess a relatively good knowledge of the client's belief system so that they are able to dispute those religious beliefs or practices that are both dysfunctional and incongruent with the client's beliefs (Tan, 2005). Therapists who are well versed in spiritual literature can recommend spiritual texts to help their clients open their eyes to multiple levels of meaning in religious texts and to realize that mystery will always be a part of our lives (Doehring, 2006).

A Humanistic Approach to Spiritually Oriented Psychotherapy

Humanistic psychology has generally accepted spirituality as an integral part of human life. Maslow had promoted spirituality as a major positive component of the humanistic approach. Unlike Freud, Maslow was convinced that it would be abnormal for a person not to be preoccupied with certain religious or spiritual issues. The humanistic approach to spiritually oriented psychotherapy is based on two assumptions: (1) that humans often suffer at the level of the soul and (2) that a psychotherapeutic relationship is a place where people's souls can be nurtured and healed. In fact, love is the most powerful healer of the suffering soul. In a therapeutic relationship, love takes the form of empathy, respect, honesty, caring, and acceptance. These factors make soul-to-soul contact possible and can have a profound effect on the client's inner life. Many prominent psychologists like Carl Jung, William James, Viktor Frankl, Gordon Allport, Abraham Maslow, Irvin Yalom, and others were convinced that psychopathology sometimes has its roots in spiritual conflicts and deprivations (Elkins, 2005).

Interpersonal Psychotherapy from a Spiritual Perspective

Whereas traditional interpersonal psychotherapy is silent on spiritual matters, the main principle of the interpersonal psychotherapy conducted from a spiritual perspective (IPSP) is that psychological events reveal a more fundamental spiritual reality and that the human psyche is linked to spiritual truth. The intention of IPSP is to address suffering and improve spiritual clarity through reshaping client's relationships, which are viewed as divine gifts and that offer an opportunity for spiritual growth and for learning spiritual lessons. For IPSP, spiritual reality is more fundamental than the psychological one so that when we suffer in relationships, there is an underlying spiritual reason. People can evolve spiritually, experiencing the unity of the universe through the love experienced in relationships. This approach can be applied to people from any spiritual tradition (Miller, 2005).

Theistic Integrative Psychotherapy

According to the Christian theistic view of personality development, people who attempt to follow God's Spirit and accept universal moral principles are more likely to develop a healthy personality. They also feel closer to God and experience a sense of strength, meaning, and fulfillment originating in their spiritual beliefs. Although therapeutic change can be facilitated by a variety of means, complete healing requires a spiritual process that includes God's inspiration and love. This often involves a deep affirmation of person's eternal spiritual identity and worth, facilitated by prayer or other spiritual experiences. Such experiences are life-transforming events and often reorient the client's values from a materialistic value system to a more spiritually oriented one. These inner changes result in alterations in the client's lifestyle, leading to healthier behaviors as well as a lessening of psychological and physical symptoms (Scott, 2005).

Intensive Soul Care

In this approach, soul and spirit are seen as essential for the development of full personhood. The psychological and spiritual dimensions are two aspects of the inner self. No personal problem can be described as purely psychological so that any pathology can be conceptualized as a certain combination of soul suffering and spirit longing. The ISC therapist will be able to search for the spiritual implication of an apparently psychological problem and vice versa. Pathology should be understood in broader terms than the *Diagnostic and Statistical Manual of Mental Disorders*, Fifth Edition (DSM-5), and always include elements such as the human experience of isolation, alienation, the sense of meaningless, and existential guilt (Benner, 2005).

An Interaction of Spiritually Integrated/Oriented Therapy within Various Spiritual Traditions

We would expect that spiritual traditions and a number of practices originating in them could enter into dialogue or even become part of the counseling process. Below, we will point out only a few examples and will develop these more in further chapters of the book.

Among all spiritual traditions, Buddhism has had the most influence on contemporary psychology. Buddhism is characterized by a clear understanding of the human mind as well as meditation practices that are useful in therapy, since they help cultivate intentional awareness and attention, leading to an efficient self-regulation of the person's behavior. Another main concept of Buddhism lies in cultivating nonjudgmental acceptance of both the self and others (Kristeller & Rapgay, 2013). According to Buddhist philosophy, life is a transient phenomenon and refusing to accept this inherent attribute of its nature leads to unnecessary suffering. In order to relieve this suffering, we are invited to seek out and accept our own fragility (Szczygiel, 2015). This way of thinking is akin to what is found in existential therapies.

We can easily imagine an effective psychotherapy based on a collaborative treatment plan that incorporates Islamic principles (Hodge & Nadir, 2008). Although little has been done to integrate the empirical findings of the psychology of Islam into treatment, research shows that this could be very successful (Abu-Rayia, 2013). In the past year alone a significant number of important publications have been published in this field. Hussein Rassool (2021) developed a synthesis of contemporary empirical psychology and Islamic psychology, or science of the soul, that includes the physical, psychological, social, and spiritual dimensions of being human. The first-ever articulation of an emerging Islamic orientation to psychotherapy can be found in the volume edited by Hooman Keshavarzi and colleagues (2021), *Applying Islamic Principles To Clinical Mental Health Care: Introducing Traditional Islamically Integrated Psychotherapy*. This approach is termed Traditional Islamically Integrated Psychotherapy (TIIP) and is based on an Islamic epistemological and ontological framework as well as on Western psychology. Abdallah Rothman (2022) attempts to reconcile the teachings of Islamic theology pertaining to human nature, the self, and the soul with contemporary notions of psychology. Similar processes are being developed with respect to Judaism (Frankel, 1998; Levin & Prince, 2011; Cooper, 2006); Hinduism (Avasthi et al., 2013; Pandurangi et al., 2014; Jegathesan & Abdullah, 2018); and First Nations spirituality (Duran, 2006, 2019; King & Trimble, 2013). We will look into these in the next chapters.

Clearly, it is impossible to overlook the heterogeneity of the Christian faith. Despite this, Christian counseling in its various forms seems to be the most developed model of a spiritually integrated-oriented therapy adjusted to a particular faith tradition. One of the authors who developed this type of approach over the last years is Mark McMinn (2008, 2011). Another is Dan Montgomery (2009, 2010), who developed *Compass Therapy*. One of the recent examples of Christian counseling is *Incarnational Psychotherapy* (Rennebohm & Thoburn, 2021). Many faculties offer excellent training for Christian counselors. A number of examples of these approaches will be examined later in this book.

Proposed Model to Integrate Spiritual Issues into Counseling

Apart from traditional forms of spiritual care such as spiritual direction or, more recently, pastoral counseling, there is a growing need for the integration of spiritual issues and processes into a secular form of therapy. As the process of therapy unfolds, the counselor may choose to make certain interventions as a response to the client's spiritual concerns and experiences. In such cases, the inclusion of spiritual content into the counseling process would be in reaction to problems brought up by the client (Piedmont & Wilkins, 2020). Sperry (2012) noted that most clients expect their counselors to do this.

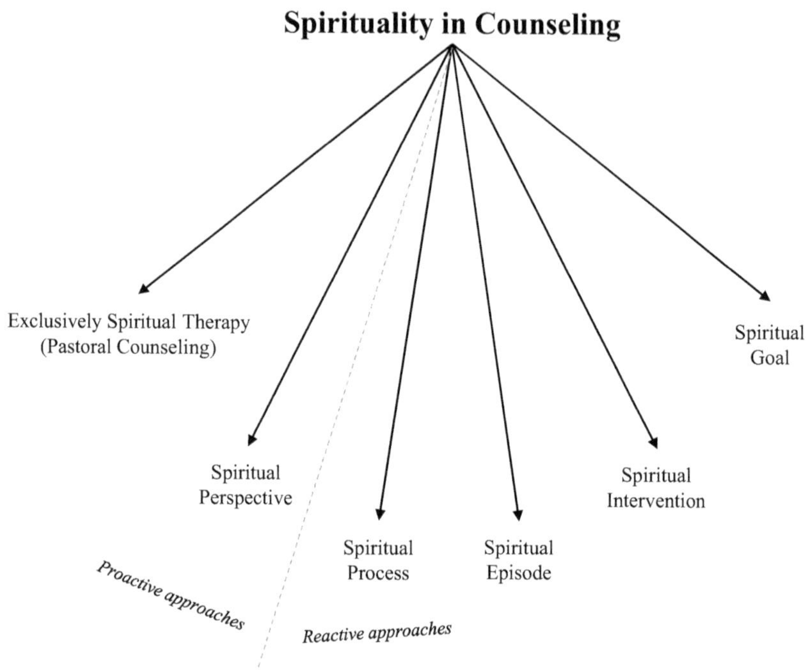

Figure 5.1 Spirituality in counseling.

In order to illustrate this challenge (Figure 5.1), I would distinguish the following options with regard to the presence of spiritual issues found in therapy (Jastrzębski, 2021):

- Exclusively spiritual therapy (pastoral counseling): therapy that is exclusively focused on spirituality.
- Spiritual process: a time of spiritual process within problem-focused therapy.
- Spiritual episode in therapy: a spiritual episode emanating from a spiritual discovery, insight, and challenge in someone's life and happening simultaneously with therapy.
- Spiritual intervention: a spiritual intervention in order to free the client from a certain blockage hindering the healing process. This might necessitate the intervention of a spiritual guide.
- Spiritual goal: such as when counseling's focal point is (or has become) the ultimate meaning of life.
- Spiritual perspective/understanding: a situation where only the therapist recognizes spiritual issues, paths, and processes in the client's life.

The first option represents an approach that is entirely spiritually oriented. Both counselor and client are aware of that dynamic and both agree to work primarily with this dimension of human life, which is imbued with faith, religiosity, or spirituality.

The second option, spiritual process, may be an unexpected development in an otherwise routine, problem-focused therapy. In this context, both counselor and client recognize that a life event, such as an unexpected death of someone close, needs to be immediately integrated into therapy as it presents a major issue to be dealt with in the here and now. It may be, for instance, a spirituality based grieving process and could take from five to eight sessions to work through.

The third option, a spiritual episode, is a similar therapeutic phenomenon, but is less dramatic and less time-consuming, usually taking two to three sessions. An example of this would be an abrupt spiritual discovery, a revelation, or an insight that needs to be integrated into the client's life.

The fourth option is spiritual intervention. Regular therapeutic work may deal with trauma, but a spiritual doubt or obstacle prevents the process from developing smoothly. Thus, we can imagine a situation where the therapist discerns that a spiritual or religious intervention may help the process even though the goal or focus of therapy or the intervention may not be religious or spiritual per se. In this event, resolving this spiritual issue may lead to the possibility of further healing. To do so, the counselor either needs to be well grounded in the spiritual tradition of the client, or would need to suggest that the client seek extra assistance from an experienced minister, priest, or other spiritual guide.

The fifth option is a spiritual goal. It means that either the client or therapist – or both – are aware that, in the final analysis, the entire therapy is spiritually oriented. We can say that in this situation, counseling has a spiritual horizon such as finding an ultimate meaning to life, but it is not the subject of direct discussion within the counseling session.

The last option is the spiritual perspective or understanding on the part of the therapist alone (Jones, 2019). This means that the therapist is a spiritually sensitive and practicing person, but will never reveal this to the client as they do not approach this question in therapy. Nonetheless, the spiritually sensitive therapist will recognize spiritual issues, paths, and processes in the client's life and will try to assist them indirectly. The ultimate spiritual horizon for a spiritually sensitive counselor may simply be their faith, which may be expressed in praying for clients outside of the session without them being aware of this fact.

The above model can also be used to understand psychological issues present in the process of spiritual direction. Nowadays, it seems almost unavoidable that people seeking spiritual direction will also bring along certain psychological problems and will want to discuss them occasionally or in more depth with their spiritual directors. For this to be successful, the therapist should have a fundamental openness to this kind of approach but must also be aware of their professional limitations and know when a referral would be more beneficial for the client.

Conclusions

In early psychological approaches, scientists tried to find ways to connect metaphysical concepts with specific psychological dynamics. It is a well-known fact that Freud saw religious strivings and behaviors as mere expressions of underlying psychological processes related to basic primal needs. Thus, Freud understood spiritual content simply as one of many attempts at gratifying underlying unconscious tensions. Such an approach made religion seem understandable to scientists, but reduced it to unhealthy or immature psychological strivings. Although this approach exists to this day and has the advantage of utilizing established psychological models that offer useful interpretive frameworks, there are serious limitations to this perspective. A reductionist approach cannot be considered as contributing to the integration of spirituality into psychology as it fails to appreciate the unique, non-reducible perspectives concerning the ultimate nature of being human. Surely, theologians and those interested in theological questions would argue that reductionism is an overly simplistic and naive view of reality (Piedmont & Wilkins, 2020).

Whichever psychological approach the helping professional chooses to provide optimum care for clients, they need to be open to using a range of tools in their therapeutic care of others, which is not limited to but should certainly include the spiritual dimension of being human.

Discussion Questions

1. Have you ever had an experience with spiritual direction, pastoral counseling, or spiritually oriented psychotherapy?
2. Can you state, in your own words, the main differences between them?
3. Do you see a possibility of collaboration between various professionals with the aim of helping people in their spiritual quest?
4. What would be the ideal way to render this collaboration possible?

References

Abu-Raiya, H. (2013). The psychology of Islam: Current empirically based knowledge, potential challenges, and directions for future research. In K. I. Pargament, J. J. Exline, J., & J. W. Jones, (Eds.), *APA handbook of psychology, religion, and spirituality (Vol. 1: Context, theory, and research*, pp. 681–695). American Psychological Association. https://doi.org/10.1037/14045-038

Avasthi, A., Kate, N., & Grover, S. (2013). Indianization of psychiatry utilizing Indian mental concepts. *Indian Journal of Psychiatry, 55*(6), 136–144.

Benner, D. G. (2005). Intensive soul care. In L. Sperry & E. P. Shafranske (Eds.), *Spiritually oriented psychotherapy*, (pp. 287–306). American Psychological Association.

Captari, L. E., Sandage, S. J., & Vandiver, R. A. (2021). Spiritually integrated psychotherapies in real-world clinical practice: Synthesizing the literature to identify best practices and future research directions. *Psychotherapy.* Advance online publication. https://doi.org/10.1037/pst0000407

Cheston, S. E. (2000). A new paradigm for teaching counseling theory and practice. *Counselor Education and Supervision, 39*(4), 254–269.

Cooper, H. (2006). Forty years of Judaism and psychotherapy: An overview. *European Judaism: A Journal for the New Europe, 39*(2), 14–19.

Corbett, L., & Stein, M. (2005). Contemporary Jungian approaches to spiritually oriented psychotherapy. In L. Sperry & E. P. Shafranske (Eds.), *Spiritually oriented psychotherapy* (pp. 51–73). American Psychological Association.

Dawbarn, K. & McQuillan, P. (2020). From better access to better outcomes: Integrating logotherapy with focused psychological strategies. *Psychotherapy and Counselling Journal of Australia.* https://pacja.org.au/2020/06/from-better-access-to-better-outcomes-integrating-logotherapy-with-focused-psychological-strategies-2/

Doehring, C. (2006). *The practice of pastoral care: A postmodern approach.* Westminster John Knox Press.

Duran, E. (2006). *Healing the soul wound: Counseling with American Indians and other native peoples.* Teachers College Press.

Duran, E. (2019). *Healing the soul wound: Trauma-informed counseling for indigenous communities* (2nd ed.). Teachers College Press.

Elkins, D. N. (2005). A humanistic approach to spiritually oriented psychotherapy. In L. Sperry & E. P. Shafranske (Eds.), *Spiritually oriented psychotherapy* (pp. 131–151). American Psychological Association.

Fox, J., & Piedmont, R. L. (2020). Religious crisis as an independent causal predictor of psychological distress: Understanding the unique role of the numinous for intrapsychic functioning. *Religion, 11*, 329.

Frankel, E. (1998). Repentance, psychotherapy, and healing through a Jewish lens. *American Behavioral Scientist, 41*(6), 814–833.

Frankl, V. E. (2006). *Man's search for meaning.* Beacon Press.

Frankl, V. E. (2014). *The will to meaning: Foundations and applications of logotherapy.* Plume.

Hodge, D., & Nadir, A. (2008). Moving toward culturally competent practice with Muslims: Modifying cognitive therapy with Islamic tenets. *Social Work (New York), 53*(1), 31–41.

Jastrzębski, A. K. (2021). Models of psycho-spiritual care: Responding to the spiritual needs of our contemporaries. *Studia Ełckie, 23*/2, 173–188.

Johnson, R. (2013). *Spirituality in counseling and psychotherapy: An integrative approach that empowers clients.* John Wiley.

Jones, R. S. (2019). *Spirit in session: Working with your client's spirituality (and your own) in psychotherapy.* Templeton Press.

Keshavarzi, H., Khan, F., Ali, B., & Awaad, R. (Eds.). (2021). *Applying Islamic principles to clinical mental health care: Introducing traditional Islamically integrated psychotherapy.* Routledge/Taylor & Francis Group.

King, J., & Trimble, J. E. (2013). The spiritual and sacred among North American Indians and Alaska Natives: Mystery, wholeness, and connectedness in a relational world. In K. I. Pargament, J. J. Exline, & J. W. Jones (Eds.), *APA handbook of psychology, religion, and spirituality* (Vol. 1: *Context, theory, and research*, pp. 565–580). American Psychological Association. https://doi.org/10.1037/14045-031

Kristeller, J., & Rapgay, L. (2013). Buddhism: A blend of religion, spirituality, and psychology. In K. I. Pargament, J. J. Exline, & J. W. Jones (Eds.), *APA handbook of psychology, religion, and spirituality* (Vol. 1: *Context, theory, and research*, pp. 635–652). American Psychological Association. https://doi.org/10.1037/14045-035

Levin, J., & Prince, M. (2011). Judaism and health: Reflections on an emerging scholarly field. *Journal of Religion and Health*, *50*(4), 765–777.

Lukas, E., & Hirsch, B. (2002). Logotherapy. In F. W. Kaslow, R. F. Massey, & S. Davis Massey (Eds.), *Comprehensive handbook of psychotherapy* (Vol. 3, pp. 353–376). John Wiley & Sons.

Marshall, M., & Marshall, E. (2017). *Anthropological basis of meaning centered psychotherapy*. Ottawa Institute of Logotherapy.

May, G. G. (1987). *Will and spirit: A contemplative psychology*. HarperCollins.

May, G. G. (1992). *Care of mind/care of spirit: Psychiatric dimensions of spiritual direction*. Harper & Row.

Maynard, E. (2017). Pastoral counseling. In A. Wenzel (Ed.), *The SAGE encyclopedia of abnormal and clinical psychology* (Vol. 1, pp. 2486–2488). SAGE. www.doi.org/10.4135/9781483365817.n998

McMinn, M. R. (2008). *Sin and grace in Christian counseling: An integrative paradigm*. IVP Academic.

McMinn, M. R. (2011). *Psychology, theology, and spirituality in Christian counseling*. Tyndale House.

Miller, L. (2005). Interpersonal psychotherapy from a spiritual perspective. In L. Sperry & E. P. Shafranske (Eds.), *Spiritually oriented psychotherapy* (pp. 153–175). American Psychological Association.

Montgomery, D. (2009). *Compass therapy: Christian psychology in action*. Compass Works.

Montgomery, D. (2010). *Pastoral counseling and coaching*. Compass Works.

Moon, G. (2002). Spiritual direction: Meaning, purpose, and implications for mental health professionals. *Journal of Psychology and Theology*, *30*(4), 264–275. https://doi.org/10.1177/009164710203000402

Muruges, D. V. (2018). Hinduism and counseling: Karma, women empowerment, grief and death, anger management, Bhagavad Gita, and psychotherapies. In A. J. Jegathesan & S. S. Abdullah (Eds.), *Multicultural Counseling Applications for Improved Mental Healthcare Services* (pp. 211–222). IGI Global. https://doi.org/10.4018/978-1-5225-6073-9.ch013

Pandurangi, A. K., Shenoy, S., & Keshavan, M. S. (2014). Psychotherapy in the Bhagavad Gita, the Hindu scriptural text. *The American Journal of Psychiatry*, *171*(8), 827–828. https://doi.org/10.1176/appi.ajp.2013.13081092

Pargament, K. I. (2007). *Spiritually integrated psychotherapy: Understanding and addressing the sacred*. Guilford Press.

Pearce, M. J., Pargament, K. I., Oxhandler, H. K., Vieten, C., & Wong, S. (2019). A novel training program for mental health providers in religious and spiritual competencies. *Spirituality in Clinical Practice (Washington, D.C.)*, *6*(2), 73–82. https://doi.org/10.1037/scp0000195

Perrin, D. B. (1998) Spiritual direction, hermeneutics, and the textual constitution of selfhood, *Église et Théologie*, *29*(1), 31–62.

Perrin, D. B. (2007). *Studying Christian spirituality*. Routledge. https://doi.org/10.4324/9780203944776

Piedmont, R., & Wilkins, T. (2020). *Understanding the psychological soul of spirituality*. Routledge.

Rassool, G. H. (2021). *Islamic psychology: Human behaviour and experience from an Islamic perspective*. Routledge/Taylor & Francis Group. https://doi.org/10.4324/9780429354762

Rennebohm, S. B., & Thoburn, J. (2021). Incarnational psychotherapy: Christ as the ground of being for integrating psychology and theology. *Pastoral Psychology, 70*, 179–190. https://doi.org/10.1007/s11089-021-00940-x

Rizzuto, A.-M. (2005). Psychoanalytic considerations about spiritually oriented psychotherapy. In L. Sperry & E. P. Shafranske (Eds.), *Spiritually oriented psychotherapy* (pp. 31–50). American Psychological Association.

Rothman, A. (2022). *Developing a model of Islamic psychology and psychotherapy: Islamic theology and contemporary understandings of psychology*. Routledge/Taylor & Francis Group.

Schulenberg, S. E., Hutzell, R. R., Nassif, C., & Rogina, J. M. (2008). Logotherapy for clinical practice. *Psychotherapy: Theory, Research, Practice and Training, 45*(4), 447–463.

Scott, R. P. (2005). Theistic integrative psychotherapy. In L. Sperry & E. P. Shafranske (Eds.), *Spiritually oriented psychotherapy* (pp. 259–285). American Psychological Association.

Shafranske, E. P. (2005). In L. Sperry & E. P. Shafranske (Eds.), *Spiritually oriented psychotherapy* (pp. 105–130). American Psychological Association.

Snodgrass, J. L., McCreight, D., & McFee, M. R. (2014). To whom shall I refer? *Counseling Today, 57*(6), 54–59.

Sperry, L. (2001). *Spirituality in clinical practice: Incorporating the spiritual dimension in psychotherapy and counseling*. Brunner-Routledge.

Sperry, L. (2002). *Transforming self and community: Revisioning pastoral counseling and spiritual direction*. Liturgical Press.

Sperry, L. (2005). Integrative spiritually oriented psychotherapy. In L. Sperry & E. P. Shafranske (Eds.), *Spiritually oriented psychotherapy* (pp. 307–329). American Psychological Association.

Sperry, L. (2012). *Spirituality in clinical practice: Theory and practice of spiritually oriented psychotherapy* (2nd ed.). Taylor & Francis Group.

Sperry, L. (2013). Distinctive approaches to religion and spirituality: Pastoral counseling, spiritual direction, and spiritually integrated psychotherapy. In K. Pargament (Ed.), *APA handbook of psychology, religion, and spirituality* (Vol. 2: *An applied psychology of religion and spirituality*, pp. 223–238). American Psychological Association.

Sperry, L., & Shafranske, E. P. (2005). Addressing the spiritual dimension in psychotherapy: Introduction and overview. In Sperry, L. & Shafranske, E. P. (Eds.), *Spiritually oriented psychotherapy* (pp. 11–29). American Psychological Association.

Stewart-Sicking, J., Deal, P., & Fox, J. (2017). The ways paradigm: A transtheoretical model for integrating spirituality into counseling. *Journal of Counseling and Development, 95*(2), 234–241.

Stewart-Sicking, J., Fox, J., & Deal, P. (2020). *Bringing religion and spirituality into therapy: A process-based model for pluralistic practice*. Routledge.

Stone, H. (1999). Pastoral counseling and the changing times. *Journal of Pastoral Care, 53*, 47–56.

Szczygiel, P. (2016). Maneuvering difficult emotional terrain in psychotherapy: A Buddhist-informed conceptual framework. *Clinical Social Work Journal, 44*(3), 241–251. https://doi.org/10.1007/s10615-015-0570-1

Tan, S-Y., & Johnson, W. B. (2005). Spiritually oriented cognitive-behavioral therapy. In L. Sperry & E. P. Shafranske (Eds.), *Spiritually oriented psychotherapy* (pp. 77–103). American Psychological Association.

6 Ethical Considerations regarding Integrating Spirituality into Counseling

Introduction

The majority of counselors are generally not spiritual counselors (e.g., spiritual directors), yet they should be able to support a client's progress in view of promoting healthy spiritual development or be able to help them to find meaning within the context of the clinical issues that they are facing. Meaning-making is one of the fundamental aspects of spirituality. Moreover, certain transformative spiritual experiences may enable clients to transcend their psychological disorder (Young, & Cashwell, 2011).

Scholars, both religious (e.g., Browning & Cooper, 2004) and atheistic (e.g., Ellis, 1980) have repeatedly noted that psychotherapy is not an endeavor devoid of relating to values. At the very least, psychotherapy is predicated upon the value that human suffering should be alleviated. But it is also true that psychotherapies implicitly work toward their distinctive visions of what it means to live a full and happy life (Stewart-Sicking, 2008).

For helping professionals who are spiritually sensitive, both theological and psychological dimensions are clearly intertwined and are difficult, if not impossible, to separate. Nonetheless, each set of concepts has its own characteristics, and functions differently in each person's mental life. In order to deal with this appropriately, we would need to have training in both areas: psychology and theology. This combination of expertise can potentially facilitate therapeutic as well as pastoral conversations with the client. However, this is not a widespread occurrence and would require many years of formation. Also, because there are different theological concepts across various denominations, finding a universal pattern that integrates theology and psychology remains greatly problematic (Piedmont & Wilkins, 2020).

Spiritually sensitive therapists are often asked to provide explanations that make sense from the theological perspective of their client. When they are not familiar with their client's religious, spiritual, or ethnic backgrounds, they must demonstrate a willingness to learn about them. They will also want to explore with clients how they practice beliefs within their unique context. Counselors should not assume that clients will teach them about their spirituality without openly asking about this topic. In such cases, the

DOI: 10.4324/9781003262145-7

counselor is invited to give up the role of an expert in order to develop an open curiosity about their clients' spiritual perspectives, their sociopolitical context, and their ethnic identification (Wiggins, 2011).

When the Sacred appears in counseling sessions, spiritual emotions are evoked, which can be challenging to deal with. Indeed, their inappropriate integration can lead to psychological and spiritual distress. Sometimes the therapist and client can interact around the client's image of the divine. At times, insights presented by the therapist can appear to the client as a divine revelation, which can easily lead to the client's dependence on the therapist and delay expected healing. In order to avoid this pitfall, therapists should be extremely careful when helping a client who comes from their own faith tradition. When this happens, there is always the temptation for the therapist to believe that other therapists would not have the competence to work with such a client. The potential magnitude of damage that can be done to this person should remind the counselor to be extremely conscious in this regard. This is also why functions that are proper to an ordained person, such as hearing a confession in the Catholic tradition, should not become a part of the therapeutic process. Ethical danger will always increase when healthy boundaries are not respected (Stewart-Sicking et al., 2020).

Sperry and Mansager's Possible Relationships between Psychology and Spirituality

There are many options of how to relate spirituality to counseling. Len Sperry and Erik Mansager (2007) propose five categories, each having a different relationship between psychology and spirituality/theology. Their proposal is based on two considerations: (1) Are they similar or different (i.e., unique) domains? (2) Which one should have primacy in the therapeutic encounter? The last group is holistic, which means that in practice, neither psychology nor spirituality has primacy, whatever their similarities or differences may be (Jastrzębski, 2018).

The Psychological and Spiritual Domains of Human Experience and Development Are Essentially the Same, But with the Psychological Having Primacy

Here, spiritual growth is linked to psychological growth and its social and interpersonal dimensions. In practice, it means that by way of effective psychotherapeutic work and personality development, one can attain a sounder spirituality. That being the case, there is little need for direct spiritual intervention. This approach is typical of the psychological reductionism that is present in the classical psychoanalytic view of Freud (1927/1995) or Rizzuto (1979), where an individual's representation of God is nothing more than a reflection of their paternal representations.

The Psychological and Spiritual Domains of Human Experience and Development Are Essentially the Same, But with the Spiritual Having Primacy

Using a common basis of psychology and spirituality, this approach could lead to spiritual reductionism; nonetheless, Jung would use this approach to some extent. He attempted to deal with religious images and processes and was, at times, accused of either 'psychologizing theology,' or of 'theologizing psychology.' These kinds of discussions only served to show that Jung was keen to alternate between the two disciplines. In doing so, Jung did develop an original approach to the psychology of religion. Some would even say that he himself was the founder of a new religion, nonetheless based on natural terms (Becker, 2001).

From the perspective of spirituality, the individuation process, so important for Jung, especially through the encounter with the shadow, bears a striking resemblance to the passive night of the senses, which, in the Christian tradition, is a necessary prerequisite for mystical transformation (Ruffing, 1990). May (1987), however, stresses the importance of not presuming that psychological development and spiritual growth are synonymous. Unfortunately, psychology, when making observations on this issue, has been inclined toward reducing spirituality to environmental, behavioral or mental phenomena (May, 1987).

The Psychological and Spiritual Domains of Human Experience and Development Are Different, Though at Times Overlapping, with the Psychological Having Primacy

Spiritual and psychological dimensions of human life are distinct realities. They can intermingle and the growth in one may be reflected in the other. In this approach, psychological development does not necessarily involve spiritual growth. Some would say that spiritual development depends on psychological development so that a person would have to develop sufficient psychological maturity before becoming able to undertake any spiritually oriented endeavor. This remains a back-and-forth process and is represented, for instance, by an existential–humanistic approach to spirituality where psychotherapy would embrace the spiritual dimensions of the human being; here, nevertheless, that primacy belongs to psychology (Sperry & Mansager, 2007).

The Psychological and Spiritual Domains of Human Experience and Development Are Different, Though at Times They Overlap, with the Spiritual Having Primacy

In this approach, spirituality is seen as distinct from psychological development so that spiritual growth does not require psychological growth. Both spiritual and psychological growth can intermingle, but there have been saints with obvious psychopathologies, as for example those of St. Theresa of Lisieux, who despite suffering from separation anxiety disorder, was able to develop a sound spiritual life (Vitz & Lynch, 2007). This leads to a more general statement that pathology may occasionally serve to boost religious experiences (Helminiak, 1984).

The implication in this case is that both spiritual direction and regular psychotherapy are required. Examples of this approach include: transpersonal psychology, a theistic spiritual strategy for psychotherapy (Richards & Bergin, 1997, 2003), integrative spiritually oriented psychotherapy (Sperry, 2012), spiritually oriented cognitive-behavioral therapy (Tan & Johnson, 2005), interpersonal psychotherapy from a spiritual perspective (Miller, 2005), and Frankl's logotherapy (Frankl, 1988).

The Psychological and Spiritual Domains of Human Experience and Development Are Different, Yet Neither Has Primacy, Nor Is Either One Reducible to the Other

Spirituality and psychotherapy are different, goal-oriented processes, each of which strives toward its own ends. Depending on the client's concern, the therapist applies either psychotherapeutically oriented methods or spiritually oriented ones. This would be a holistic orientation that moves smoothly between psychotherapy and spiritual direction, appropriately addressing psychological or spiritual issues as they arise. In practice, it may mean for example combining elements of existential psychotherapy with spiritual accompaniment. Here, psychological and spiritual dimensions are two sides of the 'inner self' with no sharp distinction between the psyche and the spirit, because both are seen as intimately linked. The holistic approach takes the view that conscious human awareness presents the link between spirituality and psychology. 'Both spirituality and psychotherapy provide methods for exploring, deepening, and expanding consciousness' (Sperry & Mansager, 2004, p. 158). Both have to be in constant dialogue (e.g., Nelson, 2009; Browning, 2010; Griffith, 2010).

Forced Westernization

Therapists may be tempted to secularize conversations with their clients and disregard their spirituality, while trying to replace it with a worldview embedded in modern Western thought and marked by positivism and materialism. It is clear that interventions that force clients in this direction should be considered unethical. Modern codes of ethics guide professions against this kind of influence. Historically, it is clear that significant prejudice has linked religious practices with symptoms of psychopathology. The truth is that it is extremely difficult to reach a perfectly objective point of view with which to judge these issues. Although it is sometimes necessary to critically examine a client's beliefs, therapists would be better off to rely on critiques from within the client's traditions rather than from without.

Skillful Socratic questioning can serve as a prudent way to avoid premature judgments (Stewart-Sicking et al., 2020).

> Should a client change their concept of God, the Sacred, or however they define the nature of ultimate reality to be more consistent with twenty-first-century science? Should a counselor encourage a couple to consider divorce, separation, or an open relationship when the partnership appears doomed even though such steps are not encouraged in their tradition or is considered a severe moral failing within their faith community? Can a client's lack of acceptance of other religions be understood as inhabiting a lower stage of psychological development? Should the client's reluctance to practice meditation or mindfulness be a sign of lack of openness or rigid beliefs?
>
> (Stewart-Sicking et al., 2020, p. 112)

When the therapist determines that a certain spiritual belief is exacerbating the pathology, they have to be extremely careful not to impose their own worldview on their client (Jastrzębski, 2010). Within great wisdom traditions, a number of useful rules can enable the counselor to confront the client without dismissing their spiritual tradition. In particular, very old traditions have developed useful and effective tools for self-correction. This can be called an internal critique. Of course, this requires the clinician to acquire more knowledge about their client's spiritual tradition, but this will be well worthwhile. In rare cases when the client remains unreceptive to this internal critique and threatens self or others, the therapist needs to challenge the client's spiritual convictions more directly, by demonstrating, for instance, how much they are harming others by their actions. Such an action is permitted only when it is obvious that clients are at odds with their core values and present a threat to society. This situation may also require a consulting with a minister or similar expert, who can provide an alternate solution to the clinician and client (Stewart-Sicking et al., 2020).

There are various concepts of personal maturity. It can be seen as courageously facing the tragic dimension of life, or alternatively as its avoidance or romanticization. Some see happiness in material wealth, whereas others underline the importance of nonattachment to material goods. All these questions make assessing spirituality a constant challenge, because the client's personal understanding of the truth is often formed within their own spiritual tradition. In fact, spiritual traditions are difficult to evaluate psychologically, as they have nonscientific origins (Stewart-Sicking et al., 2020).

Ethical Competencies

Several professional associations provide sound guidance with respect to the integration of spirituality in counseling. First is the list proposed by the Association for Spiritual, Ethical, and Religious Values in Counseling (ASERVIC, 2009; Robertson & Young, 2011), a division of the American Counseling Association. Another is Division 36 of the American Psychological Association, which published 'Spiritual and Religious Competencies for Psychologists' (Vieten et al., 2013). Finally, there are guidelines presented by the Council for Accreditation of Counseling and Related Educational Programs (CACREP, 2009, 2015).

These lists of competencies should help therapists become aware of their strengths and weaknesses while working with spirituality in counseling: conceptualizing cases, developing appropriate interventions, as well as requesting support from other experts such as clergy, spiritual directors, and religious scholars when required. Clinicians should also be aware of biases originating in their own spiritual experiences that can cause either attraction or aversion to certain forms of spiritual practices and theories. This may manifest itself as naive idealism, skepticism, and suspicion. In order to offset such pitfalls, future therapists are encouraged to get to know their own spiritual journey through the use of spiritual self-assessment or by writing their spiritual autobiographies (Stewart-Sicking et al., 2020).

ASERVIC

ASERVIC is the end result of a long process that began in the 1950s. In 1951, the Archdiocese of New York formed the Catholic Guidance Council, whose aim was to support counseling in parish schools. After New York, more diocesan councils were formed so that in 1958 the National Conference of Guidance Councils was founded. In 1955, a special group composed of Catholic members within the American Personnel and Guidance Association (APGA) created the Catholic Counselors of APGA and started publishing the *Catholic Counselor*, which later became *Counseling and Values*. In 1961, they formed the National Catholic Guidance Conference (NCGC) and met annually at the APGA conferences in order to support Catholic counselors. In 1977, NCGC became the Association for Religious Values and Issues in Counseling as it transitioned from a Christian-based organization to one open to all religions and values. Finally, in 1993, it became the Association for Spiritual, Ethical, and Religious Values in Counseling (ASERVIC), an organization that is exclusively committed to promoting the integration of spiritual, religious, and ethical values in counseling (Robertson & Young, 2011).

ASERVIC first met in 1995. At this convention, 13 experts tried to define the best ways to include spirituality and religion in counseling and education in an ethical manner. Their work was inspired by the prescriptions of the Council for Accreditation of Counseling and Related Educational Programs (CACREP, 2015). The results of this work were presented in 1996 and revised in 2009 when the ASERVIC Board of Directors adopted the 14 competencies developed in this process. These are presented below (Robertson & Young, 2011).

Culture and Worldview

1. The professional counselor can describe the similarities and differences between spirituality and religion, including the basic beliefs of various spiritual systems, major world religions, agnosticism, and atheism.
2. The professional counselor recognizes that the client's beliefs (or absence of beliefs) about spirituality and/or religion are central to his or her worldview and can influence psychosocial functioning.

Counselor Self-Awareness

3. The professional counselor actively explores his or her own attitudes, beliefs, and values about spirituality and/or religion.
4. The professional counselor continuously evaluates the influence of his or her own spiritual and/or religious beliefs and values on the client and the counseling process.
5. The professional counselor can identify the limits of his or her understanding of the client's spiritual and/or religious perspective and is acquainted with religious and spiritual resources, including leaders, who can be avenues for consultation and to whom the counselor can refer.

Human and Spiritual Development

6. The professional counselor can describe and apply various models of spiritual and/or religious development and their relationship to human development.

Communication

7. The professional counselor responds to client communications about spirituality and/or religion with acceptance and sensitivity.
8. The professional counselor uses spiritual and/or religious concepts that are consistent with the client's spiritual and/or religious perspectives and that are acceptable to the client.
9. The professional counselor can recognize spiritual and/or religious themes in client communication and is able to address these with the client when they are therapeutically relevant.

Assessment

10. During the intake and assessment processes, the professional counselor strives to understand a client's spiritual and/or religious perspective by gathering information from the client and/or other sources.

Diagnosis and Treatment

11. When making a diagnosis, the professional counselor recognizes that the client's spiritual and/or religious perspectives can a) enhance well-being; b) contribute to client problems; and/or c) exacerbate symptoms.
12. The professional counselor sets goals with the client that are consistent with the client's spiritual and/or religious perspectives.
13. The professional counselor is able to a) modify therapeutic techniques to include a client's spiritual and/or religious perspectives, and b) utilize spiritual and/or religious practices as techniques when appropriate and acceptable to a client's viewpoint.
14. The professional counselor can therapeutically apply theory and current research supporting the inclusion of a client's spiritual and/or religious perspectives and practices.

CACREP

The Council for Accreditation of Counseling and Related Educational Programs (CACREP) is the leading accrediting organization for graduate programs in counseling in the United States. Spirituality was explicitly included in its former versions as 'a sense of a relationship with or belief in a higher power or entity greater than oneself that involves a search for wholeness and harmony' (CACREP, 2009, p. 63).

Outside of specialized disciplines such as pastoral counseling, therapists have usually conceptualized spirituality as a part of their multicultural competence (Scott et al., 2016). The inclusion of training and accreditation guidelines regarding spirituality as a competency finally appeared in CACREP in 2009 and marked an important moment for those who had long advocated for the recognition of these issues in therapy (Stewart-Sicking et al., 2020).

The latest CACREP (2015) standards do not mention spirituality, which is now deemed to be part of social and cultural diversity and is related to as spiritual beliefs and worldviews. In this context, researchers found that, unfortunately, most counselors had not heard of the ASERVIC Competencies, and that counselors generally did not feel prepared to address spiritual or religious issues in therapy. This was due to lack of understanding regarding the importance of spirituality and religion in the therapeutic process. Indeed, even today, a more standardized system is needed to help prepare counselors to use religion and spirituality fruitfully in their work. As it stands now, available programs are usually restricted to one specific denomination or faith (Bohecker et al., 2017).

Lynn Bohecker and colleagues (2017) recommend that this part of the curriculum area be added to Section 2: Professional Counseling Identity of the CACREP Standards. It should include a variety of aspects, such as spirituality and identity, as well as models of faith development. Principles of spiritual wellness and strategies for counseling, interviewing, and assessing individuals, couples, and families from diverse spiritual and religious perspectives also need to be given priority. Issues related to gender, race, ability, sexual orientation, and nationality as well as how these interact with spirituality and religion should also be addressed. Finally, there should be an appropriate outline of the history of spirituality and religion including both Western and Eastern religions as well as nonreligious beliefs such as humanism, atheism, and agnosticism (Bohecker et al., 2017).

Embedded Practices versus Disembedded Tools

It seems that there is no perfect model to integrate psychological and theological approaches. Therapists usually refer to spiritual concepts because they are spiritually sensitive themselves or because they are trained to address these issues either in response to client concerns or because they are naturally interested in this dimension of human life. Nonetheless, it is important to remember that therapists should not practice outside of their sphere of competency. And since spiritual training is often not part of their professional formation, addressing these issues can prove challenging when the complexity of the client's theological concerns overwhelms the therapist's ability to manage them effectively. For many clinicians, spirituality only comes down to a cultural variable (Piedmont & Wilkins, 2020).

While embedded practices, meaning practices within a given faith community, are ethically less problematic with regard to consent and the imposition of values, they tend to create different issues. First, many spiritual practices, especially those considered supernatural, must be conducted by religious officials and most therapists are not religious leaders. Even when therapists are clergy from the client's tradition, engaging in practices such as absolution or blessing raises questions about boundaries and transference (Stewart-Sicking et al., 2020).

In practice, therapists often use techniques commonly found in spiritual direction and pastoral care interventions such as scripture reading, prayer, and meditation. This is an acceptable practice as long as the goal remains addressing the basic psychological issues of infinitude, meaning, or worthiness, and as long as they are guiding their clients psychologically and not theologically. Thus, spirituality can become a medium through which psychotherapists can access more basic psychological motivations. One has to keep in mind this subtle and yet important distinction (Piedmont & Wilkins, 2020).

To address this issue, the use of disembedded interventions has been proposed. These secularized interventions take what is most important and effective from embedded practices in all spiritual traditions and apply them without requiring the therapist or client to adhere to any particular belief system. This approach helps avoid certain sources of resistance, because it does not refer to any orthodox practice or dogma of a particular religion (Stewart-Sicking et al., 2020).

Despite their usefulness, as demonstrated very clearly in the practice of mindfulness methods, disembedded interventions have their shortcomings, one of which is of an ethical nature. Not taking into consideration either the metaphysical or the religious nature of certain interventions does not meet the criterion of informed consent. For instance, a conservative Christian client, who is encouraged by the therapist to embark on the practice of loving-kindness meditation, may feel betrayed and harmed once they find out that this practice has Buddhist origins. This omission could cause tangible therapeutic harm (Stewart-Sicking et al., 2020).

Supervision

Supervision often seems to be the last context when spiritual and religious issues appear in the therapeutic process and must be addressed or discussed (Polanski, 2003; Stebnicki, 2006). Unfortunately, supervisors often perceive themselves as incompetent to face spiritual issues. Therapists frequently find their supervisors unprepared to deal with anything transcendent or spiritual in a counseling session. Consequently, they react by downgrading the importance of such experiences or by not mentioning them at all (West, 1998).

To address this problem, we can point to cultural immersion experiences as a possible way of increasing our sensitivity to unknown belief systems. Perhaps the best way to accomplish this is by inviting the supervisees to attend a gathering of a spiritual or religious group that they are unfamiliar with. Ideally, this gathering should be part of their client's belief system. Optionally, a person can reach out to audiovisual material such as movies, songs, sermons, or lecture podcasts produced by this specific spiritual or religious group (Hull et al., 2016).

Tools facilitating the development of spiritual competencies include spiritual autobiographies or genograms. These require supervisees to recount their spiritual histories in order to gain a better understanding of how their spiritual heritage influences their work with clients. Counselors can also develop a resource list (referral network) of spiritual leaders, programs, and services that can assist their clients in their spiritual or religious needs. Finally, counselors can use some form of spiritual mentorship to help them pursue their own spiritual development through a relationship with a spiritual guide or leader. However, spiritual mentorship cannot replace clinical supervision (Hull et al., 2016).

Assessment

Therapists who want intake procedures to include spirituality are not yet well equipped to do so, since there is not much literature on this topic. This may discourage them from including spirituality in the initial dialogue with their clients (Hagedorn & Gutierrez, 2009). Consequently, spirituality receives little or no attention during the intake assessment, despite the fact that both therapist and client may view their spirituality as an important element shaping their identities (Hathaway, Scott, & Garver, 2004). Still, including spirituality in clients' assessment can prove to be important in addressing the presenting issue as well as facilitating both spiritual and therapeutic growth (Harris, Sisemore, Pargament, & Brown, 2014).

Assessing spirituality should enable the clinician to understand the client's existential realities and how the client's beliefs, values, and practices influence the way in which they deal with their presenting problem or condition. The goal of such an assessment is not to determine the accuracy of clients' worldviews but how these affect their psychological functioning. Assessment of spirituality is a two-stage process. First, a preliminary assessment focuses on four major areas: the importance of spirituality for the client, an affiliation with a given faith community, available spiritual resources, and an understanding of how their spirituality relates to the presenting issue. Second, if necessary, a comprehensive assessment can be done. At this stage the clinician is interested in obtaining more information regarding their client's spiritual and religious beliefs, practices, and experiences and understanding how these influence the client's problem as well as providing clues to possible solutions (Hodge, 2013).

C. Missy Butts and Daniel Gutierrez (2018) identified five functional tasks for an effective assessment of spiritual beliefs and practices: (1) use of nonjudgmental prescreening questions; (2) respect for the subjectivity of a client's spirituality as expressed by their personal definition of spirituality and the role it plays in their life; (3) paying attention to spiritual bypass; (4) requesting client preferences on how to integrate spirituality into the counseling process; (5) a constant monitoring for the counselor's own biases regarding spirituality and religion (Butts & Gutierrez, 2018).

Conclusions

Helping professionals are guided by many sets of ethical rules in their service to others. Integrating spirituality into the counseling process poses a distinct set of challenges. Fortunately, with the passage of time there is a slowly growing awareness of these issues. Also, an ethical reflection on how to work effectively and respectfully with our own spirituality has produced visible fruit. This has resulted in the creation of lists of recommendations that should serve professionals who are willing to include this dimension of being human in their professional work. Future research and reflection will surely fine-tune these guidelines. In the next chapters we will explore many concrete ethical issues pertaining to certain aspects of spirituality in counseling.

Discussion Questions

1. Are you able to articulate your own worldview based on spiritual concepts? If yes, take a few minutes to write a paragraph or two that express these.

2. How aware are you of the ethical challenges that are linked to the integration of spirituality in counseling?
3. Which issue concerns you the most? Explain.
4. What competency would you like to develop the most? Why?

References

Association for Spiritual, Ethical, and Religious Values in Counseling. (2009). *Competencies for addressing spiritual and religious issues in counseling*. Spiritual and Religious Competencies (aservic.org). www.counseling.org/docs/default-source/competencies/competencies-for-addressing-spiritual-and-religious-issues-in-counseling.pdf?sfvrsn=aad7c2c_10

Becker, K. L. (2001). *Unlikely companions: C. G. Jung on the spiritual exercises of Ignatius of Loyola*. Herefordshire (Gracewing) and Surrey (Inigo Enterprises).

Bohecker, L., Schellenberg, R., & Silvey, J. (2017). Spirituality and religion: The Ninth CACREP Core Curriculum Area. *Counseling and Values, 62*(2), 128–143. https://doi.org/10.1002/cvj.12055

Browning, D. S. (2010). *Reviving Christian humanism: The new conversation on spirituality, theology, and psychology*. Fortress Press.

Browning, D. S., & Cooper, T. D. (2004). *Religious thought and the modern psychologies* (Vol. 2). Fortress Press.

Butts, C. M., & Gutierrez, D. (2018). Expanding intake assessment to incorporate spirituality using five functional tasks. *Counseling and Values, 63*(2), 147–163. https://doi.org/10.1002/cvj.12085

Council for Accreditation of Counseling and Related Educational Programs. (2009). *2009 CACREP accreditation manual*. Author.

Council for Accreditation of Counseling and Related Educational Programs. (2015). *2016 CACREP Standards*. Author.

Ellis, A. (1980). *The case against religion: A psychotherapist's view*. American Atheist Press.

Frankl, V. E. (1988). *The will to meaning: Foundations and applications of logotherapy*. Meridian.

Freud, S. (1927/1995). *The future of an illusion*. Norton.

Griffith, J. L. (2010). *Religion that heals, religion that harms: A guide for clinical practice*. Guilford Press.

Hagedorn, W. B., & Gutierrez, D. (2009). Integration versus segregation: Applications of the spiritual competencies in counselor education programs. *Counseling and Values, 54*, 32–47. https://doi.org/10.1002/j.2161-007D.2009.tb00003.x

Harris, N., Sisemore, T. A., Pargament, K. I., & Brown, G. S. (2014). The relationship of decline in spiritual struggles to psychotherapy outcomes: Evidence from a large scale survey of psychotherapy clients. *Christian Psychology: A Transdisciplinary Journal, 8*, 40–48.

Hathaway, W. L., Scott, S. Y., & Garver, S. A. (2004). Assessing religious/spiritual functioning: A neglected domain in clinical practice? *Professional Psychology: Research and Practice, 35*, 97–104. https://doi.org/10.1037/0735-7028.35.1.9710

Helminiak, D. A. (1984). Neurology, psychology, and extraordinary religious experiences. *Journal of Religion and Health, 23*, 33–46.

Hodge, D., R. (2013). Assessing spirituality and religion in the context of counselling and psychotherapy. In K. Pargament, A. Mahoney, & E. P. Shafranske, (Eds). *APA handbook of psychology, religion, and spirituality* (Vol. 2: *An applied psychology of religion and spirituality*, 93–123). American Psychological Association.

Hull, C., Suarez, E., & Hartman, D. (2016). Developing spiritual competencies in counseling: A guide for supervisors. *Counseling and Values, 61*(1), 111–126. https://doi.org/10.1002/cvj.12029

Jastrzębski, A. (2010). Założenia ideologiczne szkół psychoterapeutycznych a światopogląd psychoterapeutów i pacjentów. In L. Grzesiuk & H. Suszek (Eds.), *Psychoterapia. Integracja* (pp. 331–351). Eneteia.

Jastrzębski, A. (2018). On the possibility of the psychology of spirituality. *Counseling and Spirituality,* 36/1–2 (2017), 33–49.

May, G. G. (1987). *Will and spirit: A contemplative psychology*. HarperCollins.

Miller, L. (2005). Interpersonal psychotherapy from a spiritual perspective. In L. Sperry & E. P. Shafranske (Eds.), *Spiritually oriented psychotherapy* (pp. 153–175). American Psychological Association.

Nelson, J. M. (2009). *Psychology, religion, and spirituality*. Springer.

Piedmont, R., & Wilkins, T. (2020). *Understanding the psychological soul of spirituality*. Routledge.

Polanski, P. J. (2003). Spirituality in supervision. *Counseling and Values, 47*, 131–141.

Richards, S., & Bergin, A. (1997). *A spiritual strategy in counseling and psychotherapy*. American Psychological Association.

Richards, S., & Bergin, A. (2003). A theistic spiritual strategy for psychotherapy. In S. Richards & A. Bergin (Eds.), *Casebook for a spiritual strategy in counseling and psychotherapy* (pp. 3–32). American Psychological Association.

Rizzuto, A. (1979). *The birth of the living god*. University of Chicago Press.

Robertson, L. A., & Young, M. E. (2011). *The revised ASERVIC spiritual competencies*. In C. S. Cashwell & J. S. Young (Eds.), *Integrating spirituality and religion into counseling: A guide to competent practice* (pp. 25–42). American Counseling Association.

Ruffing, J. (1990). Psychology as a resource for Christian spirituality, *Horizons, 17*, 47–59.

Scott, S. K., Sheperis, D. S., Simmons, R. T., Rush-Wilson, T., & Milo, L. A. (2016). Faith as a cultural variable: Implications for counselor training. *Counseling and Values, 61*(2), 192–205. https://doi.org/10.1002/cvj.12037

Sperry, L. (2012). *Spirituality in clinical practice: Theory and practice of spiritually oriented psychotherapy* (2nd ed.). Taylor & Francis Group.

Sperry, L., & Mansager, E. (2004). Holism in psychotherapy and spiritual direction: A course correction, *Counseling and Values, 48*, 149–160.

Sperry, L., & Mansager, E. (2007). The relationship between psychology and spirituality: An initial taxonomy for spiritually oriented counseling and psychotherapy. *The Journal of Individual Psychology, 63*, 359–370.

Stebnicki, M. A. (2006). Integrating spirituality in rehabilitation counselor supervision. *Rehabilitation Education, 20*(2), 115–132.

Stewart-Sicking, J., Fox, J., & Deal, P. (2020). *Bringing religion and spirituality into therapy: A process-based model for pluralistic practice*. Routledge.

Stewart-Sicking, J. A. (2008). Virtues, values, and the good life: Alasdair MacIntyre's virtue ethics and its implications for counseling. *Counseling and Values, 52*(2), 156–171. https://doi.org/10.1002/j.2161-007X.2008.tb00099.x

Tan, S-Y., & Johnson, W. B. (2005). Spiritually oriented cognitive-behavioral therapy. In L. Sperry & E. P. Shafranske (Eds.), *Spiritually oriented psychotherapy* (pp. 77–103). American Psychological Association.

Vieten, C., Scammell, S., Pilato, R., Ammondson, I., Pargament, K. I., & Lukoff, D. (2013). Spiritual and religious competencies for psychologists. *Psychology of Religion and Spirituality, 5*(3), 129–144. http://dx.doi.org/10.1037/a0032699

Vitz, P. C., & Lynch, C. P. (2007). Thérèse of Lisieux from the perspective of attachment theory and separation anxiety. *The International Journal for the Psychology of Religion, 17*(1), 61–80. http://dx.doi.org/10.1080/10508610709336854

West, W. (1998). Developing practice in a context of religious faith: A study of psychotherapists who are Quakers. *British Journal of Guidance & Counselling, 26*(3), 365–375. https://doi.org/10.1080/03069889800760321

Wiggins, M. I. (2011). *Culture and worldview*. In C. S. Cashwell & J. S. Young (Eds.), *Integrating spirituality and religion into counseling: A guide to competent practice* (pp. 43–69). American Counseling Association.

Young, J. S., & Cashwell, C. S. (2011). *Integrating spirituality and religion into counseling: An introduction*. In C. S. Cashwell & J. S. Young (Eds.), *Integrating spirituality and religion into counseling: A guide to competent practice* (pp. 1–24). American Counseling Association.

7 Spirituality Embedded in Culture

The Context

The context in which we live has a definite effect on our spiritual growth. We cannot separate ourselves from the flow of historical and political processes that characterize our society, nor are we unaffected by the goals related to these. Spirituality remains relative to the world, understood as the sum of human experiences that have come down to us mostly through culture and tradition. Ernst Cassirer stressed that we do not live only in the physical world, but also in world of symbols expressed through language, myth, art, religion, and spirituality. All of these impose limits on our freedom but also provide us with the opportunity for dialogue and growth. Empirical research has already demonstrated that culture influences our perception of reality. More generally, our relationship with the world is reciprocal. This means that the world shapes us just as we shape it. According to Heidegger (1962), human life is divided into the natural environment (*Umwelt*), society (*Mitwelt*), and interiority (*Eigenwelt*). Our likelihood of influencing the world is based on our capacity to take responsibility for our own actions. We can become self-aware and responsible for our own existence and, in doing so, we can shape our inner world or spirituality. This can also enable us to play our part in shaping the world around us (Jastrzębski, 2019).

Our world is constantly changing, and talking about stability can only provide us with a temporary sense of security and identity. In fact, there is continuous movement through and in our lives. We simultaneously experience both our being and the process of our becoming so that our sense of self and identity is constantly developing and, in turn, affecting the way we perceive the world and our place in it (Freshwater, 2015).

According to the *Cambridge Dictionary* (2020), culture can be:

1) The way of life, especially the general customs and beliefs, of a particular group of people at a particular time;
2) The way of life of a particular people, especially as shown in their everyday behavior and habits, their attitudes toward each other, and their moral and religious beliefs;

DOI: 10.4324/9781003262145-8

3) The art of describing, showing, or performing that represents the traditions or the way of life of a particular people or group; literature, visual art, music, dance, theater, etc.

The elements of culture include:

1) Knowledge (science, philosophy)
2) Beliefs (religion, spirituality, values)
3) Arts (literature, music, architecture)
4) Laws (political system, social organization and rules)
5) Customs (tool usage, cooking, shelter, clothing)
6) Habits (rituals, celebrations, time management)

> Culture can be described as a way of life that includes a system of shared beliefs, values, attitudes, meanings, motives, behaviors, products, and perceptions of the universe. Each area is shaped by family customs, ethnic traditions, and environmental influences. Spiritual and religious beliefs are also aspects of culture that contribute to the way someone lives his or her life.
>
> (Robertson & Young, 2011, p. 30)

Socialization is the process of absorbing various worldviews, attitudes, and norms of behavior characteristic of the specific group where one belongs. Socialization can be seen as a 'humanization' of the individual. Despite the obvious limiting dimensions of our cultural background, realizing that no one grows up in isolation allows us to accept tradition and culture with a sense of gratitude. Our existence follows a chain that began with our distant ancestors, made its way through time, and will continue through future generations. As a consequence, it would be a serious mistake to try to cut ourselves off from our cultural and traditional roots. In the end, our being is a co-being, our existence is a co-existence, and our living is a co-living. Culture is the place where our transgenerational wisdom is continually being stored and where it remains available to us so that we can exercise our gifts and potential responsibly. Although each of us must find the way to make life meaningful for ourselves, we can also be guided by the numerous generations before us who undertook this same task, leaving behind their share of universal wisdom. Freedom can be defined as a brave search for our own way of reaching human and spiritual fulfillment, while also taking into account the unquestionable wisdom that our ancestors inscribed into the culture they left us. Integrating this wisdom into our own life project allows us to contribute to the transgenerational body of wisdom for future generations. Certain spiritual paths have proven useful in the past and can help our present generation achieve its goals as well. Among these are spiritual and ascetical practices like prayer and fasting. Ultimately, we are invited to use culture and tradition in a constructive and creative way (Jastrzębski, 2019).

Therapists cannot distance themselves from their culture, language, and social positions in their evaluation of their clients' thoughts and actions, nor can they choose to become oblivious to what makes them unique in the practice of their work. Culture and counseling are so intertwined that it is impossible to separate them. Indeed, we may be tempted to impose our own cultural views on others without being aware of it (Stewart-Sicking et al., 2020). 'Exploring differing notions of culture, spirituality and religious belief can enable true insights into what it means to be human, and enable sufficient sense of what lies at the core of our all-too-brief time in the unfolding universe' (Nolan & West, 2015, pp. 233–234).

It is clear that spiritual traditions can promote cultural differences and vice versa. Yet in the case of certain minorities concerned with the survival of their religious values as cultural values, religion may become their culture. In that event, we speak of religion-as-culture (Cohen & Hill, 2007). Spiritual tradition can also be empirically inseparable from a given collectivity. For example, we generally state that Easterners are collectivist and Westerners are more individualist, but we can say the same about Buddhists and Protestants (Saroglou & Cohen, 2013). Culture may also cause groups sharing the same spiritual tradition, but coming from different geopolitical contexts, to practice their spiritual tradition in different ways as is, for instance, the case in the Muslim world (Khan, Watson, & Habib, 2005). The same geopolitical context may influence which religion will be most likely assimilated into the exiting culture (Cohen et al., 2006).

Multiculturalism and Spiritual Traditions

Spirituality is most definitely intertwined with culture. Together, with the help of other multicultural dimensions, people are able to find their identity and understanding. Nonetheless, it is not sufficient to simply borrow techniques from multicultural sources. Spirituality must be integrated into the background of other cultural elements because it invites us to venture beyond the everyday aspects of our lives and points us toward the Sacred (Stewart-Sicking et al., 2020).

For the last few decades, multicultural issues such as race, ethnicity, and culture have been progressively integrated into counseling and psychotherapy (McCabe, 2007). The trend to combine various cultural expressions and spiritual traditions is clearly visible in the New Age movement. Here we find elements of holistic medicine such as homeopathy as well as alternative methods of healing body, mind, and spirit. New Age spirituality is based on the assumption that the spirit is present in everyone and in everything. In this context, healing means connecting with some universal spiritual energy referred to as chi (Chinese), ki (Japanese), or prana (Sanskrit), and using it to maintain one's well-being. In New Age spirituality, there is considerable room made to include, accept, and celebrate the mystery of life as it borrows from great mystical traditions such as the contemplative traditions in Christianity, Kabbalah, Quakers, Shinto, Taoism, and Zen

Buddhism. A syncretic mixture of certain spiritual schools and practices such as magic, alchemy, and astrology, as well as transcendental meditation may be part of a person's background (Wiggins, 2011). Yet May (1987) warns us that amalgamating various spiritual traditions is not the best solution. In order to be able to teach us something, each tradition must preserve its integrity by following its own ways, making its own mistakes and reflecting on its own insights. Only by doing so can these various traditions shed light on the spiritual paths of others (May, 1987).

In fact, extended research on traditional healing methods across all cultures (e.g., Moodley et al., 2008) demonstrates that spirituality and spiritual experiences have taken on a central role in the healing process. Because of skepticism regarding the role of religion in therapy, this often occurs outside of institutional religion. The reasons for this distrust are legion and include the fragmentation of Christianity into diverse denominations, or the conflict and trauma caused by the differences between Sunni and Shia Islam. Yet, a more balanced approach views the links between religion, spirituality, and multiculturalism as highly complex, while simultaneously being instrumental in processing converging perspectives, depending on the specific spiritual tradition, or one's particular worldview. Taking this into account, mental health practitioners are called to accept the importance of cultural awareness and sensitivity when working with clients from different social and cultural backgrounds, including diverse religious and spiritual ones. The dogmatically negative view of religion that was promoted by Freud in psychology is increasingly interpreted as unacceptable, just as racism or sexism are. It is important, however, not to exclude the possibility that religion can compromise an individual's health and well-being when it imposes unhealthy ideological or political frameworks. Generally speaking, bringing religion and spirituality into psychotherapy also means including the ideas of multiculturalism, since religion implies the existence of a wide variety of traditions, institutions, beliefs, and practices (Moodley & Barnes, 2015). Depending on their tradition and culture, people naturally differ in their conceptions of God and transcendent reality.

> In spite of the fact that the search for the sacred unfolds in a larger social and cultural context, the influence of family, organization, institution, community, and culture on spirituality is easy to overlook. Just as we rarely notice the air that nourishes us in our daily lives, we can neglect the power of the larger context that supports our spiritual journeys.
>
> (Pargament, 2007, p. 164)

Therapists wanting to take into account their client's ethnic background, cannot do this without considering how their client's religious or spiritual background intersects with their cultural background and how it informs the client's beliefs, worldview, and sense of self. Consequently, including religion and spirituality as part of counseling requires not only an understanding of a client's religious or spiritual orientation, but also demands a more general understanding of other dimensions of their cultural identity (Vogel et al., 2013).

Existing research on religion and spirituality has shown that they can have a positive influence on an individual's health. This is particularly true in the case of ethnic minorities, where religion is deeply embedded in their cultural traditions and identities (Worland & Vaddhanaphuti, 2013). Religious frameworks are able to provide followers with meaningful ways to understand their suffering and tragedies, especially with respect to seemingly pointless and traumatic experiences. If the integrity of a given culture is threatened, religion can provide an important source of healing and reintegration. Unfortunately, both religion and culture have had an extremely powerful negative influence on global and international sociopolitical and economic events such as crimes against humanity, genocide, the Holocaust, colonialism, US imperialism, wars, and ethnic cleansing. The inclusion of religion and culture in therapy provides an opportunity to enter into the client's narrative and from there, reach their center of distress and discomfort, where their pain and suffering can be encountered, brought to consciousness, and integrated into the self (Moodley & Barnes, 2015).

In a world where there are many cultures, it is also important to take into account the cultural assumptions guiding our approaches to counseling that do not necessarily apply to all people; in these times of globalization, attempts to export Western models of therapy need to be evaluated with a critical spirit. For example, we have to admit that Western prosperity has not made people much happier. The introduction of a Western approach to psychotherapy in Africa and India was accompanied by clear signs of a postcolonial process, including a plethora of its harmful side effects (West, 2015).

The multicultural implications of integrating spirituality into counseling are that the development of a true pluralism is of prime importance; it is meant to cherish cultural differences and at the same time search for and discover ways of living peacefully and collaboratively with the differences that exist in our society. Our aim should not be a universally applicable theory that reduces spiritual traditions to their commonalities, but rather a pluralistic approach that will enable us to gain new wisdom from our differences (Eck, 2007). The foundation of multiculturalism should be the recognition of experiences of others on their own terms (Stewart-Sicking et al., 2020).

Becoming a culturally competent therapist requires the ability to integrate many dimensions that include broad theoretical, conceptual, research-based, and practical issues. The journey to cultural and spiritual competence requires good insight into one's beliefs, attitudes, and behaviors as they relate to race, culture, ethnicity, and so on. To become a culturally competent therapist requires developing an open mind for viewing and accepting cultural diversity. From the social justice point of view, we need to acknowledge the existence of political biases in Western approaches regarding race, gender, and ethnicity (Sue & Sue, 2016).

Sacredness of Space and Time

Theological–spiritual reflection indicates that in the context of spirituality, time takes on a new dimension and we can develop a new experience of time called *Kairos*, which means being aware of the fullness of the present moment. On the opposite is *chronos*, the day-to-day experience of time as we go about our business without being touched in any profound way or being transformed spiritually. *Kairos*, however, among its many definitions since its first use in ancient Greek, is called a time of grace, a time of visitation by the divine, or a moment of special illumination (Rybicki, 2020).

Spiritual development will normally lead us to be more attuned toward time and help develop a capacity to perceive or discern the blessings of the present moment. It will also be characterized by a more responsible use of time, recognized as a powerful gift in our life. The good use of time requires dedication and attentiveness as well as spiritual maturity. In fact, many spiritual traditions, through a number of meditative practices, underline the importance of mindfulness.

Most cultures have developed concepts of sacredness that are often tied to beliefs regarding the origins of the world. A very common belief is that the Sacred is to be found 'in the heavens' so that anything elevated and closer to the heavens, like mountains, is seen as more sacred. This principle is found in Judaism, Confucianism, and Hinduism as well as in other Asian religions. Aboriginal peoples around the world generally share this belief but also believe in the power of certain elemental geometrical shapes such as circles. Many spiritual traditions emphasize that the Sacred can be and is part of our daily life. Examples include shrines created to honor one's ancestors (Shinto tradition), small household prayer altars (Hinduism and Buddhism), and the existence of benevolent house gods according to the Confucian tradition. These all serve to keep the Sacred present within ordinary life. In the past, wealthy and devout Christians built chapels on their properties or within their palaces. Some sites associated with painful memories have been transformed into sacred places. One can point to Hiroshima, Japan, with its Peace Memorial, to the World Trade Center Memorial in the USA, to Auschwitz, in Poland, and many others places of remembrance all over the world (Simmins, 2008).

Architecture

It is noteworthy that over the centuries, architecture has reflected the vital importance of the Sacred in most cultures. Places of worship were often constructed in the center of communities and were designed to help people go beyond time and space when they engaged in sacred rituals. Many towns and villages have the temple in the exact geographical center. This was done intentionally to bring people into contact with the harmony of the cosmic order. Cultural life and its infrastructure, like markets, schools, and hospitals were created close by, enabling the sacred domain to penetrate into the secular world. In each of these situations, the temple was positioned in such a way as to allow people to find their inner sacred spaces and to discover a meaning to human existence by communicating with the transcendent. This central positioning protected the temple from profane use, ensuring that it remained sacred. Through the ages, the center has remained a place where transcendent reality can be encountered, where one can transcend time and enter, however briefly, into the eternal present, where one can get a glimpse of one's true self (Eliade, 1959).

Accordingly, in Judaism, and subsequently in Christianity, the temple was seen as a sacred place where God communicated with humans; churches and mosques are often located in the centers of villages or towns. In some cases, access to the temple, or a part of it, has been reserved for people with special authority, gifts, training, and for the preparation and the performing of prescribed rituals. Aboriginal peoples have continued to believe that certain places are sacred because they were touched by the Creator and these cannot be entered unless one has been adequately prepared by prayer, fasting, or abstinence. Although temples are part of their culture, Taoist and Shinto visions of nature are more universal and do not privilege one place over another; the adherents of these religions maintain that one must place their will in harmony with the natural universe. The same principles of respect for the Sacred were and still are applied when places of worship are created in people's houses or in natural environments. Unfortunately, during the course of human history, religious intolerance has manifested itself in acts of destruction or devastation of sites regarded as sacred by others. In other cases, more than one religion has claimed the right to the same sacred place. Examples of this can be found in contemporary India where both Hindu and Muslim communities have their roots, or in Jerusalem, where three major world religions try to coexist (Simmins, 2008).

For many people, sacred places can also be found almost anywhere, even in a corner of one's own backyard. For Hindus, it is common to create puja areas in their homes where the family shrine is housed. For others, more advanced architectural forms such as mosques, temples, and cathedrals are sacred places where people feel particularly close to the divine (Pargament, 2007). And yet for those who consider themselves spiritual and nonreligious, sacred places are often found in nature.

Major world religions also build 'houses where the divine dwells' where their members can worship their Creator. These places have a double function: (1) they embody a power ascribed to the mystery, beyond human potential as well as (2) serve as a place of refuge and renewal. Many such houses were built in places where the divine was thought to be more actively present or where it was said to have been gifted with certain revelations. One of the examples is the Christian monastery of St. Catherine, at the foot of Mt. Sinai, where, according to the Bible, God spoke to Moses in the Burning Bush. Another place is Fatima, where Mary, Mother of Jesus is said to have appeared to three children. There are many such temple cities in different religions worldwide, such as Varanasi, the city of temples in India. Shrines and sacred spaces can also take a variety of other forms such as enclosures, gates, altars, mountains, pillars, or caves. Many spiritual traditions associate sacred spaces with events from the lives of their founders. This sometimes can be associated with the belief that their most sacred spaces represent the center of the universe. In fact, the majority of religions assert that the world is made in the image of the divine, and therefore one can discover traces of the sacred in all of creation (Simmins, 2008).

Music and Dance

From ancient times, people have connected with the Sacred through music and dance. In the time of King David, Biblical psalms were often sung, sometimes accompanied by dance, and most certainly accompanied by percussion instruments, harps, and woodwind instruments. Most spiritual traditions have included sacred music in their worship services or other spiritual practices. It seems that people universally feel the connection between movement, music, and the sacred dimension of their lives. For example, Sufi dancers in Islam celebrate the dances of universal peace; certain Buddhists as well as the Hari Krishna Hindus use chants to achieve ecstatic union with the Sacred; cantors play an essential role in most forms of Jewish worship. Generally speaking, singing helps the congregants enter into a spirit of worship. For some people, music becomes a privileged language of spiritual experiences (Pargament, 2007; Simmins, 2008).

Early Christians used to perform a dance called the *tripudium*. As they sang, they locked arms and moved together making three steps forward and one step back, in a repetitive fashion. This form of dance was their way of declaring that Jesus Christ had conquered all evil in the world and that this victory allowed believers forward, though not without setbacks. Today, spiritual dancing can be part of either private or communal prayer (Floster, 1992).

Many prayers are set to a melody or rhythm and are usually accompanied by instruments such as pipe organs, harps, lyres, and other instruments that are considered sacred. Moreover, many forms of secular music facilitate euphoric feelings of universal connectedness. It has even been argued that contemporary pop music can take on a certain spiritual dimension. When we are touched by music, it transports us to a place beyond time and space, and we become lost in it (Cantz, 2013).

Music is so powerful that it can move us to tears. All music can make us happy or sad and bring about an encounter with the Sacred. African American spirituals are considered to be one of the most impressive expressions of sacred music because they put into words a deep spiritual longing for the Promised Land, especially consoling for the slaves who first sang them (Simmins, 2008). In the Catholic Church, the importance of sacred music was reconfirmed by the Second Vatican Council in 1963 (Sacrosanctum Concilium, 112). Cardinal Ratzinger (1986) indicated that music is one of the manifestations of the Word of God, as the song of creation that unconsciously resonates within all human beings in virtue of its order and meaning. A very compelling illustration of this is the use of music therapy in elderly people with cognitive decline. Such programs, popular in Jerusalem, take advantage of music and dance to create meaningful connections with seniors (Pargament, 2007).

Music has the potential to alter the state of mind of its listener. In practically all major world religions including Hinduism, Sikhism, and Buddhism in the East as well as Judaism, Christianity, and Islam in the West, the role of music has been crucial since their inception. Often, sacred music has been believed to have a significant transformative effect on its listeners, although the link between music and spirituality has received only modest attention across academic disciplines such as music theory, anthropology, sociology, and theology (Cantz, 2013). Religion often provides the inspiration for lyrics or musicians' ideologies. In fact, the musical culture of today sometimes incorporates language related to religion, spirituality, and mysticism (Coggins, 2018). Music and singing, similarly to meditation and yoga, connect people directly with the core of their being and transport them to their transitional space. This is also true outside of any religious context (Cantz, 2013).

From the point of view of object relations theory, music can be conceptualized as a transitional space, where we can experience our true self and feelings of self-authenticity. This transitional space, according to Donald W. Winnicott (1953), can be understood as the space between the external world and our interiority, which is especially open to creativity. Eero Rechardt (1985) says that music can evoke specific moods in the listeners that can be relaxing and soothing, exciting, or even frightening. This last dimension can be linked to negative spirituality expressed by demonic music that evokes or promotes a desire for destruction and the illusion of liberation from the ego. In terms of its effects on the listener, this kind of music can be compared to the use of drugs, and from the Christian perspective, is a harmful way of trying to express or deepen our spirituality (Ratzinger, 1986).

The sacred qualities of music originate in its ability to transform the listener's perception of time. Music gives people a unique sense of atemporality and facilitates an encounter with the infinite. An example of this can be found in the Jewish Hasidic tradition where *niggunim* (literally 'humming tune') plays an important spiritual role, allowing a reconciliation between the idealized past and the spiritual present (Koskoff, 2001).

Sacred music surpasses the limitations of rational meaning-seeking and offers transcendental experiences that reverberate within one's spiritual core. It is able to express a visceral recollection of the earliest affective attunement experiences of children with their primary caregivers. In this way, sacred music is an analogy of interpersonal fusion and bonding. Therein also lies the power of musical concerts, which captures the spiritual experience of a person in the collective as well as the collective experience within the individual (Cantz, 2013).

Key Concepts of First Nations Spirituality

First Nations hold a holistic view of the universe and believe that all life is sacred. One of the main purposes of human life is to live in harmony with the cycles and seasons of nature. There are, of course, certain differences among First Nations cultures. For example, various communities place value on certain locations because of their association with a particular spirit; others are important either because of their association with precious resources or because they are considered to be ritually significant places. Generally, every aspect of creation, be it human, animal, or plant, is sacred, because the Creator made the world to be appreciated and enjoyed by every creature, in deep and mystical harmony (Simmins, 2008). Native American traditions are centered on their respect for Mother Earth, and because all we have comes from the goodness of the Earth, we, as a human community, should honor and protect her (McGaa, 1990).

Native spiritualities invite us to look with respect toward ancient knowledge and traditional ways of understanding the world. This also applies to their understanding of healing, which is clearly illustrated in the concept of radical empathy (Smith, 2015). In fact, First Nations psychology views a healthy life as harmonious with the earth and its wholeness (Rybak, Lakota Eastin, & Robbins, 2004). Healing is seen as a path to recover one's wholeness in connection with nature (Rybak & Decker-Fitts, 2009). For First Nations peoples, all things are interconnected, all have a purpose, and hence are worthy of our respect and reverence (Hunter & Sawyer, 2006). In native cultures, a person also acknowledges the existence of the feminine energy capable of guiding people toward a productive reconstitution and reinvigoration of suppressed and alienated parts of humanity. Metaphorically speaking, each person is invited to listen to the Grandmother Spirit who leads us to acknowledge important truths about ourselves and who invites us to share them with other species in the created universe (Smith, 2015).

Most native cultures believe that there are permeable frontiers between spiritual, human, animal, and afterlife realities. Because of their privileged relationship with the spiritual realms, shamans are believed to have spirits residing in their houses. In Native spirituality, an emphasis is also put on the cardinal directions that are linked with the cycles of life. Traditionally, the East is connected with spring as a place of life and new beginnings. Indeed, most buildings on native land are sited toward the East. The South is connected with summer as a time of youth, strength, and idealism; the West is associated with autumn as a time of emotional growth and self-awareness; the North is connected with winter as the time of wisdom and one's life fulfillment. The four cardinal directions are also associated with four elements: earth, wind, water, and fire (Simmins, 2008). These are examples of transformative imagery and are quite prevalent in aboriginal cultures. Acquainting ourselves with native spirituality gives us an opportunity to broaden our perspectives around nature, the environment, the body and the sacred therein (Jenkins, 2004).

The ten Commandments of Native Americans:

- The Earth is our Mother, care for her.
- Honor all your relations.
- Open your heart and soul to the Great Spirit.
- All life is sacred; treat all beings with respect.
- Take from the Earth what is needed and nothing more.
- Do what needs to be done for the good of all.
- Give constant thanks to the Great Spirit for each day.
- Speak the truth but only for the good in others.
- Follow the rhythms of nature.
- Enjoy life's journey, but leave no tracks. (O'Murchu, 2012, p. 96)

Again, according to indigenous cultures, each human being consists of four distinct parts: emotional, mental, physical, and spiritual. These are linked with the cardinal points as well as with specific colors: (1) white with the North and the physical dimension of the human being; (2) red with the East and our spiritual dimension; (3) yellow with the South and our emotional dimension; (4) black with the West and our mental dimension. Circles of nature are of special interest because of their power to connect different dimensions of life. In native cultures, certain geographical areas are seen as an intersection between the physical and spiritual worlds. This is particularly true of mountains, rocks, caves, or springs. Moreover, certain places and activities are regarded as having a transformative energy: sweat lodges, sun dances, rain dances, as well as other ritual activities. Some areas are considered sacred because of their association with particular plants or animals used in rituals. Harvesting or killing is usually done with ritualistic care (Simmins, 2008).

Conclusions

No doubt, spirituality and culture are interconnected. We need to understand our lives as a dynamic process where interacting forces shape our identities and behaviors. Consequently, a 'pure' spirituality or spiritual tradition does not exist and we should therefore not be looking for it. There is no pure Islam just as there is no pure Indian spirituality. We are all children of our times, and the historical moment in which we live influences the ways we relate to the divine. Politics, worldviews and cultural phenomena like the New Age movement, feminism, fundamentalism, and the development of social media shape the very fabric of who we are. We will be all the wiser if we acknowledge this fact.

Discussion Questions

1. What is your favorite element of the culture that influences your positive sense of identity?

2. Are there some elements in that same culture that have a negative influence on your sense of identity?
3. In your opinion, what is the most spiritual element of your culture? Explain.
4. Which elements of this culture can be most helpful in counseling?
5. Have you ever explored a culture other than your own? What have you learned from this experience?

References

Cantz, P. (2013). A psychodynamic inquiry into the spiritually evocative potential of music. *International Forum of Psychoanalysis*, *22*(2), 69–81.

Coggins, O. (2018). *Mysticism, ritual and religion in drone metal*. Bloomsbury Academic.

Cohen, A. B., & Hill, P. C. (2007) Religion as culture: Religious individualism and collectivism among American Catholics, Jews, and Protestants. *Journal of Personality*, *75*, 709–742. http://dx.doi.org/10.1111/j.1467-6494.2007.00454.x

Cohen, A. B., Malka, A., Rozin, P., & Cherfas, L. (2006). Religion and unforgivable offenses. *Journal of Personality*, *74*(1), 85–118. https://doi.org/10.1111/j.1467-6494.2005.00370.x

Culture. In *Cambridge Dictionary*. https://dictionary.cambridge.org/dictionary/english/culture (17.10.2020)

Eck, D. L. (2007). Prospects for pluralism: Voice and vision in the study of religion. *Journal of the American Academy of Religion*, *75*(4), 743–776.

Eliade, M. (1959). *The sacred and the profane: The nature of religion*. (W. R. Trask, Trans.). Harcourt, Brace & World.

Foster, R. J. (1992). *Prayer: Finding the heart's true home*. Harper.

Freshwater, D. (2015). Foreword. In G. Nolan, & W. West (Eds.), *Therapy, culture and spirituality: Developing therapeutic practice* (pp. xi–xii). Palgrave Macmillan.

Heidegger, M. (1962). *Being and time*. Basil Blackwell.

Hunter, D., & Sawyer, C. (2006). Blending Native American spirituality with individual psychology in work with children. *The Journal of Individual Psychology*, *62*(3), 234–250.

Jastrzębski, A. (2019). *Homo Theomorphicus et Theophoricus: A receptive-responsive theory of spirituality*. Peeters.

Jenkins, P. (2004). *Dream catchers: How mainstream America discovered native spirituality*. Oxford University Press.

Khan, Z. H., Watson, P. J., & Habib, F. (2005). Muslim attitudes toward religion, religious orientation and empathy among Pakistanis. *Mental Health, Religion & Culture*, *8*(1), 49–61. https://doi.org/10.1080/13674670410001666606

Koskoff, E. (2001). *Music in Lubavitcher life*. University of Illinois Press.

May, G. G. (1987). *Will and spirit: A contemplative psychology*. HarperCollins.

McCabe, G. H. (2007). The healing path: A culture and community derived Indigenous therapy model. *Psychotherapy: Theory, Research, Practice, Training*, *44*(2), 148–160.

McGaa, Eagle Man, E. (1990). *Mother earth spirituality: Native American paths to healing ourselves and our world*. Harper.

Moodley R., & Barnes, C. (2015). Multiculturalism, religion and counselling: Freedom to heal. In G. Nolan, & W. West (Eds.), *Therapy, culture and spirituality: Developing therapeutic practice* (pp. 7–23). Palgrave Macmillan.

Moodley, R., Sutherland, P., & Oulanova, O. (2008) Traditional healing, the body and mind in psychotherapy. *Counselling Psychology Quarterly*, *21*(2), 153–165.

Nolan, G., & West, W. (2015). Conclusion. In G. Nolan, & W. West (Eds.), *Therapy, culture and spirituality: Developing therapeutic practice* (pp. 232–234). Palgrave Macmillan.

O'Murchu, D. (2012). *In the beginning was spirit: Science, religion and indigenous spirituality*. Orbis Books.

Pargament, K. I. (2007). *Spiritually integrated psychotherapy: Understanding and addressing the sacred*. Guilford Press.

Ratzinger, J.C. (1986). *A new song for the Lord: Faith in Christ and liturgy today*. Crossroad Publishing.

Rechardt, E. (1985). On musical cognition and archaic meaning schemata. *Scandinavian Psychoanalytic Review, 8*, 95–113.

Robertson, L. A., & Young, M. E. (2011). *The revised ASERVIC spiritual competencies*. In C. S. Cashwell & J. S. Young (Eds.), *Integrating spirituality and religion into counseling: A guide to competent practice* (pp. 25–42). American Counseling Association.

Rybak, C., & Decker-Fitts, A. (2009). Understanding Native American healing practices. *Counselling Psychology Quarterly*, *22*(3), 333–342.

Rybak, C., Lakota Eastin, C., & Robbins, I. (2004). Native American healing practices and counseling. *Journal of Humanistic Counseling, Education and Development, 43*, 25–32.

Rybicki, A. (2020). Time in spirituality. *Verbum Vitae*, *38*(1), 403–417.

Saroglou, V., & Cohen, A. B. (2013). Cultural and cross-cultural psychology of religion. In R. F. Paloutzian & C. L. Park (Eds.), *Handbook of the psychology of religion and spirituality* (pp. 330–354). Guilford Press.

Simmins, G. (2008). *Sacred spaces and sacred places: A comparative approach*. VDM Verlag Dr. Müller.

Smith, D. P. (2015). Listening to the grandmother spirit: The chance for prophetic change in contemporary healing. In G. Nolan, & W. West (Eds.), *Therapy, culture and spirituality: Developing therapeutic practice* (pp. 78–91). Palgrave Macmillan.

Stewart-Sicking, J., Fox, J., & Deal, P. (2020). *Bringing religion and spirituality into therapy: A process-based model for pluralistic practice*. Routledge.

Sue, D. W., & Sue, D. (2016). *Counseling the culturally diverse: Theory and practice* (7th ed.). Wiley.

Vogel, M. J., McMinn, M. R., Peterson, M. A., & Gathercoal, K. A. (2013). Examining religion and spirituality as diversity training: A multidimensional look at training in the American Psychological Association. *Professional Psychology: Research and Practice*, *44*(3), 158–167.

West, W. (2015). One Western size fits all: Counsellor training in different countries and cultures. In G. Nolan, & W. West (Eds.), *Therapy, culture and spirituality: Developing therapeutic practice* (pp. 70–77). Palgrave Macmillan.

Wiggins, M. I. (2011). *Culture and worldview*. In C. S. Cashwell & J. S. Young (Eds.), *Integrating spirituality and religion into counseling: A guide to competent practice* (pp. 43–69). American Counseling Association.

Winnicott, D.W. (1953). Transitional objects and transitional phenomena. *International Journal of Psychoanalysis*, *34*, 89–97.

Worland, S., & Vaddhanaphuti, C. (2013). Religious expressions of spirituality by displaced Karen from Burma: The need for a spiritually sensitive social work response. *International Social Work*, *56*(3), 384–402.

8 Signs of Healthy Spirituality

Introduction

We may wonder whether the contemporary conceptualizations of spirituality will allow the development of useful guidelines to assist people in their quest for spiritual maturity. Daniel Helminiak seems to be optimistic regarding that point and states that a normative dimension of spirituality can indeed be developed. He calls it 'a real science of spirituality' (Helminiak, 2008, p. 163); and more recently (2011) has referred to it as 'spiritualogy' (p. 598). This science should be able to determine 'what genuine humanness requires by way of beliefs and ethics' (Helminiak, 2005, p. 81). For the contemporary mind, spirituality pertains especially to meanings and values, which do not necessarily involve any existing spiritual tradition but rather are one of the inherent aspects of being human, which is meaning-making (Helminiak, 2005). For many people, spirituality becomes an orienting system not only providing answers to life's most urgent questions but also, and more fundamentally, shapes perceptions and thus one's subjective experience, including experiences of human suffering (Sperry & Shafranske, 2005).

Theoretical Considerations

Although spirituality is of interest to many sciences, only theology presents clear normative guidelines of how to explore its depths. Members of given spiritual traditions are expressly advised on what serves their spiritual development and what does not. In order to develop a universal approach to spirituality, we need to find a way to integrate it into a normative/prescriptive dimension beyond the usual explanatory level applied in social sciences (Jastrzębski, 2020). In this descriptive approach there is neither a question of 'why?' nor a study of 'why things are as they are.' Helminiak (2011) says that the strength of social sciences lies in their analyses and comparisons of people's convictions and commitment; their weakness is in ignoring the truthfulness and validity within human life and development since beliefs can be true or false and values beneficial or destructive. In fact, human life is hardly neutral or value free. 'Without a normative component, social science cannot address the burning issues of our times, and without a breakthrough to

DOI: 10.4324/9781003262145-9

explanatory status, social science can hardly be normative' (Helminiak, 2011, p. 598). And yet, each spirituality is value oriented, and normally proposes some rules to be lived by. In order to be helpful for counseling, psychological research would need to develop some kind of normative dimension as well (Helminiak, 2006).

Generally, every human person holds some understanding about life and shapes their own life according to that understanding. Moreover, each person normally intends to achieve some kind of 'growth' that can also be a

> deliberate commitment to self-transcendence, along the lines of the meanings and values that one holds. [...] Insistence on this concern functions precisely to specify spirituality as a deliberate dimension of living differently from the passive possibility of living without any deliberate pursuit of growth or self-enhancement consonant with one's chosen beliefs and values. Hence, spirituality is understood as an active and deliberate endeavor.
>
> (Helminiak, 2006, p. 202)

Therefore, what we need to do in order to develop a normative dimension of spirituality is 'to determine the structures, mechanisms or processes, and triggers that pertain to spiritual integration and growth' (Helminiak, 2008, p. 164). Finally, 'the legitimate scientific question about spirituality would be this: What is going on in people, how, and why, when they are engaged in spiritual pursuits, including what some might call a "relationship with God"?' (Helminiak, 2008, p. 166).

Moreover, Helminiak (2008) adds that when we consider spirituality as an essential part of the human mind, then any human functioning that involves experience, understanding, judgment, and decision must be, by definition, spiritual. We are all spiritual beings, but not every one of us makes full use of their innate spirituality, whether for good or ill (Jastrzębski, 2020).

> The human spirit shows itself in the generation of a world mediated by meaning and motivated by value. But every human being lives with some set of meanings and values, ideas and ideals, visions and virtues. In part these spiritual components are constitutive of human experience. Indeed, devoid of meanings and values, the distinctive qualities of humanity, an experience could not rightly be called human. Therefore, all human experience is spiritual. All human experience depends on the functioning of the human spirit.
>
> (Helminiak, 2008, p. 172)

The major task that lies before the new science of spirituality is to develop its normative component. To begin with, we can say that a healthy spirituality should be characterized by an appropriate balance between the various dimensions of one's life such as the self, relationships, work, and emotions. Moreover, healthy spiritual practices should help rather than hinder in developing one's humanity in all its dimensions. For example, a healthy spirituality would empower us to express our emotions. In a therapeutic context, spirituality has to be in line with psychological or therapeutic work. One of the major fruits of a healthy spirituality should be an increasing compassion for others and for ourselves. A healthy spirituality stems from a set of values embedded in a community that cherishes them. This community and its well-established rules become a guiding principle or teacher for us and accompany us in our spiritual growth. Finally, a healthy spirituality leads us to become involved in the real world with real people, helping others live a better life (Picciotto & Fox, 2018). It also allows us to become aware of and to accept the circumstances of our lives (Cashwell et al., 2010).

Healthy Spirituality in View of Spiritual Growth

No doubt, spiritual growth should be a healthy endeavor related to the advanced stages of personal development. In order to be evaluated, we need to distinguish between true and false spiritualities and determine the mechanisms or processes by which a healthy spirituality operates and distinguish them from those that are dysfunctional (Helminiak, 2006). Another guideline is that an authentic spirituality helps people be open to the demands of spiritual growth and is expressed in the willingness to accept both positive and negative life experiences (Fox & Piccotto, 2019).

Any development requires leaving something behind or giving up certain familiar ways of behavior, simply because one is not able to become everything that one thinks one could be. In psychoanalysis, the developmental work focuses on accepting reality and renouncing outdated or unattainable ways of being, especially giving up narcissistic imaginations. Our spiritual development requires us to leave some things behind and to give up familiar ways of behaving. If we have idealized expectations of ourselves and what we could be, we will need to let these go. At the same time, we must be on guard against pathological self denial and its masochistic propensities, and ensure that our spiritual development in such cases does not focus on self-destructive behaviors (Parsons, 2006).

Practical Considerations

Unfortunately, spirituality, like any other human activity, can be used in both healthy and harmful ways.

According to Lisa Cataldo (2013):

> Spirituality, as an aspect of human life, can be lived out in both positive and negative ways. On the positive side, it can lead us to good-humored acceptance of our flawed selves as both minuscule blips in a wide, wide universe and glorious examples of creativity and love. It can make us aware that 'nothing human is alien to us,' that we are as human beings capable of the most elevated acts of service and selflessness, as well as the

> most base acts of greed, hatred, and destructiveness. This is humility, and it is perhaps the greatest feeling of 'real' to which we can aspire. But if it is not experienced as inseparable from our flawed human selves and placed in the wider context of human life, including the power of culture and the reality of suffering, spiritual experience can also lead to solipsism and inflation, a kind of 'happy blindness' to our own pain and the real pain experienced in the bodies and minds of others.
>
> (p. 283)

According to the Bible, a healthy tree is recognized by its good fruit. The fruit of successful spiritual growth is concrete change in terms of knowledge, wisdom, attitude, and motivation. Normally, it leads to one's transformation. Some fruit appears rapidly while some requires time to ripen (Roy, 2001). According to William James (2010), the fruits of conversion are convictions that

> (1) the visible world is part of a more spiritual universe, from which it draws its chief significance; (2) that union or harmonious relation with that higher universe is our true end; (3) that prayer or inner communion with the spirit thereof – be that spirit 'God' or 'law' – is a process wherein work is really done, and spiritual energy flows in and produces effects, psychological or material, within the phenomenal world; (4) a new zest which adds itself like a gift to life, and takes the form either of lyrical enchantment or of appeal to earnestness and heroism; (5) an assurance of safety and a temper of peace, and, in relation to others, a preponderance of loving affections.
>
> (p. 377)

After James, Allport (1950) in his classic work *The Individual and His Religion* described a healthy or mature spirituality as open to criticism and revision, rich and flexible with respect to one's transformational motives or values. Moreover, healthy spirituality provides one with a philosophy of life or existential meaning, as well as an attitude of tolerance for diversity. Immature spirituality, however, focuses on exclusions and is self-centered. It is also prejudicial, fanatical, impulsive, and primitive. Unhealthy spirituality does not really provide us with any meaningful response to existential questions and does not equip us to revise our beliefs when necessary (Jastrzębski, 2020). For P. Scott Richards and Allen E. Bergin (2000), healthy spirituality is intrinsic, interpersonal, reconciling, actualizing, renewing, nurturing, and inspiring, whereas unhealthy spirituality is extrinsic, narcissistic, authoritarian, aggressive, perfectionist, dependent, and hyper-spiritual.

In short, spirituality can be mature or immature, healthy or unhealthy, authentic or false. Healthy spirituality is marked by compassion, love, charity, freedom, creativity, connection, morality, courage, calmness, and intuition. Unhealthy spirituality is characterized by indifference, despair, isolation, self-centeredness, self-hatred, hatred toward others, violence, anxiety, and confusion (Cataldo, 2013; Jones, 2019). Finally, healthy spirituality can be supported through a rational and empirical assessment that demonstrates its internal logical sense as it relates to adaptive functioning and well-being (Zinnbauer, 2013)

Normative Guidelines

Spiritual paths are not the same for everyone: they can be smooth or bumpy, and can lead either to growth or to decline. According to Pargament (2007), the final outcome depends on the degree spirituality is integrated into one's life situations and their larger context. The most effective spirituality is a *well-integrated spirituality*; problems arise in *dis-integrated spirituality*, where particular elements are out of balance and working against each other. In a well-integrated spirituality, all elements work well together in synchrony with each other in response to life's situations; they are flexible, embedded in a larger social context, and oriented toward spiritual goals that are capable of encompassing the full range of human potential and providing a powerful guiding vision. People living with dis-integrated spirituality fail to meet their life challenges and requirements, often clash with their social systems, and demonstrate too much rigidity or a lack of independent judgment that misdirects them in their pursuit of spiritual values (Pargament, 2007).

A well-integrated spirituality has to encompass the full range of human experiences, including the darker side of life, and should provide an overarching vision to guide our life. Nonetheless, some spiritual pathways are dead ends leading to the spiritual dis-integration of individuals and communities. We can become spiritually disoriented when our ways of thinking, feeling, acting, relating, and coping fail to reach our spiritual goals and cause us to get trapped or lost. Western culture, with its accent on freedom, tends to encourage people to construct their own personal spiritualities. Because of this 'smorgasbord approach' to spirituality, many may remain spiritually malnourished. Thus, in cafeteria-style spirituality, we can find forms of spirituality that are self-contained and focused only on personal gratification; there is often a pronounced lack of concern for others; the often-hollow practices found in this spiritual disorientation result in the absence of authentic sacred feelings and a lack of connection to the wisdom of great spiritual teachers. Most people can live with some degree of spiritual inconsistency, but when the elements of one's spirituality are in conflict with each other, these inconsistencies become more challenging (Pargament, 2007).

In the context of spiritual struggles, Kenneth Pargament and Julie Exline (2022) propose to associate healthy spirituality to the concept of wholeness, which is marked by breadth and depth, cohesiveness, and life affirmation. They present it against its opposite, brokenness, which is marked by shallowness, harshness, imbalance, and narrowness. Both wholeness and brokenness describe spiritual pathways and destinations.

Spirituality and religiosity have been identified as natural points of reference to orient people in their lives. The task of the therapist is to identify and to support the beliefs, values, and practices that enhance their client's ability to cope with life-challenging situations (Sperry & Shafranske, 2005).

Psychiatric Evaluation of Spiritual Experiences and Challenges for an Adequate Diagnosis

How to evaluate spiritual experiences? Arbitrary standards cannot be applied to evaluate such experiences. The best way to do so is by using our wisdom as well as by looking for the fruits of such experiences. While evaluating spirituality in the context of mental health, we may make errors of reductionism. The lack of appreciation for the transformational dimension of spiritual experiences may lead to a pathologization of genuine spiritual experiences. In this way, Freud described the experiences of mystics as infantile narcissism. On the other hand, a lack of appreciation for mental health issues can lead the counselor to confuse pathology with a mystical spiritual experience.

In this context, the most important issue is how to distinguish between these two different states of the human psyche. First, there is no laboratory test that can help us. Second, there is no specific symptom that could indicate the presence of a mental disorder, because some common psychiatric symptoms such as hallucinations and dissociation can occur among physiologically sound individuals with intense spiritual experiences. However, we can look at the way people process this information. In the case of mental disorders, we may observe an abnormal duration, intensity, and modulation of such processes as they are either disproportionate in their severity or inappropriate in their character. We can add to these abnormal forms of cognition such as disjuncture in the logical flow of thoughts (e.g., loose association, flight of ideas), the lack of capacity to modulate exaggerated emotional states, and the lack of concern for other persons' feelings or reactions. Finally, these inappropriate behaviors will normally diminish relatively rapidly in response to medication. In contrast, religiously induced suffering will not disappear with the use of medication. Nonetheless, one should not rely exclusively on the response to medication as a way to differentiate normal spiritual experiences from mental disorders because of the many different factors that come into play and add to the complexity of this kind of situation (Griffith, 2010).

> Psychiatric illness can malform religious experiences, amplify suffering in daily life, and create caricatures of spirituality. Assessing impacts of mental illness in religious life is a clinical challenge, however. Intense religious experiences, particularly in group contexts, can produce within a normal person literally any symptom of psychiatric illness, including hallucinations, delusional fears, dissociative trans states, or panic anxiety. Such a person is badly served by a label of mental illness. Moreover,

> a person with a *bona fide* mental illness may yet be able to elaborate a rich, complex spiritual life, in which personal spirituality helps provide resilience against the illness. A mentally ill person can have a normal religious life.
>
> (Griffith, 2010, p. 181)

It is not uncommon for spiritual practices to produce profound transformational experiences and to help people with mental disorders (Turner & Hodge, 2020). In many instances, these experiences may be episodes of spiritual emergence that encourage growth and positive transformation. They are relatively easy to integrate into one's daily life. In other occurrences, however, they can become spiritual emergencies that can give rise to mental health symptoms, such as depression, anxiety, and even symptoms of psychosis. Unfortunately, for some counselors, this transformative territory is simply unknown. Their tendency may then be to pathologize these experiences rather than to understand them within a spiritual or religious framework. When this occurs, there is always the risk that a profound transformative process may be undermined and usurped. However, counselors who are strongly drawn to spiritual experiences may focus on the positive elements of these experiences and miss the psychological issues at stake. As a common example, consider the person who spends an extraordinary amount of time serving others. It is possible, of course, that they have a personal spirituality that is oriented toward social justice and servant leadership. It is equally possible, however, that this service orientation is grounded in a very weak sense of self, a self that needs approval from others, and seeks it through caring for others. Their acts of service may be masking mental health issues such as anxiety, depression, and low self-esteem. Interpreting such behaviors as a spiritual gift may cause the therapist to miss any one of many underlying mental health issues that may be present (Cashwell & Young, 2011).

> When religion interacts with psychiatric illness, the levels of complexity multiply. Religious beliefs color a person's thoughts, feelings, and behaviors with an added hue of meaning. When a person is already depressed, religious beliefs can irrationally amplify guilt, apathy, or self-hatred. Religious beliefs can escalate the intensity of intrusive thoughts in obsessive-compulsive disorder. Religion that activates a sense of uncertainty or dread can intensify any anxiety disorder. […] Religion can transform delusions and hallucinations into psychoses. Religious beliefs have lethal consequences when used to justify suicidal or homicidal impulses. Those with psychiatric disorders suffer daily, often in ways hidden to others around them, and religious faith sometimes exacerbates this suffering instead of lessening it.
>
> (Griffith, 2010, p. 8)

Within a spiritual journey, an individual may experience either a spiritual emergence (i.e., a gradual spiritual awakening with little, if any, disruption in psychological and social functioning) or a spiritual emergency (i.e., a significant and often abrupt disruption in psychological and social functioning). In other cases, however, the emergence of a spiritual problem occurs concomitantly with a psychiatric disorder and may, in some cases, serve as a primary indicator of the disorder. In some instances, the spiritual content may be strongly, if not solely, an artifact of the psychopathology. Consider, for example, an individual who has psychotic delusions and believes he is Jesus Christ, the son of God (Cashwell & Young, 2011).

Hallucinations and Delusions

The religiously oriented hallucinations, delusions, and preoccupations that commonly appear during psychosis are usually quite easily recognized as pathological. It does not take extensive psychiatric training to see that such phenomena are nearly always self-serving and compensatory, as in many instances they represent the efforts of a wounded self-image to feel special and more powerful. They generally cause a person to feel different from and in most cases superior to other people. Unfortunately, they are very often associated with a deterioration in other areas of daily life. It is also painfully obvious that they are held together with a tension and a rigidity that are clearly defensive in nature (May, 1992).

> Grandiosity, feelings of special powers, hallucinations, delusions, and many other so-called secondary symptoms of schizophrenia serve in large part as attempts to reinforce or shore up a severely fragmented sense of self. These symptoms are psychic band-aids and baling wire that patch together the remnants of self-definition, and they can also sometimes be found in extreme forms of spiritual narcissism.
>
> (May, 1987, p. 121)

May (1987) underlines that while working on the psychiatry ward, he never encountered a single patient who reported a unitive experience linked to a psychosis. They reported only some distortion of their perception of self or time but never any experience of unconditional love. There appears to be no obvious relationship between neurosis and spiritual experience (May, 1987).

Religious Psychosis

Psychotic thinking can interact destructively with one's belief system in multiple ways. Sacred texts can easily supply the content of psychotic thinking. This can, for example, lead to an obsession with the coming of an eschatological age, attacks on others considered to be possessed by Satan, or to the presence of auditory hallucinations in which God's voice is commanding one to attack one's doctor. Other existing spiritual experiences or practices may trigger psychotic episodes in vulnerable persons. Moreover, religious convictions can potentially cause a mentally ill individual to refuse psychiatric treatment in favor of prayer or spiritual rituals, thus aggravating their situation as mentally ill individuals. In certain religious groups, mentally ill people can be judged as not having enough faith or as possessing a weak character, which only increases their suffering. Finally, psychotic persons easily fall prey to manipulation by intimidating spiritual leaders since their cognitive capacities are very limited at the time of psychosis (Griffith, 2010).

Both spiritual experiences and schizophrenia, each in its own way, can present a threat to the human self. Schizophrenia destroys one's self-definition by immersing it into a fragmented emptiness. And although a spiritual experience can immerse the self-image in mystery and dissolve it in love, it can, in certain cases, also lead to disintegration. If this unitive experience is not accompanied by the surrender of one's self to a Higher Power, it can easily lead to psychosis or suicide (May, 1987).

For some people, passing through a period of psychosis is a deeply spiritual and transformative experience. After their psychotic episode, some people became more creative, daring, and accomplished (Griffith, 2010). Some dissociation can be a fruit of spiritual transformation. In this case, it produces radically new and more accurate perceptions of reality. This could be called a 'new-order' as distinct from a psychiatric 'dis-order.' This transformation may take the form of a sudden change, or it can be a long and rather slow process. Later on, these kinds of spiritual experiences are also integrated into a new level of personal identity. However, one has to distinguish this from other dissociative experiences within the spiritual context that are neither healthy nor creative. In fact, extreme dissociation indicates an underlying psychiatric disorder and occurs if people become spiritually fanatical or defensive. The most dramatic form of dissociation is that of Satanic possession, but it is a rare phenomenon. It is usually preceded by an intense period of obsession. The signs of possession have been clearly described in Roman Catholic and Anglican theological literature, and we will talk a bit more about that in the chapter on the dark side of spirituality. Before diagnosing a possession, both a psychiatric and a spiritual evaluation are needed, because some psychological manifestations may masquerade as forces of evil. Much expertise and experience are needed in such cases. One of the possible diagnostic questions in this context relates to one's relationship to the world as a consequence of one's spiritual experience: Does a person's relationship to the world encourage them to become more committed to society for the sake of others, or is it an attempt to escape from this responsibility? (May, 1992)

There is a link between religious delusions and violence. This is because psychotic persons frequently interpret their auditory hallucinations as coming from either God or Satan and that what they hear is a direct order to execute a violent act. Religious delusions can also lead to self-injurious behaviors, which at times can be extreme. There is also a close association between membership in a religious cult and the presence of mental illness, because in both cases, people invest so much of themselves in implausible and idiosyncratic beliefs that their participation in an ordinary life becomes very difficult. The only difference is that psychotic persons do not function properly even in a religious group where some ascetic practices are encouraged. Sound spiritual beliefs should also produce good fruit in one's life and do not present a mixture of positive and negative symptoms as is often the case with psychosis (Griffith, 2010).

Religiously based psychotic delusions can be summarized in four points:

1) Misidentification with some major religious figure such as Buddha or Christ,
2) Persecutory beliefs such as being targeted for harm by the Devil or Jinn,
3) A grandiose messianic mission,
4) Self-belittlement because one is convinced of having committed unpardonable sins (Griffith, 2010).

Affective Disorders

In the case of clinical depression, religious beliefs that evoke a sense of guilt or of being condemned by God may result in a refusal of the needed psychiatric treatment. They may also lead to self-neglect, general suffering, and, finally, suicide. In the case of mania, when people have difficulty managing their psychic energy, it is difficult to distinguish it from normal religious enthusiasm, passionate commitment, or even perhaps from an ecstatic moment. Normally, religious beliefs are a buffer against committing suicide, since many spiritually oriented groups that view life as a precious gift condemn any form of willfully taking one's life. Religious beliefs can also mobilize more hope and help people find purpose in life (Griffith, 2010).

Doubts about religious beliefs are common and may sometimes cause emotional distress. At other times, religion plays a role in making people more susceptible to suicide. They may wish to die in order to be with God, to see life after death, or may even want to end their lives after breaking with their faith community. Suicidal thoughts may also be occasioned by delusions and hallucinations of a religious nature (Weber & Pargament, 2014). This may happen when someone is convinced that God is calling them 'home' and that death is just the gate to a better life, when people think this self-destructive act can have a redemptive function, when the feelings of being abandoned by God are extremely powerful, and when someone decides to sacrifice their life for their faith, as in the case of suicide bombers (Griffith, 2010).

The Spiritual Dark Night versus Clinical Depression

Another challenge facing both spirituality and psychiatry is differentiating between a spiritual dark night as an absence of any spiritual consolation or a clinical depression. The rule of thumb would be to misinterpret a dark night as a depression rather than the reverse (May, 2004). When attempts to remedy a depression are only minimally successful, one can ask whether it is not actually a spiritual dark night and opt to work with it on the spiritual level. Conversely, when one mistakes a depression for a spiritual experience, one can create unnecessary suffering and confusion regarding the nature of spiritual desolation. This is actually quite a common occurrence since many people use spirituality as a defense mechanism in order to avoid dealing with real-life problems (spiritual bypass).

There are some useful elements that help in discerning between a spiritual dark night and clinical depression:

- The dark night does not affect the quality of one's work;
- During the dark night, one does not lose one's sense of humor. In depression, one is more cynical or bitter;
- The dark night enhances one's level of compassion toward others. In clinical depression there is more self-absorption;
- One does not really want to liberate oneself from the dark night experience because it feels right;
- A person living through the dark night of the soul does not desperately seek help, but is looking for a way to understand what they are living through;
- In the presence of a person going through the dark night, one does not feel annoyed or frustrated (May, 1992).

Scrupulosity versus OCD

Scrupulosity is understood as a form of obsessive-compulsive disorder (OCD), often characterized by persistent doubts about God, one's sinfulness, and the adequacy of one's religious practices (Inozu et al., 2012). Scrupulosity is usually expressed by various forms of obsessions and compulsions with religious themes as well as hypermorality linked to guilt and shame (Cashwell & Young, 2011). The most common forms of scrupulosity are religious rituals, such as prayer or confession, in which the individual desperately seeks to achieve atonement for their perceived or imagined transgressions (Miller & Hedges, 2008). There is still a great need to develop more research regarding scrupulosity since it appears to be one of the most common forms of obsessive-compulsive disorder and causes significant mental distress (Cashwell & Young, 2011).

The primary way of helping people affected by scrupulosity is exposure and response prevention (ERP), also applied to other forms of OCD (Miller & Hedges, 2008). Its underlying principle is that when the individual confronts their fears and puts a stop to their escape response, they will experience a significant decrease in symptoms. When ERP is not applicable or too challenging, the therapist can use standard cognitive tools such as demonstrating the contradictions between the client's compulsive behavior and the teachings of their religion (Cashwell & Young, 2011). Also, some research has demonstrated that subtle differences may exist in how scrupulosity is experienced in various religious traditions as exemplified in comparisons between Islamic and Christian believers (Inozu et al., 2012).

Anxiety

When anxiety disorders color religious experiences, they add to the fear and dread that are already present. For instance, panic disorders propel people to escape from perceived dangers and push them into a frantic search for security in the divine. Moreover, anxiety disorders, when experienced within a religious frame, can cause an increase in personal suffering as well as a significant deterioration of meaningful relationships. One loses the joy of being in community, and one's personal relationship with the divine may become a source of apprehension/desolation rather than consolation (Griffith, 2010).

Self-Loss

Self-loss and a sense of self-transcendence are two of the major markers of certain spiritual experiences. There are also pathological instances of self-loss such as the depersonalization described by the *DSM-5* as a dissociative cluster, a sense of detachment from one's usual sense of self. What distinguishes depersonalization from healthy episodes involving changes in the perception of our body is the sense of isolation and alienation from other people and our environment. The pathological episodes of self-loss do not involve any relational aspect, nor do they prevent people from building meaningful relationships. Another pathological version of self-loss is visible in some cases of schizophrenia and in certain psychotic states when the usual sense of one's self fades away and produces maladaptive consequences. Also, in healthy self-loss experiences, the tendency toward psychoticism or neuroticism is no greater than in a healthy population (Yaden et al., 2017).

Conclusions

Understanding spirituality in the contemporary context has become a demanding task. Today's concept of spirituality is very broad and universal, and for this reason, very vague. If we want the notion of spirituality to include all phenomena that fall under the umbrella of spirituality, its definition will become even more vague and ambiguous. Despite these changes, people still need guidance in their lives. In the past, as well as in the present, spirituality lived in the context of a specific spiritual tradition that normally equipped people with a set of concrete rules and guidelines on how to develop spiritual maturity. For people engaged in a nonreligious form of spirituality, there is a challenge. How does one assess a given spirituality regarding its effectiveness in helping a person in becoming a better human being? William James (2010) already believed that we need more than a pragmatic spirituality that brings to light only what serves human self-actualization. We need not only a pragmatic component (self-actualization) but also a normative one, pointing the way to self-transcendence, as Frankl (1988) hoped to accomplish with his logotherapy.

From the existential perspective, a healthy spirituality should lead one to a deeper and fuller engagement with the world, with oneself, and with others, taking full responsibility for one's actions and fulfilling one's values (Vachon et al., 2016). Rollo May (1958) describes this kind of healthy spirituality as a deep, self-aware, and authentic way of existence. The healthy functioning person accepts their reality in all dimensions of their being. Other aspects of living a healthy spirituality include the ability to face existential anxiety pertaining to death as an unavoidable fact of life, the duality of meaning and meaningless. Freedom and responsibility are also both part of living a healthy spirituality (Tan & Wong, 2012). Wong (2015) further suggests that healthy spirituality leads to building meaningful relationships.

The real importance of spiritual experiences lies in their potential to introduce positive changes into one's life and remains related to one's ability to integrate these experiences and to allow them to be transformative. A rule of thumb can be put forward in the form of a question: has the person affected by a spiritual experience become more loving or more selfish, more self-aware or more self-denying, more peaceful or more anxious, and so on?

Discussion Questions

1. If someone asked you to describe healthy spirituality, how would you respond?
2. If someone asked you to describe unhealthy spirituality, what would you respond?
3. Do you think we can develop a normative approach to evaluate spirituality?
4. In your life, have you experienced that, at certain times, your mental frame of mind influenced your spiritual growth? How?
5. Which sign of a healthy spirituality speaks to you the most?

References

Allport, G. W. (1950). *The individual and his religion: A psychological interpretation.* Macmillan.

Cashwell, C. S., & Young, J. S. (2011). Diagnosis and treatment. In C. S. Cashwell & J. S. Young (Eds.), *Integrating spirituality and religion into counseling: A guide to competent practice* (pp. 163–181). American Counseling Association.

Cashwell, C., Glosoff, H., & Hammond, C. (2010). Spiritual bypass: A preliminary investigation. *Counseling and Values, 54*(2), 162–174. https://doi.org/10.1002/j.2161-007X.2010.tb00014.x

Cataldo, L. (2013). Can there be a psychoanalytic spirituality? A response to Kenneth Porter. *Psychoanalytic Perspectives, 10*, 270–284.

Fox, J., & Picciotto, G. (2019). The mediating effects of spiritual bypass on depression, anxiety, and stress. *Counseling and Values, 64*(2), 227–245. https://doi.org/10.1002/cvj.12116

Frankl, V. E. (1988). *The will to meaning: Foundations and applications of logotherapy.* Meridian.

Griffith, J. L. (2010). *Religion that heals, religion that harms*. Guilford Press.

Helminiak, D. A. (2005). A down-to-earth approach to the psychology of spirituality a century after James's Varieties. *The Humanistic Psychologist, 33*(2), 69–86.

Helminiak, D. A. (2006). The role of spirituality in formulating a theory of the psychology of religion. *Zygon, 41*(1), 197–224.

Helminiak, D. A. (2008). Confounding the divine and the spiritual: Challenges to a psychology of spirituality. *Pastoral Psychology, 57*, 161–182.

Helminiak, D. A. (2011). Spirituality as an explanatory and normative science: Applying Lonergan's analysis of intentional consciousness to relate psychology and theology. *The Heythorp Journal, 52*, 596–627.

Inozu, M., Clark, D., & Karanci, A. (2012). Scrupulosity in Islam: A comparison of highly religious Turkish and Canadian samples. *Behavior Therapy, 43*, 190–202. https://doi.org/10.1016/j.beth.2011.06.002

James, W. (2010). *The varieties of religious experience*. Library of America Paperback Classic.

Jastrzębski, A. K. (2020). The normative aspect in the contemporary understanding of spirituality. *Wrocław Theological Review, 2*(28), 95–111.

Jones, R. S. (2019). *Spirit in session: Working with your client's spirituality (and your own) in psychotherapy*. Templeton Press.

May, G. G. (1987). *Will and spirit: A contemplative psychology*. HarperCollins.

May, G. G. (1992). *Care of mind/care of spirit: Psychiatric dimensions of spiritual direction*. Harper & Row.

May, G. G. (2004). *The dark night of the soul: A psychiatrist explores the connection between darkness and spiritual growth*. Harper.

May, R. E. (1958). *Existence – A new dimension in psychiatry and psychology*. Basic Books.

Miller, C. H., & Hedges, D. W. (2008). Scrupulosity disorder: An overview and introductory analysis. *Journal of Anxiety Disorders, 22*, 1042–1058.

Pargament, K. I. (2007). *Spiritually integrated psychotherapy: Understanding and addressing the sacred*. Guilford Press.

Pargament, K. I., & Exline, J. J. (2022). *Working with spiritual struggles in psychotherapy: From research to practice*. Guilford Press.

Parsons, M. (2006). Ways of transformation. In D. M. Black (Ed.), *Psychoanalysis and religion in the 21st century: Competitors or collaborators* (pp. 117–131). Routledge.

Picciotto, G., & Fox, J. (2018). Exploring experts' perspectives on spiritual bypass: A conventional content analysis. *Pastoral Psychology, 67*(1), 65–84. https://doi.org/10.1007/s11089-017-0796-7

Richards, P. S., & Bergin, A. E. (Eds.). (2000). *Handbook of psychotherapy and religious diversity*. American Psychological Association. https://doi.org/10.1037/10347-000

Roy, L. (2001). *Transcendent experiences: Phenomenology and critique*. University of Toronto Press.

Sperry, L., & Shafranske, E. P. (2005). Addressing the spiritual dimension in psychotherapy: Introduction and overview. In Sperry, L. & Shafranske, E. P. (Eds.), *Spiritually oriented psychotherapy* (pp. 11–29). American Psychological Association.

Tan, S.-Y., & Wong, T. K. (2012). Existential therapy: Empirical evidence and clinical applications from a Christian perspective. *Journal of Psychology and Christianity, 31*(3), 272–277.

Turner, P. R., & Hodge, D. R. (2020). Spiritually informed interventions and psychotic disorders: A systematic review of randomized controlled trials. *Research on Social Work Practice, 30*(8), 895–906. https://doi.org/10.1177/1049731520946824

Vachon, M., Bessette, P.C., & Goyette, Ch. (2016). 'Growing from an invisible wound': A humanistic-existential approach to PTSD. IntechOpen. https://doi.org/10.5772/64290

Weber, S., & Pargament, K. (2014). The role of religion and spirituality in mental health. *Current Opinion in Psychiatry*, *27*, 358–363. https://doi.org/10.1097/YCO.0000000000000080

Wong, T. P. P. (2015). Meaning therapy: Assessments and interventions. *Existential Analysis*, 26(1), 154–167.

Yaden, D. B., Haidt, J., Hood, R. W., Vago, D. R., & Newberg, A. B. (2017). The varieties of self-transcendent experience. *Review of General Psychology*, *21*(2), 143–160. https://doi.org/10.1037/gpr0000102

Zinnbauer, B. J. (2013). Models of healthy and unhealthy religion and spirituality. In K. Pargament (Ed.), *APA handbook of psychology, religion, and spirituality* (Vol. 2: *An applied psychology of religion and spirituality*, pp. 71–89). American Psychological Association. https://doi.org/10.1037/14046-004

9 The Dark Side of Religion and Spirituality

Introduction

While we all accept the importance of positive spiritual growth, at times some practitioners of religion and spirituality become misguided in their pursuits despite their best intentions. We also know that distorted and misinterpreted spirituality can lead to various degrees of error and even to devastating destruction, as witnessed in the terrorist attacks of 9/11 (Helminiak, 2008; Jastrzębski, 2020).

Spirituality is part of our lives at its best and at its worst. It can foster expressions of the greatest human potential, but it can also become a latent and destructive force with the power to wreak havoc on human lives. When used well, spirituality has the potential to add color, depth, and meaning to our everyday life, but the opposite is also possible. 'Spirituality' is not always a synonym for 'goodness.' Spirituality has been used to justify forced conversions, suicide, torture, and genocide. Even today, some parents deny medical treatment to their children for religious reasons. We still see attacks on places of worship, cases of mass suicide, violent confrontations fueled by conflicting spiritual stands, and spiritual leaders who abuse their most vulnerable members in horrific ways (Pargament, 2007).

James L. Griffith (2010) summarizes this state of affairs very dramatically:

> Aggression, coercion, stigmatization, and exploitation propelled by religions have produced some of the greatest moral catastrophes and humanitarian disasters that human beings have suffered. Religious justification ideologies have helped genocide, ethnic cleansings, racism, and abusive social hierarchies to thrive.
>
> (p. 167)

Spiritual Manipulation

Spiritual beliefs and practices are normally oriented toward guiding people in the direction of a fullness of life and happiness, but they often bring opposite results. Religious beliefs can help a person endure suffering, but certain beliefs can also become a source of anguish, an obstacle to development,

DOI: 10.4324/9781003262145-10

or cause the destruction of relationships between people. Some spiritual traditions have a dark side that, in the name of preserving the sacred 'order of affairs,' stop women and young people from openly questioning anything, younger people from admonishing elders and speaking freely or 'disobeying' the rules of group leaders. Sometimes, the body is considered to be something completely negative, and which must therefore be dominated through radical asceticism. Some practices of meditation or prayer also cause complete separation of people from their community and even from themselves (Griffith & Griffith, 2003).

Negative experiences with religious and spiritual organizations may include abuse, condemnation, propagation of fear, and guilt. They may be linked to ideologies that restrict human potential and suffocate human growth, thus becoming a form of spiritual violence. This brings people to lose touch with their authentic spirituality. Some begin to see spirituality as judgmental and oppressive. Unfortunately, they may also abandon the idea of spirituality in general, thus losing the source of supportive spiritual energy. For many, this eventually leads to a withdrawal from their religious organization. Others may dismiss their inner wisdom in order to gain acceptance by their peers and avoid rejection by spiritual leaders at the cost of continuing the abusive spiritual practice. In both cases, people are traumatized and feel powerless. This can be considered to be spiritual oppression (Johnson, 2013).

Destructive behaviors occur most often, but not always, on the outskirts of mainstream religion and involve both leaders and groups who are convinced of a special mission commissioned to them directly by God. Such persons will not only refuse to listen to therapists but also disregard the advice of their own religious authorities. Leaders of destructive groups are most often convinced of their uniqueness and infallibility. For this reason, their behavior can easily spiral out of control and lead to acts contrary to healthy morality, including bombings, collective suicides, and other acts of violence. One of the signs of a leader's narcissism is their self-designation as having unique access to some Higher Power that endows them with exceptional privileges. Such leaders willingly blame others, point their fingers, and judge; they use spirituality to manipulate others. It is also imperative for them to impose their own spiritual experience on others as the only true path of spirituality for everyone. Such an attitude should raise skepticism. When there is a risk of abuse or violence on the part of the spiritual leader, the best form of defense is social control. Unfortunately, in similar situations, only external, objective observers can adequately assess the situation. Those who are involved are very often convinced that they are making good conscious choices, guided by the voice of the divine. In addition, many spiritual traditions emphasize the necessity of obedience and promote the acceptance of suffering in the name of faith (Griffith & Griffith, 2003).

Some leaders of religious groups gain respect through their manipulation of others. Such persons are hungry for admiration and submission from others, and are not eager to deal with the needs of their subordinates. Such relationships are the antithesis of spirituality. Unfortunately, these people often hold managerial positions in communities and use the phraseology of spiritual enlightenment and the glory of the divine to mask their methods of seducing others (Griffith & Griffith, 2003). Spiritual leaders can be dishonest and conceal prejudice and bigotry to outsiders behind the appearance of spiritual tolerance. The only reason they participate in spiritual practices is to allay the guilt that accompanies their immoral behavior; they appeal to spiritual doctrines to justify their authority and power. Such behaviors become even more reprehensible when the leader lays claim to a personal aura of spiritual holiness. Spiritual hypocrisy can be understood as a deliberate misuse of spirituality in order to achieve not only nonspiritual but even anti-spiritual goals. It is often accompanied by spiritual inauthenticity (Pargament, 2007). 'Because of their sacred mission, religious institutions, clergy, and leaders are generally held to a higher standard. And when they fall short, many people struggle with disappointment, anger, hatred and resentment towards religious hypocrisy' (Pargament & Exline, 2022, p. 306).

Spiritual Narcissism

Unfortunately, as soon as a person becomes aware of their spiritual growth, there is a risk of them falling prey to spiritual narcissism. This is the unconscious or conscious use of one's spiritual development to increase self-importance in order to feel more special or holier than others. It seems that our ego can very easily convince us that we have already become holy. When this occurs, the spiritual journey that normally should lead to the deepening of our humility transforms itself into a path of growing pride. When spiritual narcissism takes over the entire spiritual process, it will very probably sabotage it. This can take two forms. First, narcissism forces spiritual leaders to believe that they are growing spiritually thanks to their own efforts. Second, there is a conviction that they have been selected above other human beings and granted supernatural gifts or abilities. Either way, the narcissist becomes self-engrossed (May, 1987; Picciotto et al., 2018).

Spiritual Intolerance, Violence, and Extremism

Although it is normal for people to want to preserve and protect the values that they cherish, spiritual extremism can result when the extraordinary measures that are taken to protect these values turn into extreme measures. Spiritual dedication can thus turn into a fanatical pursuit that justifies extreme measures such as acts of cruelty to others and to oneself. In spiritual extremism there is no place for humility, mercy, and compassion, thus leading people away from a healthy spirituality. Spiritual extremism can foster a spiritual intolerance that is expressed as shunning, faith-based prejudice, fanaticism, and finally, as participation in religious wars. In spiritual intolerance, people try to deal with spiritual differences by simply destroying anyone who is not part of their spiritual group (Pargament, 2007).

Furthermore, religious beliefs may influence medical decision-making. When medical advice is refused, this can create a conflict between a doctor's and a spiritual leader's opinions. But before coming up with a definitive judgment in such instances, one has to be very careful. For example, when a woman chooses to give birth to a child while risking her own life, we should see an intentional sacrifice and a courageous act of heroism, rather than any kind of manifestation coming from the dark side of spirituality. Sometimes, religious affiliation causes delays in seeking treatment for mental illness. For example, some members of certain faith traditions (e.g., Christian) are convinced the cause of schizophrenia is possession by evil spirits or is a punishment that comes directly from the divine, hindering people with religious delusions from receiving the support they need (Weber & Pargament, 2014).

Many spiritual leaders gain power and personal profit by using spiritual rhetoric. Spiritual vocabulary, thanks to its powerful metaphors, touches people, but once stripped of its original meaning, can give a distorted, perverted message when it is used for hateful, egoistic objectives. For example, in the mid-twentieth century, the Yugoslav and Serbian politician Slobodan Milošević, used Slavic myths to arouse hatred among his soldiers, prompting them to carry out acts of mass genocide in the name of the Holy Trinity. We often hear about pastors stealing from their own communities, or about charismatic leaders maintaining abusive sexual relations with their members, and becoming sexual predators. Spiritual vocabulary may also be used for manipulation. For example, Serbian psychiatrists Jovan Rašković and Radovan Karadžić used their knowledge of the mechanisms of paranoia for political purposes. They wanted to induce indignation and fear in order to fuel nationalistic attitudes. This led to a rekindling of people's primitive suspicions and fears, to the extent that their long history of mutual kindness and goodwill was destroyed (Griffith & Griffith, 2003). During the same conflict, Ratko Mladić, the commander of the Serbian forces, decreed that Bosnian Muslims were no longer fellow members of a once-shared country but rather the worst enemies of his nation. He was convinced that liberating the sacred land for his own people was his holy mission (Halberstam, 2001).

> When killing for God, one may even feel righteous or contemptuous of less zealous individuals who have qualms. The social impact is profound. Individuals are motivated to find, even manufacture, religiously grounded justifications for violence. The religious call to action provides cover for moral accountability. The religiously violent can act out freely their darkest, most suppressed impulses to maim, to prey upon, to punish, to exact revenge, while feeling themselves only to be closer to God in the process.
>
> (Griffith, 2010, p. 167)

Spiritual Oppression

Social emotions evoked in religious groups, such as pride, honor, guilt, and shame serve to keep members aligned with group values and agendas as well as with the expectations of their spiritual leaders. Using this mechanism, they create a group-oriented self in each of their followers. Personal objections are silenced, and all forms of opposition disarmed. Another dark side of this process is the dissociation that is required to suppress incongruent opinions. This process restricts one's personal self and moral reasoning. Humiliation is a kind of emotional aggression that openly lowers the other person's social status or dignity in the presence of others. It is a violation of the victim's self-respect and causes immeasurable resentment and bitterness that can be difficult to forget. An act of humiliation can lead to low self-esteem and powerless rage (Griffith, 2010), thus turning a potential survivor into a victim.

When researchers applied a feminist perspective to the codependency problem linking victims to perpetrators of domestic violence and abuse, they highlighted the role victims inadvertently played in these relationships, as some of their behaviors actually served to perpetuate their problem. Victims often seem reluctant to take any action to stop the cycle of violence because they are not willing or able to take a stand against their abuser for fear of losing the relationship, and then not being able to take care of themselves and their children in the future. Some of them tolerate mistreatment because they are taught in their faith traditions to be humble and to fight their pride. As a consequence, they deny their own dignity, which leaves their manipulator unchallenged. Practical support is definitely needed, and can usually be found in compassionate therapists working in agencies specialized in helping survivors escape situations of domestic violence. However, another tool in resolving this situation is found in regaining one's spiritual strength by developing such a relationship with God that it will support the establishment of a healthy sense of self and personal autonomy, as well as affirm the individual as being capable of living in union and co-stewardship with God (Mahoney & Pargament, 2004).

Manipulated members of religious sects can end up denying to themselves that they are in a situation of spiritual oppression and defending their spiritual leaders despite having uncovered their manipulative strategies. This phenomenon is called silencing of the personal self. When this occurs, an individual's moral self becomes suppressed; the moral dilemmas that ensue can result in physical or psychological symptoms of varying degrees of severity. This can be accompanied by other dissociative attitudes such as bad faith and doubling, which can justify acts of violence against outgroups. Doubling relates to both conscious and unconscious strategies used to find a way through an unmoral world while preserving some sense of personal morality. It is a form of chosen self-deception that allows the individual to perform acts that they would otherwise consider to be immoral. These mechanisms create a situation where the individual experiences emptiness and emotional distancing from others while simultaneously taking part in the group's abusive, sadistic, or exploitive behaviors that, in different circumstances, would never even have come to their mind (Griffith, 2010).

Spiritual Stigmatization

Research and the media have demonstrated that across the world, members of many faith groups including Muslims and Christians are stigmatized because of their faith. This can lead people to try to hide their spiritual identity and has important implications for counseling. Indeed, these clients will most probably be hypersensitive and prone to interpreting even the most innocent of situations as harboring aggression or a lack of acceptance by their counselor. Unfortunately, some counselors may not be aware of this reality (Stewart-Sicking et al., 2020). Moreover, many clinicians are biased by the assumptions that originated in the early days of psychology of religion as well as by their subsequent developments. They see the spirituality of religious people as being opposed to science and reason, and perhaps also as something that encourages them to make neurotic choices and to suffer more than necessary. As soon as they detect any sort of religious narrative, belief, or ritual, a spontaneous and negative emotional response is triggered within them and may cause them to unwittingly become more distant and disinterested in their client. This, combined with a possible inability to be sincerely empathetic and compassionate with their client because of their bias, often diminishes the effectiveness of the therapeutic process (Griffith, 2010).

In addition, at any given moment during therapy, the spiritual identities of either the counselor or the client, or both, can cause them to take on a role of being more privileged (or marginalized) than the other; this may heavily influence the process of therapy. The counselor should be aware of these potential barriers as they may hinder the establishment of a therapeutic relationship and prevent the counselor from fostering change (Stewart-Sicking et al., 2020). In such cases, the counselor is reminded of the critical importance of seeing the client as a complex human person rather than as someone determined exclusively by their spiritual identity. This is the only way the therapy can turn out successfully (Griffith, 2010).

From a social vantage point, by keeping strict boundaries with the outside world, many fundamentalist religious groups find themselves stigmatized. This process is supported by imposing a special dress code, shaving heads, chanting, and other rituals. Spiritual leaders often use this to their advantage in order to strengthen in-group identity and solidarity as well as to assure themselves that outsiders will be kept at a safe distance (Griffith, 2010).

Trauma and Spirituality

Recent research in the area of trauma and spirituality has focused on the way in which spirituality may either serve as a coping mechanism or as a factor fostering resilience – or both – when people face traumatic events

(Farley, 2007). Probably the most harmful form of trauma is that caused by misusing and manipulating spirituality, as we presented above. Researchers have also looked into the effects of traumatic events on people's spiritual lives. They have discovered that spirituality can either increase or decrease survivors' stress or distress because traumatic events force these individuals to reexamine their previously held values and beliefs as well as their fundamental sense of purpose in life (Park et al., 2017).

It is highly probable that any immature religious belief will increase the negative effects of the trauma. This happens, for instance, when people think that they have been punished or abandoned by God. When subjected to trauma, people tend to interpret the traumatic event in a way that shakes their beliefs in a secure and loving relationship with God. The healing must then come from a reappraisal of this interpretation, followed by the restoration of their sense of being loved and protected by God. This meaning-making process between trauma and spirituality seems to be a reciprocal interplay of influence. On the one hand, spirituality influences responses to trauma and, on the other, trauma can also influence and transform one's spirituality. No doubt, trauma can disrupt one's belief system, and recovery often needs to happen by creating new, more mature ways of understanding one's place in the world, including one's relationships with other people, and with God (Park et al., 2017).

Superstition and Magical Thinking

In the pursuit of ascetic practices such as fasting and self-deprivation, spiritually inclined people may seek some form of purification. Unfortunately, this spiritual discipline can be easily exaggerated and people start to see themselves as strong spiritual warriors who are convinced of their own self-mastery in spiritual growth. Practices of spiritual willfulness such as magic, witchcraft, and sorcery are an attempt to influence or control the spiritual realm; the goal here is to gain authority over spiritual powers and use them either to harm (black magic) or help (white magic) other people. Sometimes magic involves surrendering to an evil spirit for personal gain. All these actions are based on a conviction that

> spiritual understanding is like other understandings, that it can be described, delimited, objectified, and – most importantly – acquired and used. It is therefore no surprise that this leads one to view the mystery of life as a thing, a place to be attained, or a source of power to be tapped. This is not a surprising attitude; it is encouraged by our society for all activities. One should know what one wants, how to get it, and what to do with it.
>
> (May, 1987, p. 34)

For the most part, superstition is a matter of ignorance and it leads to regressive, childish behaviors. A certain mild form of superstition is widely present in our society and to some extent it can be considered a form of harmless play. However, it has to be noted that when facing stressful situations, we tend to become more receptive to superstition. The aim of superstition is to gain fortune, luck, or special graces from the divine. If practiced in a more sophisticated way, it can become a way to bargain with the divine as well as a quest for supernatural gifts, such as prophetism. In many ways, superstitious actions resemble those of children trying to manipulate their parents in order to obtain certain goods (May, 1987).

Spiritual Bypass

Magical thinking is only one of the forms of spiritual bypass. Craig S. Cashwell and colleagues (2007) state that 'spiritual bypass occurs when a person attempts to heal psychological wounds at the spiritual level only and avoids the important (albeit often difficult and painful) work at other levels, including the cognitive, physical, emotional, and interpersonal' (p. 140). Gabriela Picciotto and Jesse Fox (2018) define spiritual bypassing as 'the use of spiritual beliefs and practices to avoid dealing with psychological issues or trauma, relationship difficulties, emotional hassles, and developmental tasks' (p. 73).

According to Robert Masters (2010), spiritual bypassing can also be called a tendency to 'fast-track spiritual progress' or to take a 'spiritual shortcut' (p. 37). In reality, we should not try to cut corners in our spiritual growth. Skipping necessary steps in spiritual development, trying to take only big steps or leaps will sidetrack us and can generate enough suffering to force us to return to square one and work through what has been left unresolved, and eventually search for, accept, and acknowledge our vulnerability. Some examples of spiritual bypass include the following:

Anger-Phobia and Dissociation

This occurs when people refuse to honestly confront others when appropriate, or if they consider anger to be unbecoming of spiritual people like themselves. They are also fearful of confrontation because they do not want to disappoint others and are afraid to challenge or to disagree. The consequence of this approach is emotional dissociation and anger-phobia, which lead to the disconnection of the person from their emotional life; this, in turn, makes it very difficult for them to get in touch with their emotions and to express them (Picciotto & Fox, 2018; Picciotto et al., 2018).

Relying on a Spiritual Leader

Another form of spiritual bypassing is found in those who blindly follow a charismatic spiritual leader (Picciotto & Fox, 2018; Picciotto et al., 2018). This relationship may take on the characteristics of codependency, child-parent transference, or even cultism (Masters, 2010).

Blind Compassion

A symptom of spiritual bypassing is blind compassion, understood as exaggerated tolerance. Using this kind of spiritual bypass, people tend to be overly permissive toward others (Picciotto & Fox, 2018). Spiritual bypassing can reveal itself as compulsive goodness or an exaggerated caring for others that can indicate a low sense of self-worth and an unhealthy desire to be accepted (Cashwell et al., 2004; Cashwell, 2005).

Avoiding Responsibilities

One of the ways spiritual bypass manifests itself is through a powerful external locus of control and abdication of personal responsibility (Cashwell et al., 2010). This bypass often involves the avoidance of responsibilities associated with work or money (Picciotto & Fox, 2018; Picciotto et al., 2018).

Exaggerated Optimism

Overstated optimism is characterized by a dramatically unrealistic outlook that focuses on the bright side of problems as well as a refusal to acknowledge the darker parts of one's personality or personal history. People often encourage others to look at the positive side of life or events, and view optimism as a way of avoiding the more troublesome realities of their life. This stops them from dealing with their core pain, which is, in the final analysis, the most important challenge in life (Masters, 2010).

Misuse of Meditation and Prayer

Meditation can be termed a lifelong work in progress. After an initial period of enthusiasm, there are usually moments of boredom, discouragement, and confusion. As the journey of meditation progresses, one will certainly have to face disturbing emotions, difficult memories, and distracting thoughts. Authentic meditation is definitely not a flight from reality. On the contrary, it should bring us into the very heart of our existence (Finley, 2005).

To explain the role of prayer, Paul E. Johnson (1959) uses the example of an airplane pilot facing an in-flight mechanical emergency to explain the role of prayer. He states that prayer will not work as a substitute for a malfunctioning wing, nor does it obviate the need for a rapid assessment by the pilot. To use prayer for such reasons is to totally miss the point. Nonetheless, prayer may help calm the pilot's nerves so that the plane can be landed safely.

The Developmental Role of Spiritual Bypass

Spiritual bypassing distorts long-term spiritual growth because it impedes the process of spiritual development. Unresolved psychological problems can result in spiritual distress or impairment (Hill & Kilian, 2003). Nevertheless, in certain circumstances people can come to realize that they are using spiritual bypassing. Picciotto and colleagues (2018) presented four ways in which this discovery can happen: through living a deep feeling of existential crisis, by feedback or help from others in their social group, by living through a concrete experience of nonspiritual activity that makes the exaggerated focus on spiritual practices clearly visible, and finally, through relational conflict or distress in a relationship.

Probably everyone who embraces a spiritual journey will at some point use spiritual bypass since it can be useful as a short-term coping strategy when dealing with high-stress or difficult situations (Picciotto & Fox, 2018). Some researchers like Mark D. Forman (2010) and Masters (2010) consider spiritual bypassing to be a common process for those who pursue spiritual paths. In some cases, it seems to be an inevitable and natural stage of spiritual development, though it needs to be outgrown. Spirituality is not a way of escaping reality but rather of transforming it.

Spiritual Underdevelopment

One of the major spiritual problems of our times is that religious and spiritual education ends just when it is supposed to begin. For Christians, confirmation is often the last stage of a youth's religious education, which leaves them with their child like conceptions of divinity and prevents them from developing a more mature understanding of spirituality that would better serve them as they navigate the complexities of adult life. Pargament (2007) calls these conceptions 'small gods' as they fail to shed enough light on the most challenging dilemmas of life. This can lead to a false conviction that one possesses exclusive access to the ultimate truth or divine revelation (Pargament, 2007).

> Both religion and science can trivialize the territory of the sacred, and both regularly do. The God who is manipulated in the sports arena, the God to whom both sides in every war pray for victory, the God whose blessings are tied to the free-market economy – these and much more are the scandal of religion. The spiritual living, and the healing that equates Botox, body sculpting, and clear financial profits to those who organize and support similar healing efforts – these too are scandals.
>
> (Hefner, 2006, p. 131)

In the process of normal spiritual growth, one would expect to develop more mature images of divinity, but there is also a possibility that we will turn to inadequate substitutes for God to fill our spiritual void. One such substitute is food, when eating is an attempt to dull our spiritual hunger; other common substitutes are alcohol, drugs, sex, and material gain. In our Western culture, we tend to worship our own selves in place of the divine. This is manifested in our unrelenting desire to satisfy our personal needs or when we try to fill the emptiness within ourselves by idolizing celebrities (Pargament, 2007).

Working with the Shadow

The shadow is composed of all the emotions and thoughts that we do not accept on a conscious level. Left unattended, the shadow part of our personality will unconsciously develop into an independent psychic reality that can potentially bring about psychosomatic illnesses, random accidents, and self-negating behaviors. In order to actively integrate our shadow, we must be able to express anger or hatred as well as our creativity and childlikeness. This is certainly challenging, but at the same time is a necessary commitment for soulful work to be successful. When the shadow of our personality is repressed or denied, it can become dangerous and violent; when it is integrated, it supplies us with additional energy with which to develop our human potential (Clarke, 2011).

According to Jung, the human personality takes root in both the collective and personal unconscious, which subsequently shapes one's conscious life. All of these facets must be integrated into one's self in order for one to become a responsible human being. This process is not without challenges, since one will have to face uncomfortable feelings. These, if not properly dealt with, can lead to desperation and sadness, discouraging further shadow work. If this is the case, the shadow becomes divided and alienated, with its egoistic propensities, uprootedness, and blindness. As well, even if one tries to deny the existence of these unconscious forces, this will not make them disappear; consequently, one will be even more enslaved to them. For Jung, the shadow is the 'negative' side of the personality, the insufficiently developed functions and contents of the personal unconscious. In practical terms, this is the sum of all the unpleasant attributes that one tries so desperately to hide (Jung, 8: 409).

Psychic powers of darkness, revenge, and destruction are hidden in all of us, and the process of individuation leads to reconciling the opposites in our personalities. Ideally, these opposites should function as poles between which psychic energy can flow. The shadow has blurry boundaries, is usually underdeveloped, and negatively perceived; nonetheless, it lies at the bottom of the conscious ego structure. In fact, humanity has a naive faith in the constant progress of the human mind, and remains unaware that the foundation of human pride is the illusion of limitless power. This pride prevents humanity from recognizing that there is also darkness in us (Becker, 2001).

When we refuse to acknowledge the existence of our dark side, we actually amplify this darkness. It can express itself in a black mood, psychosomatic disorders, or even 'accidents' triggered by our unconscious. Our society praises positive thinking and is very reluctant to enter into an honest dialogue about the dark side of who we are. This lack of courage is at the root of wars, economic exploitation, racial intolerance, and many human-caused disasters (Johnson, 1991)

Confronting our shadow is a necessary process, both psychologically and morally. There are some things that one can learn only in the dark (Taylor, 2014). We have to confront all the powerful unconscious elements in our psyche because, otherwise, we can be swept away by the chaos in our personality and end up being guided exclusively by unconscious forces. Facing our shadow is an experience that touches the very core of our being, where the very value of our life is at stake and can be either affirmed or threatened. We have to be extremely careful in dealing with this mystery, by taking into account both its positive and destructive tendencies, and treating it so that it becomes as strongly life-giving as possible. Not being attentive to this mystery may result in an extremely negative outcome, that of disconnecting from ourselves, losing the meaning, direction, and fulfillment of our life, and taking the risk of becoming totally annihilated. A wise life is a life of reconciliation between opposites, where the individual reaches a higher unity within themselves through consciousness, intelligence, and responsibility. A wise life is a balanced life where both the conscious and unconscious sides of the soul are able to cooperate (Becker, 2001).

Spiritual Projection

Projection is the process of unconsciously transferring our shadow side somewhere beyond our personality because of our inability to deal with it within ourselves. For a well-integrated person, work with the shadow occurs within the framework of one's personality, which is the appropriate place for this process to unfold. When a person projects their darkness onto the outer world, this illusion becomes so real that it appears to be an independent reality and one easily forgets that it originates in one's personality. To be spiritually mature means to be able to deal with these projections consciously, courageously, and honestly (Becker, 2001).

This defense mechanism is often used to deny the reality of evil or the shadow within oneself and to project it onto others. It is particularly obvious in terrorist acts where the terrorist has gone from 'projecting evil onto others' to 'attempting to eliminate those others' perceived as the very source of evil. Mature spirituality requires that we not eliminate the dark parts of ourselves but rather integrate them into our personality (Pargament, 2010; Moghaddam et al., 2013; Pargament & Exline, 2022).

Jung adds an interesting remark in this context. He considered that, in our day, we drastically narrow the scope of symbolic expression. He referred to this as 'impoverishment of symbols' or 'withdrawal of projection.' He saw the reformation and the development of Protestantism as key events in this process, with the destruction of Catholic images and the rejection of the cult of saints as mere superstitions. This deprived people of many projection mechanisms for their primal instincts, which inevitably led to lost contact with their unconsciousness (Lindenfeld, 2009).

We need to be extremely attentive and responsible, because the human ego naturally tends to bolster up its pride. Sometimes this means projecting our ego into substitutes where our personal attributes become a part of our own image. They are our security but at the same time they are our prison. They include power, beauty, intelligence, or social position. Projecting our soul in this way hinders our spiritual growth. In this context, material poverty has more potential to boost one's spiritual growth, although not automatically, and can lead to full spiritual freedom. One of the challenges in this regard is the kind of relationship that we entertain with our belongings, and the psychic consequences of saying 'my.' When things are 'mine' we invest our life in them and they become part of who we are. We are projected into these objects. When we withdraw the psychic investment from the objects of projections and recognize what is happening in our own souls, the psychic energy that had been bound by these projections is liberated and we discover the new life that can now flow more freely from its source (Becker, 2001).

We have to recognize our dangerous and dark unconscious as well as the influence it exerts on our lives. Through 'taming' the unconscious, we come to understand the wholeness of our personality. Light cannot exist without casting shadows. Every person has a shadow. Denying this leads to denying real life, remaining superficial, and projecting all evil into fellow human beings.

Demonology

In various ways, people try to explain the evil that is present in their lives as well as in humanity. But sometimes, after having considered all accessible logical, historical, or other scientifically gained evidence, one is forced to conclude that there exists a certain level of destructiveness and cruelty that defies any reasonable explanation. People can be aggressive; they do bad things to others as a consequence of complex inclinations or attitudes fueled by their self-importance and attachment, but there seems to be something more than that at play, something that is essentially malevolent. It appears as a driving force or magnetic energy that gives impetus to our most malicious thoughts and actions. We come to sense that perhaps neither mystery nor spirit is always from a benevolent source. We can almost sense this spiritual influence that is able to affect the course of a single life as well as world history.

Although psychology finds this challenging, religion teaches that there are evil spiritual beings that negatively influence our lives (Brown, 2022; Pargament & Exline, 2022). Many people confess their sins to pastors or priests on a regular basis. Usually, they receive good advice, encouragement to change their thoughts and actions, and a 'penance,' which can be as simple as a suggestion to pray certain prayers. But this does not always bring about the desired healing. After having tried these spiritual tools, some people choose to go for psychotherapy. But despite the known benefits of sharing with wise counselors who listen and understand, some have been in counseling for a very long time and have to admit that very little has changed. In a religious setting, we can look for yet another way of helping people. Many spiritual traditions indicate the existence of a devil or of a malevolent being or spirit, an enemy, who wants to keep people from living out their destiny to become fully functioning and flourishing human beings. According to religious teachings, evil spirits gain influence in our life through doorways that are opened to their influence, by us or by other people, and because of this, lies and deceptions produced by their influence limit our access to the blessings of life. Many spiritual traditions offer concrete means to help us close the doors through which evil exerts its influence so that we can regain the freedom of a fully functioning self. This liberation and healing is a lifelong process of releasing people from bondage at ever-deeper levels. Special rituals of liberation, exorcism, and blessing may be used for this kind of spiritual healing in a variety of spiritual traditions (Lozano, 2010).

The most extreme cases of supernatural evil are termed demonic possessions and are known across various cultures. Individuals possessed by demons believe that a demon has actually entered their person and taken some or full control over them (Pargament & Exline, 2022). From the therapeutic perspective, some say that people who believe in supernatural evil may postpone their treatment, believing that a special deliverance prayer will solve their problems. At other times, some may be stigmatized by the deliverance ministry. Others state that therapists should take a more collaborative stance toward spiritual interventions of this kind (Exline & Rose, 2013).

From the mental health perspective, clinicians often link demonic possession to hallucinations or delusions; these occur within the context of psychotic disorders and dissociative states as expressed by frightening visions and malevolent voices. However, the faith-based perspective points to the possible presence of evil accompanied by feelings of being persecuted (Gearing et al., 2011). Under these circumstances, adequate discernment is a major challenge.

> One extreme response would be to automatically pathologize any and all perceptions of demonic activity even among people who otherwise appear psychologically and physically healthy. But at the other extreme, a clinician could too readily accept reports of demonic activity at face value and risk overlooking a serious medical or mental health condition. When such conditions are uncovered, especially if they are serious, they will likely become high priorities for treatment.
>
> (Pargament & Exline, 2022, p. 291)

The energy of evil has come to be qualified as *demonic*, and it refers not only to supernatural beings but also to some propensity for destructiveness that is to be found both in the human mind as well as in society. Is it a separate agency of evil that cannot be explained solely by human tendencies of self-importance and greed? Some psychologists, such as Jungians, underline that this kind of energy can also be used creatively if used properly. For Jungians, evil is an archetype, embedded in the collective unconscious and as such is not an independent reality. Similarly, for psychodynamic psychology, evil signifies inefficient or distorted interactions between id, ego, and superego. In this approach, a demonic possession is seen as a metaphor used by the human psyche in order to avoid one's real-life responsibility (May, 1987). As Pargament and Exline (2022) say: 'Anything that goes against life, in all of its fullness – anything that deadens the soul – could be seen as evil' (p. 275).

There are also more modern ways of conceptualizing this kind of evil in our world. Christopher MacKenna (2013), relating spirituality to the interpersonal psychic world, writes:

> [Through] feelings that get projected into us [...] we are dealing with the insertion of non-physical, alien and possibly intensely destructive psychic contents into another person. From a psychological point of view, this bears an uncanny resemblance to the traditional understanding of possession by evil spirits.
>
> (p. 81)

According to this mechanism, a person may become physically or mentally ill, but the source of this illness is spiritual in nature. In any case, this is still very much an uncharted territory.

Many spiritual traditions have established ways to distinguish right from wrong, creative undertakings from destructive inclinations, and to discern the difference between true or false spiritual directions. In the Christian tradition, the very core of this process is called the discernment of spirits. With the development of Christian teachings, three kinds of spirit were defined: those coming from God, those coming from one's own psyche (self-importance tendencies and attachments), and those coming from the evil one. Today, some will say that the last kind is only a projection of our own psyche, but others still agree with the wisdom of the ancients acknowledging the presence of certain spiritual powers that sway us in various directions, away from self-surrender to God. Discernment methods may be dualistic and analytic or unitive in nature. The dualistic tend to be rather complex, and the unitive simpler. Probably the most widely recognized analytic system is the one bequeathed to future generations by Saint Ignatius of Loyola. Methods of spiritual discernment, such as this one, rely predominantly on basic common sense and recognize good fruits such as peace and humility versus bad fruits such as distress and confusion (May, 1987).

Conclusions

The dark side of spirituality and religion can easily overwhelm us and give rise to the hasty and erroneous conclusion that we should avoid any kind of spiritual engagement in order to stay safe. But as a result, we take the risk of depriving ourselves of an extremely meaningful component of who we desire to be. We definitely have to be vigilant when embarking on a spiritual journey. We do not know where it will take us. The naivete of seeing only positive sides of religion and spirituality should not blind our critical view. Yet, there are many witnesses who illustrate by their lives that spirituality, when integrated into our life in a mature way, brings more life than death, more light than darkness. At the least, it is a context and an opportunity for growing in being human.

Discussion Questions

1. Are you surprised by the title of the chapter? Have you ever thought before about the possible misuse of spirituality?
2. How does the information contained in this chapter affect your view of spirituality?
3. Do you think that people might be generally reluctant to acknowledge that they are using spirituality or religion to meet their own egoistic needs?
4. Identify a time in your life when you consciously or inadvertently made use of spiritual bypass.
5. In today's world, what are the collective signs that people rely on spiritual bypass to remedy their feelings of emptiness?

References

Becker, K. L. (2001). *Unlikely companions: C. G. Jung on the spiritual exercises of Ignatius of Loyola*. Gracewing and Inigo Enterprises.

Brown, G. C. (2022). Christian perspectives on praying for deliverance from demons. In T. G. Plante & G. E. Schwartz (Eds.), *Human interaction with the divine, the sacred, and the deceased: Psychological, scientific, and theological perspectives* (pp. 104–120). Routledge/Taylor & Francis Group.

Cashwell, C., Bentley, P., & Yarborough, J. (2007). The only way out is through: The peril of spiritual bypass. *Counseling & Values*, *51*, 139–148. https://doi.org/10.1002/j.2161-007X.2007.tb00071.x

Cashwell, C., Glosoff, H., & Hammond, C. (2010). Spiritual bypass: A preliminary investigation. *Counseling and Values*, *54*(2), 162–174. https://doi.org/10.1002/j.2161-007X.2010.tb00014.x

Cashwell, C. S. (2005). Spirituality and wellness. In J. E. Myers & T. J. Sweeney (Eds.), *Counseling for wellness: Theory, research, and practice* (pp. 197–206). American Counseling Association.

Cashwell, C. S., Myers, J. E., & Shurts, M. (2004). Using the developmental counseling and therapy model to work with a client in spiritual bypass: Some preliminary considerations. *Journal of Counseling & Development*, *82*, 403–409. http://dx.doi.org/10.1002/j.1556-6678.2004.tb00327.x

Clarke, J. (2011) *Creating rituals: A new way of healing of everyday life*. Paulist Press.

Exline, J. J., & Rose, E. D. (2013). Religious and spiritual struggles. In R. F. Paloutzian & C. L. Park (Eds.), *Handbook of the psychology of religion and spirituality* (pp. 380–398). Guilford Press.

Farley, Y. R. (2007). Making the connection. *Journal of Religion & Spirituality in Social Work: Social Thought*, *26*(1), 1–15. https://doi.org/10.1300/J377v26n01_01

Finley, J. (2005). *Christian meditation: Experiencing the presence of God*. Harper.

Forman, M. (2010). *A guide to integral psychotherapy: Complexity, spirituality, and integration in practice*. State University of New York Press.

Gearing, R. E., Alonzo, D., Smolak, A., McHugh, K., Harmon, S., & Baldwin, S. (2011). Association of religion with delusions and hallucinations in the context of schizophrenia: Implications for engagement and adherence. *Schizophrenia Research, 126*(1–3), 150–163. https://doi.org/10.1016/j.schres.2010.11.005

Griffith, J. L. (2010). *Religion that heals, religion that harms*. Guilford Press.

Griffith, J. L., & Griffith, M. E. (2003). *Encountering the sacred in psychotherapy*. Guilford Press.

Halberstam, D. (2001). *War in a time of peace*. Scribner's.

Hefner, P. (2006). Spiritual transformation and healing: An encounter with the sacred. In J. D. Koss-Chioino & P. Hefner, *Spiritual transformation and healing: Anthropological, theological, neuroscientific, and clinical perspectives* (pp.119–133). Altamira.

Helminiak, D. A. (2008). Confounding the divine and the spiritual: Challenges to a psychology of spirituality. *Pastoral Psychology, 57*, 161–182.

Hill, P. C., & Kilian, M. K. (2003). Assessing clinically significant religious impairment in clients: Applications from measures in the psychology of religion and spirituality. *Mental Health, Religion & Culture, 6*, 149–160.

Jastrzębski, A. K. (2020). The normative aspect in the contemporary understanding of spirituality. *Wrocław Theological Review, 2*(28), 95–111.

Johnson, P. E. (1959). *Psychology of religion*. Abingdon Press.

Johnson, R. A. (1991). *Owning YOUR OWN SHADOW: Understanding the dark side of the psyche*. Harper.

Johnson, R. A. (2013). *Spirituality in counseling and psychotherapy: An integrative approach that empowers clients*. John Wiley.

Lindenfeld, D. (2009). Jungian archetypes and the discourse of history. *Rethinking History, 13*(2), 217–234.

Lozano, N. (2010). *Unbound: A practical guide to deliverance*. Baker Publishing Group.

MacKenna, C. (2013). Exorcism: Some theological, psychoanalytic and cultural reflections on the practice of deliverance ministry in the light of clinical and pastoral experience. In C. C. H. Cook (ed.), *Spirituality, theology and mental health: Interdisciplinary perspectives* (pp. 75–93). SCM Press.

Mahoney, A., & Pargament, K.I. (2004). Sacred changes: Spiritual conversion and transformation. *Journal of Clinical Psychology, 60*, 481–492. https://doi.org/10.1002/jclp.20007

Masters, R. A. (2010). *Spiritual bypassing: When spirituality disconnects us from what really matters*. North Atlantic Books.

May, G. G. (1987). *Will and spirit. A contemplative psychology*. HarperCollins.

Moghaddam, F. M., Warren, Z., & Love, K. (2013). Religion and the staircase to terrorism. In R. F. Paloutzian & C. L. Park (Eds.), *Handbook of the psychology of religion and spirituality* (pp. 632–648). The Guilford Press.

Pargament, K. I. (2007). *Spiritually integrated psychotherapy: Understanding and addressing the sacred*. Guilford Press.

Pargament, K. I. (2010). *Religion and coping: The current state of knowledge*. Oxford University Press. https://doi.org/10.1093/oxfordhb/9780195375343.013.0014

Pargament, K. I., & Exline, J. J. (2022). *Working with spiritual struggles in psychotherapy: From research to practice*. Guilford Press.

Park, C. L., Currier, J. M., Harris, J. I., & Slattery, J. M. (2017). *Trauma, meaning, and spirituality: Translating research into clinical practice*. American Psychological Association. https://doi.org/10.1037/15961-000

Picciotto, G., & Fox, J. (2018). Exploring experts' perspectives on spiritual bypass: A conventional content analysis. *Pastoral Psychology*, *67*(1), 65–84.

Picciotto, G., Fox, J., & Neto, F. (2018). A phenomenology of spiritual bypass: Causes, consequences, and implications, *Journal of Spirituality in Mental Health*, *20* (4), 333–354. https://doi/org/10.1080/19349637.2017.1417756

Stewart-Sicking, J., Fox, J., & Deal, P. (2020). *Bringing religion and spirituality into therapy: A process-based model for pluralistic practice*. Routledge.

Taylor, B. B. (2014). *Learning to walk in the dark*. HarperOne.

Weber, S., & Pargament, K. (2014). The role of religion and spirituality in mental health. *Current Opinion in Psychiatry*, *27*, 358–363. https://doi.org/10.1097/YCO.0000000000000080

10 Spiritual Struggle and Transformation

Introduction

We live in a time of excessive rationalism, where we praise empirical learning and intellectual analysis. Many consider these to be the only valid ways of attaining true knowledge. Generally, the academic community does not value faith-based, experiential, and intuitive forms of knowing and states that these cannot be used to scientifically prove any belief system. This contemporary approach to religion and spirituality may lead people to become spiritually lost.

We are surrounded with all manners of environmental pollution, and our concerns range from those felt on the global stage, be they overpopulation, racism, the plight of climate refugees, global health, and widespread violence, pandemics such as COVID-19, and fear of the future, worry about personal health, financial instability, and employment insecurities. It is no surprise that life itself can be assaultive and disorienting.

In addition to having to confront these challenges, people are often oppressed by the pressures created by their own needs and even more by their spiritual hunger; they live with the deep conviction that there has to be something more meaningful than the current state of their life (Johnson, 2013). They learn that despair, meaninglessness, and sadness interfere with their ability to take on new challenges. In such states of mind, it is easy to succumb to chaos and to become vulnerable to illnesses of all sorts. Throughout their lives, they must face many kinds of suffering for which there are no magical cures.

To briefly summarize, we are living in a destabilized and chaotic world that yearns for grounding and meaning. Spirituality as well as theology are challenged to find a cure for this state (Neff & McMinn, 2020), while we must boldly face our existential situation and accept its potential for developing our humanity and spirituality (Watts, 2017).

Phillip Hefner (2006) gifts us with a challenging reality-based way of seeing our way through this chaos:

> Many a successful surgery has not prevented the patient from dying, just as many well-reasoned therapeutic interventions have produced

DOI: 10.4324/9781003262145-11

> little lasting effect or even worsened the conditions of life; pharmaceutical wonder drugs sometimes go awry, contrary to our best knowledge. Vulnerability and uncertainty in our sailing over rough water are to be expected and acknowledged. Religion is dedicated to celebrating such voyages. It is an indication that the sacred accompanies us on our travels.
>
> (p. 131).

Many spiritual traditions such as Buddhism, Christianity, and Judaism underline that spiritual growth happens especially in times of suffering, when people can develop their virtues and coping skills, thus enabling them to be stronger when facing new challenges in the future (Park, 2013).

Finding meaning in suffering and struggle are at the center of authentic spirituality. Normally, people expect to find answers to their existential questions pertaining to death and other life challenges in their religion or spirituality.

> Suffering is a universal and unavoidable experience. Suffering may emerge from a tragic event, the death of loved one, personal illness, pain and disability, unrelenting loneliness, effects of war, financial ruin, persistent mental illness, oppression, and myriad other circumstances and nameless situations. Suffering is a holistic experience: it is beyond the physical experience, and captivates the psychological, emotional, social, and spiritual dimensions also
>
> (Nelson-Becker & Sangster, 2019, p. 157)

Clinging to the idea of a benevolent God in a world full of pain often brings about cognitive dissonance for believers. It is hard to live with such tension. How can God be loving and yet allow so much suffering in the world? How can people make sense of it? One possibility is to ignore the suffering and preserve the faith. On the other hand, some will interpret the suffering of others as a consequence of their behavior and will judge them accordingly. Another possibility is to deny that God is actually loving or powerful. We can simply abandon our faith. The third, and most desired, option would be to hold on to the dissonance, allowing mystery and lack of strict logic to be part of our faith. We can hold onto faith in a loving God and, at the same time, lament our suffering (Neff & McMinn, 2020).

> Spiritual struggles can be found among people from past and present, from diverse religious and nonreligious groups, from the most ordinary to the most exemplary, from all walks of life, from all cultures, and among those facing the full of life experience, including individuals with psychological problems.
>
> (Pargament & Exline, 2022, p. 15)

Contemporary authors see religion and spirituality as constructs that are so closely related they do not distinguish between religious struggles and spiritual struggles. They simply seem to consider them to be one and the same (Wilt et al., 2018). Because of this tendency, we also will continue to use the expression 'spiritual struggles.'

The Variety of Spiritual Struggles

Spiritual life does not always follow an even, smooth trajectory. The world's great religious figures like Buddha, Jesus of Nazareth, or Muhammad, all had to face spiritual trials and struggles. Such struggles are pivotal moments as they may lead the struggling person on or off the path of their spiritual growth. Spiritual struggles may take on a variety of forms. Researchers have developed models in which to frame them. Pargament and colleagues (2011) developed the model of negative religious coping, Arndt Büssing and colleagues (2013) talked about spiritual dryness, and Exline and colleagues (2014) proposed multiple dimensions of the spiritual struggle model. There has also been a consistent line of research proving a correlation between spiritual struggle and psychological problems such as depression, anxiety, and global distress. Spiritual struggle is also found to predict paranoid ideation, obsessive compulsions, and somatization. It also seems to be correlated with poor physical health outcomes (Fox & Piedmont, 2020). In a study focusing on Roman Catholic priests, spiritual struggles were correlated with depression and anxiety, and stress as well as burnout (Büssing et al. 2013).

Psychologists have articulated several types of spiritual struggle, including interpersonal struggle related to tension within the faith community, intrapersonal struggle such as questioning one's faith or moral code of action, and struggles with deity, which involves questioning one's relationship with the divine (Exline, Yali, & Sanderson, 2000; Pargament, 2010). This last type of spiritual struggle often results in anger toward God, fear of possible divine punishment, and alienation from God. It has to be underlined that some of these struggles with the divine may be placed on the unconscious level (Pargament & Exline, 2022).

Among interpersonal struggles, some distinguish between those pertaining to family and others involving the faith community (Neimeyer & Jordan, 2002). People may perceive conflicts with spiritual beings be they divine or demonic. They can also experience personal turmoil around their morality, doubts regarding their own faith, and difficulty in finding the ultimate meaning in life (Exline et al., 2014).

Interpersonal struggles involve religious conflicts between the individual and a member or members of their social context: a spouse; family members; members of the congregation, clergy, or other church leaders; or between themselves and members of other religious groups. Struggle can also occur internally, as illustrated by the tensions people experience between the virtues they want to develop, the values they cherish, and their actual behavior. People may also struggle with the divine, questioning God's presence, benevolence, or omnipotence. Religious and spiritual struggles of these kinds may have important and distinctive implications for one's health and well-being because they touch upon the ultimate questions and concerns that we mentioned above. Disappointments with one's congregation and clergy can raise basic doubts about the trustworthiness and faithfulness of others and of God (Krause, Chatters, Meltzer, & Morgan, 2000; Pargament & Exline, 2022).

Internal religious conflicts can lead us to pose fundamental questions about our self-worth, self-control, and self-efficacy. Intrapersonal spiritual struggles can be linked to moral questions, to doubts, and to searches for ultimate meaning. Moral struggles appear when we fail to meet our personal standards and are usually fueled by idealism, perfectionism, and scrupulosity. Doubts arise when we question our spiritual convictions. Struggles related to our ultimate meaning come to the forefront when we lose our life purpose (Stewart-Sicking et al., 2020).

Even healthy spiritual development may become a source of fear for some persons. We all fear change to some extent. Certain people are afraid to fully embrace their developing spirituality because it may require them to carry out difficult changes in their lives. They are daunted by the emergence of moral imperatives such as attaining sobriety, or simply becoming a better person. This fear can be connected to past negative experiences with organized religion; in certain circumstances, it can prevent the realization of the desired spiritual development (Johnson, 2013). Spiritual struggle can definitely become a source of suffering, but we need to get to know more about the spiritual aspect of people's lives before reaching more precise conclusions. Only then will we be able to point them toward available resources that can help them in their spiritual struggle (Weber & Pargament, 2014).

According to Pargament and Exline (2022), spiritual struggles will most likely appear when a person experiences a dramatic life event that challenges their core beliefs or deepest convictions. This prevents them from finding satisfactory answers to the challenges they are facing, with the result that their internal spiritual compass ceases to work properly. The same authors also distinguish between primary and secondary spiritual struggles. Primary struggles trigger certain mental disorders such as those mentioned above. On the other hand, secondary spiritual struggles appear to be an end result of psychological distress. Of course, primary and secondary spiritual struggles may function together and form a vicious circle. Clinicians who want to work effectively with persons dealing with spiritual struggles will need to take into account this distinction (Pargament & Exline, 2022).

Exline and colleagues (2014) have developed the Religious and Spiritual Struggles Scale, where they propose a conceptualization of spiritual struggles similar to that of Pargament's. They name these supernatural struggles and list: (1) those related to conflict with supernatural beings; these can include either the experience of negative emotions toward a deity or demonic struggles with the devil, (2) interpersonal struggles, meaning conflicts with others regarding certain spiritual beliefs, and (3) intrapersonal struggles, meaning conflicts with oneself regarding faith, morality, or the meaning in life.

Different types of struggles can raise different spiritual and existential questions. They can be divided into six categories: divine struggles, demonic struggles, interpersonal spiritual struggles, struggles with doubt (feeling confused regarding certain religious teachings), moral struggles, and struggles with ultimate meaning. Sometimes spiritual struggles are rather brief, in other cases they can last many years. Some spiritual struggles may remain unconscious for a long time because of the guilt and shame associated with them (Pargament & Exline, 2022).

Questions about God's nature and relationship with the individual can lead to fear, disillusionment, and distrust in divinity. Indeed, religious and spiritual struggles may be especially distressing because they challenge those aspects of life that are most essential for discovering truths about our human condition and our ultimate destination. Nonetheless, spiritual struggle understood as the process of doubting, searching, and questioning can also be a necessary part of spiritual growth (Batson et al., 1993).

Problems with the Image of God

People's images of God are indicators of how they experience spiritual and psychological problems (Hoffman, 2010). A distorted image of God may cause unnecessary psychological and spiritual suffering (Moriarty & Hoffman, 2007). Many studies have demonstrated that there is a link between our concept of God (our intellectual definition of God), our God image, our subjective emotional experience of a relationship with God, and our psychological and spiritual wellness. It has been proven that self-esteem is positively correlated with positive images of God, and low self-esteem negatively with punitive ones (Neff & McMinn, 2020).

There is also research indicating how attachment styles developed in childhood shape the way we relate to God (e.g., Counted, 2016; Granqvist, 2020). Using this frame of conceptualization, one can better understand the complexity of human relationships with God. For instance, a secure attachment style applied to God will mean that the person experiences that God is present and responsive when called upon. In such a relationship there is little anxiety. In contrast, an anxious attachment style will produce feelings of uncertainty about God's willingness to intervene in the person's favor. Similarly, the avoidant style of attachment does not support the development of an appropriate relationship with God; in such cases, the person will turn to God in situations of extreme danger or need. The consequence of a dismissive–avoidant attachment style is the conviction that God is distant and does not care about the person. The fearful–avoidant attachment style causes a lot of fear and uneasiness since the person wants to escape from God, who seems too close and too menacing. It has to be noted that these attachment styles are present in all relationships and not only in the relationship with God (Griffith, 2010).

People who develop a positive and accepting image of God during their lifetime demonstrate fewer symptoms of anxiety or depression. Belief in a benevolent God leads to a decrease in social anxiety, paranoia, obsession, and compulsion, while punitive images of God have more significant symptoms of depression, anxiety, paranoia, obsession, and compulsion. As for being part of a religious community, an appropriate level of faith and trust buffers this group against psychological distress, whatever its cause; it is conducive to greater life satisfaction and can also give rise to a heightened moral compass (Weber & Pargament, 2014).

Spirituality can lead to internal conflicts. Negative images of God can turn religion from a potential healing resource into a source of spiritual struggle and increase feelings of guilt and discouragement (Weber & Pargament, 2014). People can also hold very different images of divinity simultaneously. For example, they can view God as either loving and close, or punitive and distant, depending on the situation. This is probably due to the fact that this image of God is composed of elements coming from different sources, such as the representations of parents, organized religion, personal needs, culture, temperament, as well as one's spiritual experiences and longings. Sometimes these different spiritual perspectives collide with each other and create a sense of unease (Pargament, 2007).

Alexis Drutchas and Anandarajah (2014) trace the evolution of the image of God in a person's life from childhood onward. First, there is a petitionary approach: the child asks God for something; then, there is a collaborative approach: the child interacts with God and God is believed to reciprocate and to offer support to the child. Here, God is given more control. Eventually, the child may perceive God as a punishing God, who has the power to punish the child for every sin. At this point, there is the potential for disconnecting from God, because the child believes that God could have helped but did not, and that God can heal but does not always do so. All these variations in one's relationship with God will be mirrored in spiritual struggles.

Reducing God to a masculine figure hinders the development of a healthy attitude toward God. When picturing God as Father, all people, regardless of their gender, are taken back, consciously or not, to their experiences with their human fathers. If their father was very judgmental, they will most likely project this characteristic onto their image of God. In this case, they will most likely reject God. Another possibility is that they will project completely opposite qualities to those found in their natural fathers onto their image of God in the hope of some consolation. Furthermore, if someone's father was emotionally cold, they may develop a fear of abandonment. Although the mother usually plays a more crucial role in human development because of the intimacy of her relationship with her child, people still tend to link their image of God with their fathers (May, 1987).

Sometimes people project their relational conflicts onto their conceptions of a higher power, which manifests itself in dynamic changes of attitudes between denying/rejecting and accepting/embracing a loving higher power. Therapists can nonjudgmentally assist clients in their dynamic relationship with God, in whatever form clients picture the Sacred. Once the person feels understood and respected, they are more likely to risk exchanging their spiritually defeating templates for ones that can provide meaningful corrective experiences of peace, centeredness, clarity, and connectedness, resulting in decreased feelings of anxiety, depression, fear, and alienation (Johnson, 2013).

Perception of Divine Help

Acknowledging divine intervention may be psychologically valuable as it relates to one's well-being and can be experienced as a significant source of help in dealing with stressful situations; it can also help in fostering post-traumatic growth. Perceived help from the divine seems to be of crucial importance for a spiritual struggle to have a positive outcome in the form of spiritual transformation. Among earlier mentioned attitudes, the collaborative approach is related most consistently and positively with spiritual growth and transformation, whereas passive religious deferral can lead to either spiritual growth or decline. Generally speaking, the most positive outcomes of spiritual struggles are reported by people who adopt a collaborative attitude with the divine and engage in religious forms of coping while at the same time trusting in divine interventions (de Castella & Simmonds, 2013).

A recent study of Joshua Wilt and colleagues (2018) confirms these preliminary findings. For example, perceiving God's interaction predicts a good prognosis for the spiritual struggle, and also makes the actions of the person involved in a struggle an integral part of the solution. This type of partnership (collaborative attitude) seems to work better than when the person takes on an active or passive role unilaterally. Active religious surrender does not predict a positive spiritual struggle outcome as much as a collaborative attitude does, because the latter is bolstered by the belief that God will provide aid. Usually, spiritual growth increases one's perception of divine help during a struggle and strengthens one's belief that God will continue to provide assistance in the future. Finally, passive religious deferral was seen to have the weakest and most inconsistent effects on spiritual growth and was also positively related to spiritual decline. In short, placing trust in God can help one find the strength necessary to confront life's challenges confidently, but further research is needed to examine these mechanisms more closely (Wilt et al., 2018).

Struggling with Meaning

Traditionally, finding meaning has been linked to our efforts to address the most essential existential questions, such as 'Why am I here?' and 'What is my ultimate goal?' Meaning-making can be understood as our ability to make sense of the world we live in as well as to create our own belief systems (Wong, 2015), to find purpose in life, and to feel that our existence really matters (Pargament & Exline, 2022). Research has found that meaning is a contributor to resilience, itself a contributing factor to mental health and well-being (Wong, 2011). And yet struggles with meaning may be easily overlooked because clinical work focuses more on 'what's the matter' than on 'what matters' (Cf. Pargament & Exline, 2022, p. 200). Things that matter can surface in soulful stories, sacred memories, moments of introspection or insight, as well as in dreams that express hidden longings (Pargament & Exline, 2022).

Crystal Park (2013) proposes to view spirituality as both a meaning-making process as well as a global meaning system that allows finding satisfactory answers to questions related to the ultimate purpose of life. Pargament and Exline (2022) term it a spiritual orienting system that includes beliefs, practices, and emotions attached to the relationship with the Sacred. This system helps an individual take pathways that lead them to their chosen life destinations. In this way spirituality allies itself to the existential approach in counseling. In fact, Frankl (2006) asserted that one of the primary ways of discovering meaning in deep challenges and recasting a meaningful life is by showing courage in difficult times. Paul Wong (2012) suggests that meaning consists of four essential elements along with their corresponding psychological processes: purpose or motivation, understanding or knowledge, responsibility or moral action, and enjoyment or affective evaluation. He states that a meaningful life has to include all of these elements.

In the context of finding meaning, Frankl describes an empty self and the existential frustration related to the lack of meaning that may cause certain mental disorders. He terms this disorder 'noogenic neurosis' (German: *noogenne Neurose*) to distinguish it from neurosis in the more traditional sense. Noogenic neuroses have their source in the 'noological' or meaning-oriented dimension of human existence. They do not appear in situations of intrapsychic conflict but rather within human existential problems, where losing the meaning of life, moral conflicts, and existential crises are of particular importance (Frankl, 2006). The challenge lies in finding a way to remove emptiness and suffering from the human soul. This kind of spiritual disorder manifests itself when people do not find the meaning of their existence, experience a lack of fulfillment, and abandon any further effort to search for meaning in their lives.

Making sense out of difficult life experiences is not an easy task, and many people find themselves in a crisis of meaning, because they are not able to understand painful life events through the lens of their worldviews. They often struggle with the question 'why?' Sometimes they get trapped in unhelpful explanations that leave them even more confused, or that stop them from achieving closure. In such moments, spiritual reframing, otherwise known as the process of spiritual meaning-making, can help many of them reappraise traumatic events. They learn to place these into a larger, more meaningful, and often more benevolent contexts made up of stories, symbols, and inspiring role models that bring new hope (Pargament, 2007).

Struggling with Death

In confronting the fear brought about by the fragility of our existence, we have developed conceptual frames that help us understand our world, ourselves, and what the space beyond death may contain. One of these conceptual frames is religion, with the belief in the transcendent elements that are responsible for our existence, as well as the hope that our individual consciousness will endure beyond physical death (Zinnbauer & Pargament 2005; Snook et al., 2019).

Ernest Becker (1973) argued that humans have the capacity to be aware of their own mortality, and that this awareness engenders a basic death anxiety, which underlies other forms of anxiety. Becker theorized that humans mitigate death anxiety by adhering to worldviews that promise immortality, either literally (e.g., an afterlife) or figuratively (e.g., a legacy), allowing them to effectively cope with this anxiety. While some amount of death anxiety is a normal response to death awareness, excessive death anxiety may result in avoidance behaviors and a decreased life satisfaction (Furer & Walker, 2008).

> The incorporation of death into life enriches life; it enables individuals to extricate themselves from smothering trivialities, to live more purposefully and more authentically. The full awareness of death may promote radical personal change. Yet death is a primary source of anxiety; it permeates inner experience, and we defend against it by a number of personal dynamisms
>
> (Yalom, 1980, pp. 54–55)

A significant number of people believe in the afterlife. US statistics place this number at 79%. Belief in the afterlife is lower in Europe, but in both places it has recently increased. This increase is attributed to various religious groups including members of the Jewish faith, even though traditionally and contrary to the Christian New Testament or Covenant, the Torah is silent on the afterlife. What is even more interesting is that some people tend to believe in the afterlife but not in God, which mirrors the new trend of being spiritual but not religious (Hood et al., 2009). A spiritual outlook on the afterlife helps people sustain hope, meaning, and comfort in stressful situations. Belief in the afterlife helps people carry on, even after their loved ones have died. This is expressed in practices such as visits to the grave to converse with the deceased, rituals that venerate the memory of loved ones, as well as asking them for guidance (Pargament, 2007). Although therapists that have a more secular outlook may see any attempt to sustain a connection with a loved one who has died as a sign of pathology, such experiences are very common and contribute to integrating the essence of who the deceased was for the client (Pargament & Exline, 2022).

Belief in an afterlife seems to incite people to believe in angels, ghosts, and evil spirits. Belief in disembodied spirits seems to be natural for humans, as confirmed by the cognitive science of religion (Barrett, 2013). Although this belief remains culturally impregnated, there seems to be a shared concept of 'intuitive dualism' in which our bodies and minds are understood as distinct entities that can exist without one another. So far, belief in angels, spirits, and the afterlife has not received significant attention in research, compared to, for instance, meditation. Yet these topics are gaining more and more attention in general society, and despite the fact that they are a traditional part of Christianity, academic theology sometimes seems embarrassed to engage in any reflection of this kind (Watts, 2017).

> Many religious people would respond to a visitation from the spirits of a loved one with excitement and gratitude. However, the very same experiences could become a source of distress, disorientation, and struggle to someone with a more secularized worldview or a religious individual who is wary of reports of encounters with spirits.
>
> (Pargament & Exline, 2022, p. 218)

Spiritual Struggles and Spiritual Growth

The potential for spiritual struggles to stimulate spiritual growth has often been the subject of theological discussions across faith traditions as well as in philosophical and psychological circles. As we have already indicated, the outcome of spiritual struggles may vary from individual to individual and from situation to situation. Among possible outcomes, we can single out three in particular. The first is an active religious surrender that combines efforts initiated by the person with a reliance on God's help. The second is a collaborative approach, where the person assumes responsibility for some aspects of the problem and leaves the rest up to God. Both strategies seem to be correlated with well-being and are signs of a healthy spirituality. There is also a third called 'passive religious deferral' where the person assumes very little responsibility and expects that God will take control of the situation (Pargament et al., 2000). In the case of passive religious deferral, there is also some empirical evidence of positive outcomes, though the associations with well-being are weaker. All of these coping strategies emphasize personal actions, but with varying degrees of responsibility shared between the person and God for solving a problem. In each of these, God is perceived as playing an active part in the problem-solving (Wilt et al., 2018).

Some spiritual struggles may boost spiritual growth, expressed in the perception that one's faith is becoming stronger or more mature and that God intervenes for a person during a time of trial. This kind of conviction may appear during prayer but also in daily life: (1) internally, in silence, thoughts, emotions, imagination, visions, or dreams; (2) externally, through religious texts, serendipitous events, or other people as well as by discovering the beauty of nature; and finally, (3) through otherworldly or supernatural experiences. God's presence can take the form of practical advice, insight into an emotionally stressful situation, or guidance regarding future events. Sometimes, people perceive God's interventions in their lives or in the world when they see that positive outcomes can arise even out of negative events (Wilt et al., 2018).

Spiritual Struggle and Health

Empirical studies have found that spiritual struggles are linked to both negative and positive health outcomes. On the negative side, spiritual struggles have been associated with a number of indicators of psychological distress, including anxiety, depression, negative moods, a poorer quality of life, panic disorder, and suicidal ideation (Exline et al., 2000; Hays, Meador, Branch, & George, 2001). With respect to physical health, spiritual struggles have also been associated with a delayed physical recovery in medical rehabilitation, longer hospital stays, and a greater risk of mortality following a medical illness (Pargament, Koenig, Tarakeshwar, & Hahn, 2001).

Spiritual struggles have also been associated with positive outcomes, such as stress-related growth, spiritual growth, open-mindedness, self-actualization, and lower levels of prejudice (Calhoun, Cann, Tedeschi, & McMillan, 2000). These findings seem to support the conclusion that spiritual struggles represent an essential part of human life and can either lead toward spiritual growth or significant health problems.

Spirituality can provide a frame through which people who are ill can integrate their difficult experiences. At the same time, some aspects of religion and spirituality such as spiritual struggle may be associated with greater distress and a poorer sense of well-being. Thus, assessing the impact of spiritual struggle on human life has to take into account a complex matrix of varying spiritual dimensions and a variety of physical and mental health outcomes (Salsman et al., 2015). Evidence from longitudinal studies on patients with cancer suggests that experiencing spiritual struggle may become a predictor of emotional distress. Analyzing demographic factors, religiosity, and personality indicates that anger toward God is a predictor of a poorer quality of life and more depressive symptoms (Salsman et al., 2016).

Generally, a spiritual struggle that leads to poorer mental health outcomes can be categorized as one of three types: divine, such as anger toward God; interpersonal, such as negative relationships with other believers; and intrapsychic, which fosters guilt and doubt within (Weber & Pargament, 2014).

Spiritual Transformation

As a consequence of spiritual struggle, people can experience spiritual growth and, in some cases, attain spiritual transformation. They can also succumb to spiritual despair to the point of losing sight of their faith (de Castella & Simmonds, 2013). In order to shed more light on this process, Polish psychiatrist Kazimierz Dąbrowski (1964) proposed a theory of 'positive disintegration' by which he explains how every human person is invited to pass through a series of alternate periods of disintegration and integration, every time on a higher level, to achieve their full human potential. However, spiritual transformation is not an automatic process, because people often have to confront the limits of certain of their ways of life and let go of old sources of meaning or pleasure. They then have to reorient their lives according to newly accepted values. Research on spiritual transformation is only in its infancy, but it seems to suggest that people are capable of undergoing profound spiritual transformation. They are then left with the task of sustaining its fruits (Pargament, 2007). This process can be seen as 'the movement from brokenness to greater wholeness in the search for significance' (Pargament & Exline, 2022, p. 105).

Spiritual transformation can be understood as a fundamental change pertaining to the place the divine holds in one's life. It may also signify a change in how a person characterizes their relationship with the Sacred but also the way in which they practice or develop their spirituality (Pargament, 2006). Transformation is reversible. What has become conscious or integrated may disintegrate. Spiritual transformation does not come without a price and the ongoing journey is not always successful. Nonetheless, spiritual transformation seems to be a natural and normal part of spiritual growth. The major spiritual traditions propose a variety of methods that are specifically designed to initiate and accompany spiritual transformation. Some forms of spiritual transformation are sacred transitions, altering a person's vision of divinity and making spirituality more central in their life (Pargament, 2007).

Spiritual transformation is more than just cognitive changes and is often accompanied by a restructuring of one's hierarchy of significant values and strivings. It can result in the shift from self-centered pursuits to a desire to work charitably for the whole of humanity, in a change of focus from anger and bitterness to forgiveness and peace, and in a gradual detachment from pleasurable but unhealthy dependencies such as substance abuse. At times, spiritual transformation may involve a spiritual conversion from a life devoid of faith in divinity to a life with God as its center. Generally, spiritual transformation brings about some essential movement of the Sacred from a marginal position to the very center of one's life. There are three important steps in this process: recognizing the limitations of one's current strivings, deciding it is time to change, and replacing old values with new spiritual ones (Pargament, 2007).

Although we naturally search for ultimate meaning, there is no guarantee that once we have discovered it, we will make it part of our life and be faithful to it. For example, our dependencies can include alcohol and drug abuse, materialism, and self-aggrandizement. All this can, and in fact does, take us away from more virtuous and healthy strivings. Fortunately, powerful experiences, such as a close encounter with suffering or death, may challenge our existing harmful priorities. For some people, repeated experiences of frustration and failure must occur before they are able to recognize that they have betrayed their most profound values. Andrew Newberg (2006) explains this process from a neurobiological point of view:

> The ability of neural connections to change does take some time and usually some degree of repetition. How then can we explain a momentary experience that results in a lifetime of change? The nerve cells could not break old connections and make new ones in such a

> short period of time. So there must be existing connections that are either not activated, are suppressed, or are excluded from primary modes of consciousness that suddenly become activated and, in some sense, overpower the existing neural connections. If this is the case, then one might argue that we all harbor within us the potential for transformative experiences. At this time, no research has shown that this is the case, but at the moment it is difficult to find an alternative explanation.
>
> (p. 201)

Unfortunately, some people never reach this point, and forever deceive themselves.

People who do reach this transformational moment may experience an epiphany that helps them face their human fragility. Spiritual transformation can also occur gradually through a process of introspection and self-discipline. The fruit of this process is always the same: spirituality or God moves from the periphery to the center of one's life. It may include reaching the point of self-as-transcendent, a stable and immutable self that is capable of accepting all thoughts or feelings without being determined by them. It can also mean a shift from a life preoccupied by selfish interests to a life that focuses on charity. One of the fruits of spiritual transformation is a sense of deep connection with others and a desire to be of service to them. Another positive outcome may also be participation in spiritual group practices, thus creating identity and spiritual support. With a new sense of motivation after transformation, many people feel more empowered to reach their goals (Pargament, 2007).

Conversion and Deconversion

Conversion and deconversion are the most researched kinds of spiritual transformations. According to social psychologists, any transformative experience must occur within the context of socialization. Conversion is rarely limited to a change in religious beliefs; social and cultural transformation usually accompany it. In particular, the affective bonds between the group and the individual play a vital role in conversion. Only by entering the group dynamics can social influence and social learning activate transformation in a new member. The social influence theory also indicates how individual experiences bring gradual transformation through relationships when this person is under stress or on a quest for meaning. Nonetheless, the social influence theory only partially explains the origins of conversion, because it does not refer to a sudden conversion or conversion in isolation, without any group context. Generally, people attribute more significance to the divine–human encounter in conversion (Iyadurai, 2020).

Lewis Rambo (1993) indicates seven stages of conversion: context, crisis, quest, encounter, interaction, commitment, and consequences. The context has both macro- and micro-dimensions. On a macro-level, it includes the wider world; on micro-levels it includes one's family and friends, neighbors, as well as one's ethnic group or religious community. Crisis may be catalyzed by mystical or near-death experiences, illness and healing, or even a simple dissatisfaction with one's life. Interaction includes the four following dimensions: relationships, rituals, rhetoric, and roles. Finally, testimonies of conversion generally demonstrate language transformation and biographical reconstruction (Rambo, 1993).

According to John Lofland and Norman Skonovd (1981) there are six types of conversion: (1) intellectual conversion, which involves the seeking of knowledge without significant social contact; (2) mystical conversion, as in the early days of psychological study of conversion, characterized by a dramatic insight, induced by visions, voices, or other paranormal experiences; (3) experimental conversion, meaning an active pursuit of different religious groups, their theologies, and rituals in order to find a best fit for oneself; (4) affectional conversion, with the accent put on personal experience of being loved and affirmed by a religious group or leader; (5) revivalist conversion, relying on crowd conformity that induces conversion behavior; (6) coercive conversion, involving external pressure exerted on the person to convert to a given spirituality.

Each world religion has its own theological view of conversion, unique to its beliefs, as well as a set of criteria to assess a valid and good conversion. People converting to a particular religion will be influenced in the way they perceive and interpret their conversion. Consequently, the nature of a person's conversion is at least somewhat shaped by the religion to which they are converting (Rambo, 1993).

Conversion can help people align themselves with purpose, meaning, and identity in connection with the divine (Zinnbauer & Pargament 1998). It would be unwise to underestimate the role of religion in studying conversion as this can improve assessments of the process of conversion (Snook et al., 2019). Although some mental health professionals regard conversion with suspiciousness, research in this field has suggested that conversion can have psychological and social benefits. When therapists help people sort out their values and provide new pathways to reach their chosen destinations in life, they are aware that religion is an essential part of many life journeys. They should pay close attention to the role conversion plays in uncovering people's strivings, as well as to the pathways that are chosen to achieve their goals. A careful assessment of conversion experiences can be helpful in discovering new sources of hope and inspiration (Mahoney & Pargament, 2004).

Deconversion is a rather new concept, though it is related to some older ones such as: apostasy, defection, disaffiliation, falling from the faith, and so on. Normally, deconversion is associated with negative connotations linked to leaving one's faith. It may mean abandoning a former religious system or religious belief and actively opposing it. When a person commits apostasy or defection, they are usually blamed by their faith group for being disloyal to it. Prima facie, deconversion is associated with intellectual doubt, emotional uneasiness or distress, as well as criticism of a given spiritual tradition and its concrete incarnation within a group of believers (Streib

& Keller, 2004; Paloutzian et al., 2013). On the flip side, deconversion can have positive consequences. People who deconvert may gain a new identity and change their lifestyle and their membership in social groups. The trigger of deconversion may be despair and wanting more meaning in life (Everson, 2019).

Spiritual Surrender

A benefit of spiritual transformation can be spiritual surrender. According to May (1987, p. 308), the following criteria describe true spiritual surrender:

- It is *conscious*, wide awake, and aware. There is no dullness or mindlessness.
- It is *intentional* as it is the result of a free choice. It is never forced.
- It is a *responsible* act, of which multiple consequences are accepted in advance, such as the possibility of a misguided surrender and its possible destructiveness, without blaming anyone else.
- It is *not directed toward anything or anyone* and thus it does not reinforce one's self-importance or self-definition. It is directed toward the divine mystery, beyond any image or conceptualization.
- It is a *willingness to engage the fullness of life with the fullness of oneself* without any escape or avoidance. It is a profoundly positive change of direction, leading one toward a more mature spirituality.

May (1987) describes true surrender as hope for the ultimate homecoming: 'When, if even for an instant, we die to our self-images and awaken to even a partial vision of Universal Truth, it becomes clear that we are already Home.' (p. 310).

Conclusions

Spiritual struggles, like any other issue that is the subject of counseling work, can and should be part of therapeutic dialogue (Pargament & Exline, 2022). Therapists who want to deal effectively with a client's spiritual struggles should first of all be sensitive and tolerant toward the individual themselves. The difference between spiritual and secular approaches to personal transformation is sometimes a subtle one, and counseling normally proceeds outside of a spiritual or theological attributional framework. This difference can be seen in the degree to which explicitly spiritual attributions are used, either by the therapist or the client (Watts, 2006).

In the context of spiritual struggles, it would be useful for therapists to understand how their clients perceive their relationship with the divine. For example, therapists might be open to discussing how their believer-clients can develop an attitude of collaboration with the divine. When therapists observe that a client wants to rely solely on the divine, they can explore the reasons for such an attitude as a more collaborative approach has been demonstrated to have greater potential for spiritual growth and transformation. Interventions facilitating positive interactions with the divine lead to psychological improvement and better spiritual health. Therapists may also encourage clients to discover the ways the divine is helping them in times of struggle, as such perceptions normally predict better struggle-related outcomes (Wilt et al., 2018).

While working with the image of God, counselors should not limit themselves to the cognitive level, and certainly not attempt to correct people's theology. Rather, they should attempt to create a godly relationship with them, because in order to shift a menacing image of God toward a more benevolent one, it takes both an emotional and therapeutic bond, where the client can attune their relationship with God toward a more empathetic and secure connection (Neff & McMinn, 2020).

All these suggestions might be helpful in fostering spiritual growth, preventing spiritual decline, and facilitating spiritual transformation.

Discussion Questions

1. Can you describe a spiritual struggle coming from your own experience?
2. How can the therapist, as a *fellow human being*, help people who struggle spiritually?
3. What can a counselor do to help a person who has a negative image of God?
4. Do you believe the therapist can help people achieve spiritual transformation? If yes, how?

References

Barrett, J. L. (2013) The cognitive science of religion. In R. P. Paloutzian & C. L. Park (Eds.), *Handbook of the psychology of religion and spirituality* (2nd ed.). (pp. 234–255). Guilford Press.

Becker, E. (1973). *The denial of death*. Free Press.

Büssing, A., Gunther, A, Baumann, K., F. Eckhard, & Jacobs, C. (2013). Spiritual dryness as a measure of a specific spiritual crisis in catholic priests: Associations with symptoms of burnout and distress. *Psychology of Religion and Spirituality*, *9*(1), 46–55. https://doi.org/10.1037/rel0000063

Calhoun, L. G., Cann, A., Tedeschi, R. G., & McMillan, J. (2000). A correlational test of the relationship between posttraumatic growth, religion, and cognitive processing. *Journal of Traumatic Stress*, *13*, 521–527.

Counted, V. (2016). God as an attachment figure: A case study of the God attachment language and God concepts of anxiously attached Christian youths in South Africa. *Journal of Spirituality in Mental Health*, *18*(4), 316–346. https://doi.org/10.1080/19349637.2016.1176757

Dąbrowski, K. (1964). *Positive disintegration*. Little, Brown.

De Castella, R., & Simmonds, J. G. (2013). 'There's a deeper level of meaning as to what suffering's all about': Experiences of religious and spiritual growth following trauma. *Mental Health, Religion & Culture*, *16*, 536–556. http://dx.doi.org/10.1080/13674676.2012.702738

Drutchas, A., & Anandarajah, G. (2014). Spirituality and coping with chronic disease in pediatrics. *Rhode Island Medical Journal*, *97*(3), 26–30. http://search.proquest.com/docview/1506145764/

Everson, K. K. C. (2019). Becoming religious disbelievers: Retrospective viewpoints. *Pastoral Psychology*, *68*, 157–170.

Exline, J. J., Pargament, K. I., Grubbs, J. B., & Yali, A. M. (2014). The Religious and Spiritual Struggles Scale: Development and initial validation. *Psychology of Religion and Spirituality*, *6*(3), 208–222. https://doi.org/10.1037/a0036465

Exline, J. J., Yali, A. M., & Sanderson, W. C. (2000). Guilt, discord, and alienation: The role of religious strain in depression and suicidality. *Journal of Clinical Psychology*, *56*, 1481–1496.

Fox, J., & Piedmont, R. (2020). Religious crisis as an independent causal predictor of psychological distress: Understanding the unique role of the numinous for intrapsychic functioning. *Religions (Basel, Switzerland)*, *11*(7), 329.

Frankl, V. E. (2006). *Man's search for meaning*. Beacon Press.

Furer, P., & Walker, J. R. (2008). Death anxiety: A cognitive-behavioral approach. *Journal of Cognitive Psychotherapy*, *22*(2), 167–182. https://doi.org/10.1891/0889-8391.22.2.167

Granqvist, P. (2020). *Attachment in religion and spirituality: A wider view*. Guilford Press.

Griffith, J. L. (2010). *Religion that heals, religion that harms*. Guilford Press.

Hays, J. C., Meador, K. G., Branch, P. S., & George, L. K. (2001). The Spiritual History Scale in four dimensions (SHS-4): Validity and reliability. *Gerontologist*, *41*, 239–249.

Hefner, P. (2006). Spiritual transformation and healing: An encounter with the sacred. In J. D. Koss-Chioino & P. Hefner (Eds.), *Spiritual transformation and healing: Anthropological, theological, neuroscientific, and clinical perspectives* (pp.119–133). Altamira.

Hoffman, L. (2010). Working with the God image in therapy: An experiential approach. *Journal of Psychology & Christianity*, *29*, 268–271.

Hood, R. W. Jr., Hill, P. C., & Spilka, B. (2009). *The psychology of religion: An empirical approach* (4th ed.). Guilford Press.

Iyadurai, J. (2020). Religious conversion and personal transformation. In D. A. Leeming (Ed.), *Encyclopedia of psychology and religion* (pp. 1992–1994). Springer.

Johnson, R. (2013). *Spirituality in counseling and psychotherapy: An integrative approach that empowers clients*. John Wiley.

Krause, N., Chatters, L. M., Meltzer, T., & Morgan, D. L. (2000). Negative interaction in the church: Insights from focus groups with older adults. *Review of Religious Research*, *41*, 510–533.

Lofland, J., & Skonovd, N. (1981). Conversion motifs. *Journal for the Scientific Study of Religion*, *20*(4), 373–385.

Mahoney, A., & Pargament, K. I. (2004), Sacred changes: Spiritual conversion and transformation. *Journal of Clinical Psychology*, *60*, 481–492. https://doi.org/10.1002/jclp.20007

May, G. G. (1987). *Will and spirit: A contemplative psychology*. HarperCollins.

Moriarty, G. L., & Hoffman, L. (Eds.) (2007). *God image handbook for spiritual counseling and psychotherapy: Research, theory, and practice*. Routledge.

Neff, M. A., & McMinn, M. R. (2020*). Embodying integration: A fresh look at Christianity in the therapy room*. IVP Academic.

Neimeyer, R. A., & Jordan, J. R. (2002). Disenfranchisement as empathic failure: Grief therapy and the co-construction of meaning. In K. J. Doka (Ed.), *Disenfranchised grief: New directions, challenges, and strategies for practice* (pp. 91–117). Research Press.

Nelson-Becker, H., & Sangster, K. (2019). Recapturing the power of ritual to enhance community in aging. *Journal of Religion, Spirituality & Aging, 31*(2), 153–167. https://doi.org/10.1080/15528030.2018.1532858

Newberg, A. (2006). The neurobiology of spiritual transformation. In J. D. Koss-Chioino & P. Hefner, *Spiritual transformation and healing: Anthropological, theological, neuroscientific, and clinical perspectives* (pp. 189–205). Altamira.

Paloutzian, R. F., Murken, S., Streib, H., & Rößler-Namini, S. (2013). Conversion, deconversion, and spiritual transformation: A multilevel interdisciplinary view. In R. F. Paloutzian & C. L. Park (Eds.), *Handbook of the psychology of religion and spirituality* (pp. 399–421). Guilford Press.

Pargament, K. I. (2006). The meaning of spiritual transformation. In J. D. Koss-Chioino & P. Hefner (Eds.), *Spiritual transformation and healing: Anthropological, theological, neuroscientific, and clinical perspectives* (pp. 10–24). Alta Mira Press.

Pargament, K. I. (2007). *Spiritually integrated psychotherapy: Understanding and addressing the sacred*. Guilford Press.

Pargament, K. I. (2010). *Religion and coping: The current state of knowledge*. Oxford University Press. https://doi.org/10.1093/oxfordhb/9780195375343.013.0014

Pargament, K. I., & Exline, J. J. (2022). *Working with spiritual struggles in psychotherapy: From research to practice*. Guilford Press.

Pargament, K. I., Koenig, H. G., & Perez, L. M. (2000). The many methods of religious coping: Development and initial validation of the RCOPE. *Journal of Clinical Psychology, 56*, 519–543. http://dx.doi.org/10.1002/(SICI)1097-4679(200004)56:4_519::AID-JCLP6_3.0.CO;2-1

Pargament, K. I., Koenig, H. G., Tarakeshwar, N., & Hahn, J. (2001). Religious struggle as a predictor of mortality among medically ill elderly patients: A two-year longitudinal study. *Archives of Internal Medicine, 161*, 1881–1885.

Park, C. L. (2013). Religion and meaning. In R. F. Paloutzian & C. L. Park (Eds.), *Handbook of the psychology of religion and spirituality* (pp. 357–379). Guilford Press.

Rambo, L. R. (1993). *Understanding religious conversion*. Yale University Press.

Salsman, J. M., Fitchett, G., Merluzzi, T. V., Sherman, A. C., & Park, C. L. (2015). Religion, spirituality, and health outcomes in cancer: A case for a meta-analytic investigation. *Cancer, 121*(21), 3754–3759. https://doi.org/10.1002/cncr.29349

Salsman, J. M., Pustejovsky, J. E., Park, C. L., Sherman, A. C., Merluzzi, T. V., Danhauer, S. C., Jim, H. S. L., & Fitchett, G. (2016). Reply to the association between religion/spirituality and mental health in cancer. *Cancer, 122*(15), 2441–2442. https://doi.org/10.1002/cncr.30019

Snook, D. W., Williams, M. J., & Horgan, J. G. (2019). Issues in the sociology and psychology of religious conversion. *Pastoral Psychology, 68*, 223–240.

Stewart-Sicking, J., Fox, J., & Deal, P. (2020). *Bringing religion and spirituality into therapy: A process-based model for pluralistic practice*. Routledge.

Streib, H., & Keller, B. (2004). The variety of deconversion experiences: Contours of a concept in respect to empirical research. *Archive for the Psychology of Religion, 26*(1), 181–200. https://doi.org/10.1163/0084672053598030

Watts, F. (2006). Personal transformation: Perspectives from psychology and Christianity. In J. D. Koss-Chioino & P. Hefner, *Spiritual transformation and healing: Anthropological, theological, neuroscientific, and clinical perspectives* (pp.152–167). Altamira.

Watts, F. (2017). *Psychology, religion, and spirituality: Concepts an applications*. Cambridge University Press. https://doi.org/10.1017/9781107360549.009

Weber, S., & Pargament, K. (2014). The role of religion and spirituality in mental health. *Current Opinion in Psychiatry, 27*, 358–363. https://doi.org/10.1097/YCO.0000000000000080

Wilt, J. A., Stauner, N., Harriott, V. A., Exline, J. J., & Pargament, K. I. (2018, August 23). Partnering With God: Religious coping and perceptions of divine intervention predict spiritual transformation in response to religious−spiritual struggle. *Psychology of Religion and Spirituality*. Advance online publication. http://dx.doi.org/10.1037/rel0000221

Wong, P. T. P. (2011). Positive psychology 2.0: Towards a balanced interactive model of the good life. *Canadian Psychology/Psychologie Canadienne, 52*(2), 69–81.

Wong, P. T. P. (2012). Toward a dual-systems model of what makes life worth living. In P. T. P. Wong (Ed.), *The human quest for meaning: Theories, research, and applications* (2nd ed., pp. 3–22). Taylor & Francis.

Wong, T. P. P. (2015). Meaning therapy: Assessments and interventions. *Existential Analysis*, 26(1), 154–167.

Yalom, I. D. (1980). *Existential psychotherapy*. Basic Books.

Zinnbauer, B. J., & Pargament, K. I. (1998). Spiritual conversion: A study of religious change among college students. *Journal for the Scientific Study of Religion, 37*(1), 161–180.

Zinnbauer, B. J., & Pargament, K. I. (2005). Religiousness and spirituality. In R. F. Paloutzian & C. L. Park (Eds.), *Handbook of the psychology of religion and spirituality* (pp. 21–42). Guilford Press.

11 Prayer

Introduction

Prayer has probably been a part of human behaviors since the earliest of times. For many centuries, a great body of literature on prayer has been produced, which of itself is worth studying (Ladd & Spilka, 2013). Major spiritual traditions understand prayer as a state where one's heart is touched in a variety of ways. Prayer has been advocated by all monotheistic traditions in the West as well as in several of the Eastern traditions (e.g., Hinduism, Mahayana Buddhism). Many forms of communal and private prayer are practiced within Christianity; there are Jewish prayer recitations (*davening*), and in Islam, we find the requirement to pray five times a day (*Salah*). Prayer involves verbal or nonverbal communication with the divine in view of some kind of transformation or change (Walker & Moon, 2011). We can talk about mental prayer and oral prayer; we can offer prayers for someone or something; we can participate in meditation, mindfulness practices; we can enjoy simple moments, silence, or reading a sacred text.

A coherent description of the practice of prayer remains a challenge. Generally, prayer is seen as a process and a means of connecting to one's self, to others, and especially to the divine. Prayer is probably the most common method used to experience the Sacred and it covers many forms such as silent prayer, chanting, formal prayer, spontaneous prayer, prayer born of joy and of suffering, conversational prayer, and intercessory prayer (Pargament, 2007). The 2014 General Social Survey found that 29.5% of respondents in the US said that they prayed once per day, and 27.4% prayed more than once per day. These figures are distributed differently across faith traditions: 39.2% of Protestants, 21.5% of Jews, and 20% of Roman Catholics prayed several times a day. Also, age, race, and sex influence how often one prays (Smith, 2019). As Adam B. Seligman and colleagues (2008) stated, not all prayers are ritualistic. There are supplicatory, intercessory, and event-responsive prayers. Ritual prayers are more performative, repetitive, objective, and anti-discursive. Prayer is used to sustain and strengthen people's connection with God as well as to respond to many human needs and aspirations. This makes it very difficult to discern if the prayer is apt to facilitate both the spiritual and the psychological well-being of the client in therapy (Pargament, 2007).

DOI: 10.4324/9781003262145-12

Kevin L. Ladd and Bernard Spilka (2002) proposed three categories of prayer: inward, outward, and upward. Inward prayers entail connecting with oneself and are a spontaneous part of one's spirituality, especially including the experience of abandonment, honest self-evaluation, and admission of personal faults. Outward prayers, because they focus on other people and the external world, are expressed as petitions or intercessory prayers for others. Upward prayers are directed toward the divine and their favored expressions are resting in the moment, meditation, or contemplation (Ladd & Spilka (2002).

To distinguish prayer from other human activities, we normally would relate it to the Sacred or Transcendence. But even then, it does not resolve the problem of defining prayer since there is much dispute around how to understand Transcendence. When we introduce a theological concept of the divine, we find ourselves in a territory that is considered not to be amenable to scientific study. Yet, if we do not define prayer in theological rather than psychological terms, we will not be able to operationalize the prayer in a way that distinguishes it from other psychological processes (Dein et al., 2012).

Faced with such a variety of definitions concerning prayer, it is reasonable to consider the suggestion of Fraser Watts (2001), who says that prayer is theistically oriented behavior. This definition does not refer to the content or function of prayer but gives us a tool to separate prayer from meditation. This is of crucial importance for the research on prayer, as it would be very unprecise to confuse prayer with any of the various forms of meditation. Although prayer often includes such elements as rest, quietude, waiting, or listening, meditation usually remains unrelated to the divine (Ladd & Spilka, 2013).

Meditation and Mindfulness

Despite its long history in the Christian tradition, meditation gained its popularity thanks to the infusion of Asian disciplines into the Western world during the second half of the twentieth century. Meditation within Hinduism, Buddhism, and Taoism is not usually focused on experiencing the divine. Rather, this type of meditation is a pathway to achieving inner illumination or enlightenment. It offers a way to dismantle deceptive appearances and to access deeper truths in order to attain fully open human consciousness (Pargament, 2007). Many of our contemporaries do not necessarily tie their meditative practices to any particular spiritual tradition (Hilert & Gutierrez, 2020).

What nowadays is popularly called meditation, and was called contemplation or contemplative prayer in the Christian tradition, is the last stage of prayer development. In the Christian view, a person might start with spiritual reading or *lectio divina*, which is a prayerful reading from the Bible or other spiritual writings with the aim of finding inspiration and guidance. The next stage is discursive meditation. This is where the term 'meditation' is used and it refers to a prayerful reflection on what the person has read. This reflection includes thinking about the content as well as making use of their imagination or spiritually inspired images. The third stage is prayer where the person expresses their feelings, emotions, pleas, and deepest yearnings in the presence of God. The last stage is contemplation, which is a grace of realized oneness with God or resting in God. This stage is purely receptive, and is sometimes also called a mystical experience (Finley, 2005). It leads to love as the highest state of being and to a deeper way of perceiving the nature of reality (Stewart-Sicking et al., 2020).

Generally speaking, without reference to a specific spiritual tradition, meditation has two forms: concentration and mindfulness. In concentration forms of meditation, the person is invited to focus on an object, while always refocusing on this object when their mind wanders. This object may take on a variety of forms. It can be a mantra as in the case of transcendental meditation (TM), a phrase, a song, an emotion, or the rhythm of their breathing. In mindfulness meditation, they are expected to engage in a nonjudgmental observation of the present moment and all phenomena contained therein. The main challenge here is to sustain attention, witnessing and accepting rather than avoiding or interpreting the stream of their consciousness without rejecting anything that appears in it. Some contemporary forms of mindfulness meditation (MM) invite practitioners to attend both to their breathing and to their experiences (Pargament, 2007). In recent times, many counselors practice various forms of mindfulness. The increasing popularity of mindfulness has given rise to contemplative psychotherapy, which attempts to combine the principles of religious mysticism and the Western counseling tradition (Stewart-Sicking et al., 2020).

In both contemplation and meditation, we have to remain present and awake to all contents of consciousness. These include feelings or thoughts no matter what kind: sad, angry, or peaceful. They all need to be noticed but not clung to. We have to be open and awake to each of them as they arise, remain for a time, and then pass away. One simple, but difficult step to achieve, is to be present in the present moment of our life and mind. This implies accepting the restless nature of human minds as they wander away from the present moment and gently return to being awake. We do not let the thoughts and feelings take control, but do not resist them either when they appear. They are allowed to come and freely go. Our goal is not a total absence of thoughts, but at the same time, we do not dwell on them either (Finley, 2005).

'Mindfulness' is the English translation of the word 'sati,' which originates in the language of Theravada Buddhism and means 'bare attention.' It is a direct awareness of reality without any preconceived notions, distortions, stereotypes, or judgments. Strictly speaking, mindfulness is not a meditation practice, because meditation practice is only one of many techniques used to attain the state of mindfulness. It can be achieved by a practice of observing one's experience without attachment to any particular point of view. The fruit of these practices is a mindful awareness, which is a way of being characterized by clear seeing and receptivity (Greason, 2011).

The Effects of Prayer in Human Life

In general, research on the relationship between prayer and health has demonstrated that prayer is an especially effective coping mechanism and has beneficial effects on both mental and physical health (Poloma & Pendleton, 1989). Nonetheless, prayer should not be regarded as a clinical intervention designed to improve personal well-being. Its primary end is helping believers communicate with the divine. In a psychotherapeutic context, prayer may be a potentially powerful resource of healing for clients and a way of deepening the bond between a psychotherapist and their client (Walker & Moon, 2011).

An enormous amount of empirical research on prayer has been done in medical contexts and has demonstrated that prayer possesses a great amount of latent possibility as a health care strategy, which could potentially revolutionize the medical field. One can even extrapolate this conclusion from the specific practice of prayer to the wider concept of faith in which prayer occurs, as faith is thought to affect healing in ways similar to prayer. This occurs by promoting healthy behavior, creating a positive cognitive schema, enhancing social support, and stimulating positive psychophysiological responses. In this context, prayer is perceived as one way in which faith is expressed in behavior. Such an approach allows more theological input into the discussion, referring to such concepts as a perceived relationship with the divine rather than reducing prayer to a tool to control one's immediate environment. In this broader context, faith and prayer are seen as a way of living that is cultivated over time. No doubt, prayer may affect people's lives in both a positive and a negative manner, although the negative effects of prayer have received little formal attention in research. This may be because people are naturally reluctant to discuss negative experiences with prayer. It seems that researchers have only just begun to discover the complexity of prayer as a spiritual practice (Ladd & Spilka, 2013). This research is considered a preliminary framework for further studies.

Pargament (2007) aptly summarizes:

> Because prayer takes so many forms and serves so many spiritually related functions – comfort, gratitude, forgiveness, protection, guidance, compassion, connection, meaning, support, pain tolerance, empowerment, transformation – it can be applied to a wide variety of people and problems. Unfortunately, researchers have yet to evaluate the efficacy of prayer as a resource in psychotherapy [...] I hope that this picture will change in the next few years.
>
> (p. 256)

Meditation has shown its positive effects on the human brain associated with structural changes to the hippocampus, prefrontal cortex, cingulate cortex, and insula, which were linked to a relief of stress, improved emotional regulation, and enhanced mental clarity (Gotink et al., 2016). People who meditate report significantly fewer headaches, a reduction in negative moods and anxiety, and generally experience greater existential well-being. Some findings suggest that the effects of at least some types of meditation are more visible when the spiritual dimension is more engaged (Wachholtz & Pargament, 2005). In fact, there are a number of studies relating prayer to human health, but they often miss the point as they do not take into account the most essential function of prayer, which is communion with the Sacred as a way to enter into a relationship with the divine, or, as Thomas Merton (1969) put it, a 'yearning for the simple presence of God' (p. 82).

In the general population, there exists a modest correlation between the frequency of prayer and life satisfaction. This information, however, does not help a clinician who needs more contextualized information about the kinds of prayer that could be most helpful in a given case (Pargament, 2007). There is also a body of empirical research on meditation. In the beginning, its focus was mainly on Transcendental Meditation and yoga. The results emerging from research on meditation are quite clear with respect to its mental health benefits (Seeman et al., 2003) such as stress management, diminished anxiety and depression, as well as a decrease in drug and alcohol abuse. Recently, there has been an increased interest in mindfulness. Its use in combination with cognitive-behavior therapy has shown positive results in the treatment of depression (Williams & Kabat-Zinn, 2013). However, opinions remain divided in this area and are at times skeptical (Flanagan, 2011). For example, there has been a lack of clarity on how to evaluate the clinical benefits of both meditation and mindfulness when separated from their religious origins (Watts, 2017).

Prayer as Part of Therapy

For therapeutic purposes, Donald F. Walker and Gary W. Moon (2011) define prayer in the following manner:

> In the context of psychotherapy, we define prayer as an intervention involving communication with the divine for the purpose of meeting a psychological or spiritual treatment goal. Such communication can be initiated by (a) the psychotherapist alone, (b) the client alone, or (c) the psychotherapist and client together. Furthermore, prayer can occur either in session or out of session. The specific form that prayer takes is dependent on the theoretical orientation and practice setting of the psychotherapist and on the religious background of the psychotherapist and client, as well as on the presenting problem of the client.
>
> (p. 141)

Prayer is one of the essential practices in almost all Western and Eastern religions, but its forms vary broadly between them. Prayer is an essential part of life for many people (Worthington, 2008), even though a great number of counselors ignore this fact. Nevertheless, many clients continue using prayer as a preferred means of coping with life's challenges. A client's prayer may occur

> whether the counselor believes in it or not, whether the counselor thinks it is important or not, or whether the counselor wants to discuss it or not. Clients may pray while in session, asking that the counselor understand what they are saying or that the counselor can help them.
>
> (Cheston & Miller, 2011, p. 244)

Peter Madsen Gubi (2004) and similarly Mark McMinn (2011) distinguished two kinds of prayer within counseling: covert and overt prayers. A prayer in one's heart, without another's awareness is considered covert. An overt prayer means a prayer that is consciously used during the counseling session by either the counselor or the client or both. It can also be a silent prayer but acknowledged by both parties (Gubi, 2008). Also, the counselor may pray for insight or guidance during challenging moments in the therapeutic process. For both counselor and client, a prayer during the session can involve breath control, mantras, and focusing. It has been demonstrated that activities such as reciting mantras or the rosary prayer have a positive impact on respiration rate, which reduces anxiety through relaxation and improves one's overall health. Nonetheless, the therapeutic efficacy of prayer in general will require more research (Cheston & Miller, 2011).

Ethical Considerations

There are, of course, ethical considerations related to the use of prayer in psychotherapy. McMinn (2011) suggested that prayer may not be equally applicable in every form of therapy. Prayer easily fits into the cognitive–behavioral approach when employed as a coping resource; and the educational component of CBT is congruent with the use of prayer as a homework assignment. However, using prayer in psychodynamic or humanistic approaches seems to be more challenging as these typically work exclusively with the relationship and do not use other types of interventions (McMinn, 2011).

The APA Ethics Code advises therapists to be aware of cultural and individual differences that are attributable to religion and ethnicity. In fact, many religiously committed clients may view a psychotherapist's attempts to use a spiritual intervention coming from a different spiritual tradition with suspicion, and might well conclude that the therapist is not able to understand their specific religious views (Walker & Moon, 2011). In this context McMinn (2011) suggests that psychotherapists should consider the following points: (a) whether using prayer in psychotherapy will lead to a healthier sense of the client's self, (b) whether using prayer will foster client's healthy relationship with God, and (c) if using prayer will help establish a healing psychotherapeutic relationship. This can be accomplished in different ways and degrees: one can pray for clients outside of sessions, silently pray for clients during sessions, propose a meditation assignment for client, try an in-session meditation or in-session prayer training, occasionally pray in-session with the client, and, finally, regularly pray in-session with the client (McMinn, 2011).

Nonetheless, the therapist should be very careful. One of my friends shared this experience with me (personal communication):

> A few years ago, I sought help for a particular aspect of my personal growth, and had a first meeting with three therapists. One of them was recommended to me for his deep faith. Knowing that I was a religious, he asked me if I was comfortable praying during our meetings. I had never done therapy, so I didn't know what to expect, but I was open, so I said yes. At one point during the meeting, I exposed some of my reluctance to start this therapeutic process. He then said to me: 'If you want, we will pray a little' … and he started: 'Lord I pray for my sister, give her your Spirit so that she can make the best decision for her, for her well-being.' I felt very uncomfortable. I had the impression that the therapist wanted to use the authority of God to convince me to continue the therapeutic process. In the end, I chose another therapist. With hindsight, today if I was asked if I am comfortable praying in therapy, I would say that I prefer to keep prayer for another context and devote this time to regular therapeutic work.

Richards and Bergin (2005) advise psychotherapists against incorporating prayer into psychotherapy in certain specific cases. The first is when clients do not pray as part of their regular spiritual life; the second, when they do not want to include prayer in their psychotherapy at that particular time. Moreover, praying may be inappropriate in some secular settings (Richards & Bergin, 2005).

Also, psychotherapists should not pray with clients who are misusing prayer within their own tradition, such as praying scrupulously for the forgiveness of sins that have already been officially (sacramentally) forgiven. This can occur in clients who have an obsessive–compulsive disorder or a diagnosis of an obsessive–compulsive personality. Moreover, psychotherapists should not support the prayer of clients who use this practice to make themselves appear highly spiritual to others. Praying with clients who are experiencing psychotic symptoms will also be problematic and is usually contraindicated. Some of these clients may 'pray' to hallucinations and even harm themselves or others (Walker & Moon, 2011).

From a psychological perspective, meditation lowers our customary defenses so that some memories from a distant past may surface in our minds. The same applies to a gamut of feelings, from soothing and pleasant to sad, angry, or lonely. Meditation can reveal our poverty and brokenness, which some will repress immediately. One has to be wary of meditation if one has experienced trauma that has not yet been dealt with properly. In serious situations, the content that shows up in meditation may require professional help such as psychotherapy. This is especially important in situations where opening up the boundaries of self-consciousness and identity puts someone at risk of major instability. This may happen in cases of depression, personality disorders, post-traumatic stress disorder (PTSD), and anxiety (Finley, 2005; Surmitis et al., 2018).

McMinn (2011) also suggested assessing the potential risk of using prayer in therapy, which ranges from low risk such as the psychotherapist praying for clients outside of session, through medium risk such as assigning prayer as homework outside of sessions but reviewed in session, to high risk such as praying routinely in session together with the client. Consequently, there is a low level of risk in misapplying prayer if it is just a homework assignment outside of session, because such practice reinforces the personal and spiritual nature of prayer. On the other hand, if psychotherapists regularly engage in intercessory prayer on behalf of the client during the session, clients might become dependent on the prayer life of the psychotherapist or have the psychotherapist's personal religious practices forced upon them and, by consequence, lose the opportunity to develop their own prayer life to appropriately meet their spiritual and psychological goals (McMinn, 2011).

Michael E. McCullough and David B. Larson (1999) suggested that with highly religious clients who pray regularly, encouraging prayer will result in more efficient coping. Moreover, the clinician may learn some important information about the client's self-talk, as well as their concept of the divine and religious coping style while listening to their prayers (McCullough & Larson (1999). Conversely, the potential harm of an open in-session prayer is an exacerbation of transference and countertransference as well as a blurring of the boundaries between counseling and spiritual direction that we have discussed in an earlier chapter. In some explicitly religious settings, praying with clients, for example at the end of each session, may be done routinely. This, however, runs the risk of becoming mechanical and somewhat meaningless.

Recently McMinn (Neff & McMinn, 2020) confessed:

> But one thing that remains crystal clear in my mind is that silent prayer is a beautiful part of the work we do in our counseling offices. I sometimes tell my students that my favorite prayer is a brief, one-word utterance: 'Help!' And the thing is, God does help. Time after time I have sensed the sustaining, encouraging presence of God's Spirit as I recognize the limits of my own abilities and call out to God for sustenance and direction. God with us is not at all a sterile theological concept to me, but a lived reality experienced year after year, session after session, while sitting with people in anguish and suffering.
>
> (p. 227)

Walker and Moon (2011) offer three broad recommendations for psychotherapists to consider prior to praying with clients. First, psychotherapists should do a self-assessment as well as a client assessment in view of using prayer; second, they should discuss with clients the use of prayer in psychotherapy before actually praying; third, they should obtain informed consent from their clients prior to doing so.

> To work ethically with prayer as a therapeutic tool, counselors need not only practice prayerful activities themselves but explore and understand their own religious, spiritual, and faith beliefs and practices, including personal prejudices, to avoid unwittingly imposing their beliefs on clients and doing harm.
>
> (Cheston & Miller, 2011, p. 254)

Therapists who are not comfortable praying with their clients, may refer them to a religious leader or spiritual director, and in this way respect their client's goals for psychotherapy as well as their religious values. This is especially important when the psychotherapist and the client come from different spiritual traditions, such as an evangelical Christian client working with a Buddhist psychotherapist. It is possible that some clients may test their therapist to see whether the latter will respect the formers' spiritual tradition if a request to pray is made. In such situations, it is important that psychotherapists consider their own comfort in praying with a client from a different religious background. It would be better for psychotherapists to remain true to their own spiritual tradition rather than pretend that they are comfortable in a different tradition (Walker & Moon, 2011). Pargament (2007) presents this challenge very clearly:

> Clinicians should also work within their own personal boundaries as they help clients draw on their spiritual resources. For example, though I encourage many of my clients to pray, I do not pray together with my clients in therapy – not because I believe prayer has no place in counseling, but because one-to-one prayer is not a part of my own religious tradition and background. To pray together with a client would be inauthentic for me. Though therapists can find ways to expand their own spiritual comfort zones, they should not try to help their clients in ways that feel 'spiritually dystonic.'
>
> (p. 245)

Practical Considerations

Clinicians should discern what kind of prayer, if any, would be most helpful for their clients in a given situation (Weld & Eriksen, 2007). Some clients can be encouraged to write their own prayers, others can be advised to ask for prayers from their religious leaders or congregations (Pargament, 2007). Psychotherapists should be aware that clients have different ways of praying. For example, Protestant clients generally pray directly to God whereas Catholic clients may do so through the intercession of Mary or the Saints. Thus, psychotherapists should be aware of the possible differences depending on which Christian denomination a client belongs to (Richards & Bergin, 2000). Regarding other religions, prayer in the Jewish religion is communal rather than individual and is typically learned in childhood. For prayer to occur, a quorum of at least ten Jewish males aged 13 or older, called a minyan, is needed. Normally, the prayers are chanted and are scripted and organized in a prayer book called a siddur. The prayer can also be recited privately when one cannot attend the prayer of the community in the synagogue. Even if prayers are recited individually, they remain identical to the prayer recited communally. There are only a few minor sections that must be recited with a minyan (Milevsky & Eisenberg, 2012). Orthodox Jews may view praying during the therapy session as inappropriate because Jewish law specifies the setting for traditional prayers. However, some Jewish clients may benefit from in-session experiences using their traditional prayers (Miller & Lovinger, 2000). Finally, for some nontraditional Jews, some form of prayer in the psychotherapeutic session may be beneficial but should be done with the client's cooperation in order to be sensitive to their prayer tradition (Milevsky & Eisenberg, 2012).

In one study, elderly Jewish people, including less religious ones, found the traditional Jewish prayers to be an activity that gave structure and orientation to their daily lives. Apart from that, some participants were comforted by the prayers, and others found these to be emotionally soothing. All participants retained a deep emotional connection to these prayers and approached them with a sense of reverence (Pargament, 2007).

In traditional Islam, five prayers are required daily: at dawn, noon, midafternoon, sunset, and evening. Before praying, one must engage in a ritual cleansing to achieve a state of purity. Muslims can pray anywhere and be either alone or in a group as long as they face the direction of Mecca during the time of prayer. On Fridays, a special time of group prayer takes place inside a mosque. It involves reciting the Koran out loud and must be led by a man, who serves as imam (leader) and who stands in front of others. Women who want to participate in Friday prayers do so in a separate room (Hedayat-Diba, 2004).

Aisha Hamdan (2007) presented a study of a Muslim client, Fatima. She suffered from depression, which she considered to be a punishment from Allah. To help the client, Hamdan first reframed her psychiatric condition in a more benign way, explaining that it was a spiritual test coming from Allah, and included the five required daily prayers as an essential part of the treatment plan. Because regular prayer is fundamental for any Muslim wanting to connect with the Creator, Hamdan encouraged Fatima to be faithful to prayer time even if she did not do it willingly. This served to maintain her relationship with Allah and greatly improved her spiritual functioning thereafter (Hamdan, 2007).

Prayer is also an important resource in the Alcoholics Anonymous (AA) movement. A basic prayer for members of AA is the Serenity Prayer: 'God grant me the serenity to accept the things I cannot change; courage to change the things I can; and wisdom to know the difference' (Pargament,

2007, p. 162). This prayer has become an interreligious, universal tool for the healing of many.

For some people, the prayers they recite are not associated with much depth and meaning and do not have a great impact on their beliefs. During their early religious education, many people memorize prayers from their particular religious tradition, but are often unaware of the underlying foundations (Pargament, 2007). When a client recites a prayer without it being connected to their deepest feelings or to their relationship with the divine, the experience can be a very shallow one. The therapist would need to encourage a shift from a monologue to a spiritual dialogue, which means a shift from not only speaking to the divine but also listening for divine response (Griffith & Griffith, 2002).

Some people reach a point where a particular mode of praying that was once exceptionally satisfying, ceases to be so. Being unable to pray in the previously comfortable way may result in discomfort, since previously effective mechanisms for coping have vanished. This phenomenon requires special attention from the clinicians or spiritual advisers if they want to help their clients discover other meaningful ways of praying. Examples of this type of shift include changing from using mainly spontaneous prayers to more codified prayers, changing postures during prayer such as going from kneeling to standing or finally from being physically still to walking or using other bodily types of movement, in order to help the person stay focused (Ladd & Spilka, 2013).

Methodological Challenges in Researching Prayer

It seems that in some ways contemporary psychotherapy has returned to the concept of soul care. In the past decade, several publications, including theoretical articles, case studies, as well as a handful of empirical studies have examined the use of prayer in psychotherapy and serve to prove this point. However, in many ways, prayer has remained a challenging topic for psychologists, because it is personal, difficult to define across spiritual traditions, and equally complicated to measure in an effective way. This is why prayer has not been a widely explored subject of study (Walker & Moon, 2011). Empirical studies of prayer and coping use measures of prayer that are quite efficient but also tend to simplify this complex phenomenon (Ladd & Spilka, 2013).

Psychological research on prayer, especially in relation to mental health, has typically utilized relatively simple questionnaires asking participants to report their frequency of prayer. Nonetheless, we need to take into account the complex challenge of defining prayer and avoid watering it down to yet another psychological trait of our human life such as simple relaxation. When our definition of prayer is based uniquely on psychological terms, we are not able to distinguish prayer from other psychotherapeutic processes or interventions. What makes people know that they are praying and not doing other things? Can we measure prayer or observe whether it is authentic or not? These are questions that beg resolution (Dein et al., 2012). There is a need to clearly articulate the aspects of prayer that are being studied and the conditions under which these studies are done. At the present time, this is not often the case in the existing literature. A number of studies are only concerned with a specific way of praying called 'intercessory' prayer, which means praying for the well-being of someone or for something one needs (Ladd & Spilka, 2013).

Studies focused on the relationship between prayer and health have tried to evaluate the extent to which prayers can influence physical realities such as healing from a disease. Unfortunately, these studies frequently confuse psychological and theological levels of measurement. From a faith perspective, prayer is a spiritual discipline with a spiritual goal, which emphasizes spiritual effects as its primary outcomes. When the physical effects of prayer become the main focus, we will not be able to adequately grasp the full range of prayer content and its meaning. This kind of approach to researching prayer has produced results that have missed the point stressed across faith traditions, that prayer expresses the human condition, but people believe that the outcomes of prayer are both physical and spiritual. For example, prayer can change the experience of pain by providing a sense of meaning and purpose, by serving as a distraction and relaxation, and it can also provide a means of receiving social support (Ladd & Spilka, 2013).

There are some studies linking prayer with personality traits, which use robust indexes of prayer's multiple dimensions. There are still many psychometric and interpretive challenges in this context but this field of study seems promising. Other studies on developmental features have focused on ways of understanding and engaging in prayer. This developmental perspective on studying prayer seems to be a helpful way of linking cognitive and emotional development and the practice of prayer. For example, studies involving children put an emphasis on the cognitive complexity of prayer and relate it to the emerging theories of the mind. Meanwhile, research on older adults remains largely focused on health outcomes. The future developmental research will need to expand the scope of correlational designs, look at all ages, and study prayer across the life span using longitudinal designs. Another option may include exploring the ways in which younger and older people think about their prayers and how this aligns with other cognitive processes (Ladd & Spilka, 2013).

An additional direction of empirical research on the role of prayer in human life is in the context of relationships. For example, one studies how prayer functions within intimate contexts and how it shapes the relationship of a couple. In this context, prayer can help some couples see their problems from a larger, more empathic perspective, to become more sensitive to their spouse's point of view and to decrease the feelings of hostility, contempt, and negativity between them. Clinicians can potentially integrate prayer into their work with religious couples who are experiencing serious conflict (Pargament, 2007). Future research will need to include families and larger groups of people (Ladd & Spilka, 2013).

No doubt, prayer and psychotherapeutic interventions such as mindfulness may look very similar to each other and we can give in to the temptation of losing faith in the possibility of any scientific research on prayer. We would need to be more explicit about what people are doing when they pray and work on identifying different kinds of prayer. For example, we can correlate personality types with different kinds of prayer (Francis & Robbins, 2008). We can research the images of the divine people have and how they influence their mental health (Francis et al., 2001). There is still much to be done in this regard.

Conclusions

Prayer is an integral part of human life. People coming to counseling offices very often have a regular prayer life. Statistically speaking, many counselors do not harbor much enthusiasm about prayer. Nonetheless, the variety of forms that prayer can take gives a favorably disposed counselor a rich choice of tools that can foster the therapeutic process both during and between the sessions with their clients. Although there are clear ethical constraints on how to use prayer or meditation in the context of counseling, it should not be rejected without honest consideration because its contribution to the healing process may be crucial.

Discussion Questions

1. Is prayer a part of your everyday life? If yes, what are your preferred forms of praying?
2. Do you think that praying can be helpful in any way?
3. When should prayer be avoided in the counseling relationship?
4. Have you had any bad experiences with certain kinds of prayer?
5. Would you feel comfortable including prayer into your counseling style? Explain.

References

Association of Religion Data Archives. (2014). Frequency of prayer. www.thearda.com/quickstats/qs_104.asp

Cheston S. E., & Miller, J. L. (2011). *The* use of prayer in counseling. In C. S. Cashwell & J. S. Young (Eds.), *Integrating spirituality and religion into counseling: A guide to competent practice* (pp. 243–260). American Counseling Association.

Dein, S., Cook, C., & Koenig, H. (2012). Religion, spirituality, and mental health: Current controversies and future directions. *Journal of Nervous & Mental Disease, 200*, 852–855. https://doi.org/10.1097/NMD.0b013e31826b6dle

Finley, J. (2005). *Christian meditation: Experiencing the presence of God.* Harper.

Flanagan, O. (2011) *Bodhisattva's brain: Buddhism naturalised.* MIT Press.

Francis, L. J., & Robbins, M. (2008). Psychological type and prayer preferences: A study among Anglican clergy in the United Kingdom. *Mental Health, Religion & Culture, 11*(1), 67–84.

Francis, L. J., Gibson, H. M., & Robbins, M. (2001). God images and self-worth among adolescents in Scotland. *Mental Health, Religion & Culture*, *4*(2), 103–108.

Gotink, R. A., Meijboom, R., Vernooij, M. W., Smits, M., & Hunink, M. G. M. (2016). 8-week mindfulness-based stress reduction induces brain changes similar to traditional long-term meditation practice – A systematic review. *Brain and Cognition*, *108*(5), 32–41. https://doi.org/10.1016/j.bandc.2016.07.001

Greason, D. P. B. (2011). Mindfulness. In C. S. Cashwell & J. S. Young (Eds.), *Integrating spirituality and religion into counseling: A guide to competent practice* (pp. 183–208). American Counseling Association.

Griffith, J. L., & Griffith, M. E. (2002). *Encountering the sacred in psychotherapy: How to talk with people about their spiritual lives*. Guilford Press.

Gubi, P. M. (2008). *Prayer in counselling and psychotherapy: Exploring a hidden meaningful dimension*. Jessica Kin.

Hamdan, A. (2007). A case study of a Muslim client: Incorporating religious beliefs and practices. *Journal of Multicultural Counseling and Development*, *35*, 92–100.

Hedayat-Diba, Z. (2000). Psychotherapy with Muslims. In P. S. Richards & A. E. Bergin (Eds.), *Handbook of psychotherapy and religious diversity* (pp. 289–314). American Psychological Association. https://doi.org/10.1037/10347-012

Hilert, A. J., & Gutierrez, D. (2020). Jewish meditation in counseling. *Counseling and Values*, *65*(2), 126–136. https://doi.org/10.1002/cvj.12133

Ladd, K. L., & Spilka, B. (2002). Inward, outward, and upward: Cognitive aspects of prayer. *Journal for the Scientific Study of Religion*, *41*, 475–484.

Ladd, K. L., & Spilka, B. (2013). Prayer: A review of the empirical literature. In K. I. Pargament, J. J. Exline, & J. W. Jones (Eds.), *APA handbook of psychology, religion, and spirituality* (Vol. 1: *Context, theory, and research*, pp. 293–310). American Psychological Association. https://doi.org/10.1037/14045-016

McCullough, M. E., & Larson, D. B. (1999). Prayer. In W. R. Miller (Ed.), *Integrating spirituality into treatment: Resources for practitioners* (pp. 85–110). American Psychological Association.

McMinn, M. R. (2011). *Psychology, theology, and spirituality in Christian counseling*. Tyndale House

Merton, T. (1969). *Contemplative prayer*. Herder & Herder.

Milevsky, A., & Eisenberg, M. (2012). Spiritually oriented treatment with Jewish clients: Meditative prayer and religious texts. *Professional Psychology: Research and Practice*, *43*(4), 336–340. https://doi.org/10.1037/a0028035

Miller, L., & Lovinger, R. J. (2000). Psychotherapy with conservative and reform Jews. In P. S. Richards & A. E. Bergin (Eds.), *Handbook of psychotherapy and religious diversity* (pp. 259–286). American Psychological Association. https://doi.org/10.1037/10347-011

Neff, M. A., & McMinn, M. R. (2020). *Embodying integration: A fresh look at Christianity in the therapy room*. IVP Academic.

Pargament, K. I. (2007). *Spiritually integrated psychotherapy: Understanding and addressing the sacred*. Guilford Press.

Poloma, M. M., & Pendleton, B. F. (1989). Exploring types of prayer and quality of life research: A research note. *Review of Religious Research*, *31*, 46–53.

Richards, P. S., & Bergin, A. E. (2000). *Handbook of psychotherapy and religious diversity*. American Psychological Association. https://doi.org/10.1037/10347-000

Richards, P. S., & Bergin, A. E. (2005). *A spiritual strategy for counseling and psychotherapy* (2nd ed.). American Psychological Association. https://doi.org/10.1037/11214-000

Seeman, T. E., Fagan-Dubin, L., & Seeman, M. (2003) Religiosity/spirituality and health: A critical review of the evidence for biological pathways. *American Psychologist, 58* (1), 53–63.

Smith, T. W. (2019, February 10). General Social Survey 2014 Cross Section and Panel Combined. https://doi.org/10.17605/OSF.IO/KB9S6

Stewart-Sicking, J., Fox, J., & Deal, P. (2020). *Bringing religion and spirituality into therapy: A process-based model for pluralistic practice.* Routledge.

Surmitis, K. A., Fox, J., & Gutierrez, D. (2018). Meditation and appropriation: Best practices for counselors who utilize meditation. *Counseling and Values, 63*(1), 4–16. https://doi.org/10.1002/cvj.12069

Wachholtz, A. B., & Pargament, K. I. (2005). Is spirituality a critical ingredient of meditation? Comparing the effects of spiritual meditation, secular meditation, and relaxation on spiritual, psychological, cardiac, and pain outcomes. *Journal of Behavioral Medicine, 28*, 369–384.

Walker, D. F., & Moon, G. W. (2011). Prayer. In J. D. Aten, M. R. McMinn, & E. L. Worthington Jr. (Eds.), *Spiritually oriented interventions for counseling and psychotherapy* (pp. 139–167). American Psychological Association. https://doi.org/10.1037/12313-006

Watts, F. (2001). Prayer and psychology. In F. Watts (Ed.), *Perspectives on prayer* (pp. 39–52). SPCK.

Watts, F. (2017). *Psychology, religion, and spirituality: Concepts and applications.* Cambridge University Press. https://doi.org/10.1017/9781107360549.009

Weld, C., & Eriksen, K. (2007). Christian clients' preferences regarding prayer as a counseling intervention. *Journal of Psychology and Theology, 35*, 328–341.

Williams, J. M. G., & J. Kabat-Zinn. (2013) *Mindfulness: Diverse perspectives on its meaning, origins and applications.* Routledge.

Worthington, E. L. Jr. (2008). Prayer and marital intervention: Can it be long and strong enough to matter? *Journal of Social and Clinical Psychology, 27*, 686–692. https://doi.org/10.1521/jscp.2008.27.7.686

12 Rituals

Introduction

Along with prayer, rituals are one of the most important parts of religious and spiritual practices, yet their healing potential is still to be fully uncovered. World spiritual traditions have long valued the importance of rituals and continue to do so. Elements found in rituals include bells to call congregants to prayer, singing bowls in meditation, water for washing or baptism, lighted candles, and the burning of incense to indicate the presence of the Sacred (Nelson-Becker, 2018). They provide a form of holistic knowledge as well as a way of acquiring and transmitting it. Rituals teach lessons on how best to function and to act, thus shaping new attitudes toward life and creating a sense of belonging (Taylor, 2021).

Rituals stem from centuries of traditional wisdom and use the language of our souls. We have mostly forgotten the many ancient ways that enabled us to reconnect with our true selves: storytelling, music, silence, images, art, dreams, and memories have all served to express our deepest longings (Clarke, 2011). It is interesting to note that in the scientific study of religion during the twentieth century, rituals were either analyzed at length as in the case of Émile Durkheim, Arnold van Gennep, and Anthony Wallace, or totally absent as in works of James or Allport. Be that as it may, new interest has recently grown in the research of rituals originating in more recent interdisciplinary studies of religion (Idler, 2013).

The Contemporary Landscape

An interesting dichotomy has emerged in our postmodern society. On the one hand, many people are drawn to shallow rituals and ceremonies with little significance. On the other, the prevailing tendency is to view traditional rituals with suspicion, distrust, and disbelief. These are often ridiculed and dismissed as having a narrow purpose (Nelson-Becker & Sangster, 2019). Perhaps this is because most people have never experienced good rituals or because the ones that they have access to are distorted. Some rituals have been unfairly linked with unhealthy religious practices (Clarke, 2011).

DOI: 10.4324/9781003262145-13

Religious rituals have been practiced by most people around the globe as a characteristic of human activity since the earliest human societies were formed (Idler, 2013). There exists a variety of religious rituals. Some of them mark certain times of the week or year, such as Easter or the various Harvest Festivals; some celebrate sacred events, such as the birthday of the Buddha or of Jesus of Nazareth; and some commemorate events such as the destruction of a demon by the deity Krishna in Hinduism (Pargament, 2007). Some spiritual traditions such as the Anglican Church use many rituals and others, such as the Quakers, very few (Nelson-Becker & Sangster, 2019). And what was once the domain of organized religions has become more and more part of our secular ceremonies.

For the most part, outside of religious gatherings, the effectiveness of ritual is not well recognized. The traditional venues for ritual once found in religion are changing. The percentage of people who consider themselves to be atheists or agnostics is growing and for this reason, ritual as experienced in a religious context is becoming less accessible. In fact, rituals are in danger of losing their power to heal:

> We live in an age that has seemingly lost its capacity to engage in the rituals that bring us back to the center of who we are. Instead of participation in rituals that help quell anxiety, remotivate purpose, forge a collective identity and a sense of belonging, many individuals have lost connections with ceremony. They feel abandoned, empty, purposeless, and alone. They may have participated in religious rituals in their youth or engaged in community memorial rituals through the lifespan. They may participate in sports and ad hoc daily rituals. However, the power of ritual remains largely unexplored, unrealized, and unavailable to individuals, families, and communities in a post-modern age where the pace of society allows scant space for ritual inclusion.
>
> (Nelson-Becker & Sangster, 2019, p. 153)

We can perceive a certain shortage of meaningful rituals in our contemporary way of living. Pargament (2007) calls it 'underritualization' and blames this on the frantic pace of today's life. As a result of social and technological change, we are encountering profound shifts in our lives without the appropriate rituals to help us through them. Situations such as divorce, unemployment, blended families, adoption, the return of an adult child to the family home, retirement, and entering a nursing home are all circumstances that we often have to face unprepared and unaccompanied. The stress of rushing to meet day-to-day demands makes it increasingly difficult to take a step back from all the chaos and to mark the most important moments of our life. Those who are caught in the rat race of this world may even regret spending time to welcome a new baby into the world or to grieve a death. At other times, rituals are avoided because they can create painful memories. Whatever the reason may be, when we are incapable of making room for the special moments in our life, our world loses its vibrancy and everything within it becomes dull and lackluster (Pargament, 2007).

Conceptual Clarifications

Ritual can be defined as a repeated pattern of behavior performed at specified times (Scott, 2014), though not all would agree with such definition as some rituals mark very specific and unique moments in a person's life. Usually, ritual is composed of tangible symbols and actions; these may serve to uphold social goals. Today, rituals are not only performed within the boundaries of formal religion, but may nonetheless still refer to the Sacred. Humans from all over the world are predisposed to using rituals that are expressed in a culturally specific way. Rituals may have either religious or secular roots, but both can express sacred meaning. Rituals often mark important events in communal and personal life (Nelson-Becker & Sangster, 2019).

Various levels of ritual expression exist in our lives and come under different forms such as ceremonies, ritualizing behaviors, customs, habits, and routines. These all possess certain elements of a ritual, but, because they do not share the same complexity and fullness, cannot be considered to be a stand-alone rituals. Ceremonies often mark a personal accomplishment, but usually lack a deeper level of meaning and effect on our lives: graduations, retirement, political events, and so on. In ceremonies, the abundance of formality expressed through etiquette and polite gestures often eclipses the deeper meaning of the celebration. This is because, unlike rituals, ceremonies are not intended to be transformative, although this does not exclude the person who is at the center of the ceremony from experiencing it as transformative. The difference is that in a ritual there is no division between the audience and the participants and everyone experiences this transformative effect. Ceremonies use many more words and fewer actions, whereas in a ritual there is more action and only few important symbolic words. Rituals also include the shadow, the dark side of being human (Clarke, 2011). The performance of religious rituals involves every participant and gives them an active role in the ritual, even if this participation is sometimes simply being an active witness to the action being performed. In comparison, theater performances or sporting events do not come under the definition of ritual as they do not actively involve their audience; in these venues, audience members are simply considered to be spectators (Idler, 2013).

Pargament (2007) explains that through rituals, participants shift from the role of distant bystanders to that of actors, vitally engaged in ritual actions. Christians reexperience Christ's sacrifice on their behalf and receive the spiritual gifts of redemption. During Passover, Jews retell the story of the Exodus of the Hebrew people from slavery to freedom as participants who were, and continue to be a part of these redemptive events. Such rituals bring sacred history into the present time (Pargament, 2007).

The construction of our nervous system predisposes us to utilize ritualization. Some rituals are not healthy since they do not lead us to any transformation. These are behaviors that can be identified as obsessions, compulsions, addictions, or other neurotic behaviors that prevent us from dealing with legitimate suffering and hinder our potential for decoding its message for us. The purpose of ritualizing behavior is to help us face the chaos in our life. One can think of a simple and ordered action such as weeding the garden in the midst of an emotional crisis. Restoring order to a physical aspect of our life also helps us regain balance in its affective and cognitive dimensions; it allows us to move forward during a challenging period and can prevent a major crisis (Clarke, 2011).

Routines are not the same as rituals. They are established procedures or habitual activities such as drinking our morning cup of coffee or taking a shower. These routines are performed without much awareness or insight into them. But they can give us a sense of comfort. Finally, habits are recurrent behavior patterns that help us cope with the challenges of everyday life. For example, some people go shopping in order to decrease their level of stress (Clarke, 2011).

According to Alan Basham (2011), a ritual is 'a symbolic experience or action that connects individuals to a deeper meaning or truth, enabling them to encounter that for which words alone are insufficient' (p. 210). Rituals enable people to feel a connection with the transcendent, with nature, or with others. Usually, rituals speak to the individual's cognitive, emotional, and behavioral dimensions and help them experience a connection with all parts of their being (Basham, 2011). G. C. Kenney (2000) added that religious ritual: (a) creates an emotional connection to certain religious events, (b) allows us to reenact them, (c) reveals our commitment to our faith community, (d) enables reexperiencing the foundational events of our chosen community.

Radha Parker and Sheldon Horton (1996) identified three types of rituals related to one's spirituality: liberational, transformational, and celebrational. Liberational rituals help people let go of any form of oppression, such as a toxic relationship, or an unhealthy social environment. Transformational rituals concentrate on transitional life events such as birth, adolescence, and engagement. Among them are the sacraments in Christianity, the funeral rites of Zoroastrians, Jewish bar and bat mitzvah traditions, and many others. Celebration rituals are associated with the cycle of seasons such as religious holidays, birthdays, and all kinds of anniversaries. Many of these rituals are culturally or socially sanctioned events (Parker & Horton, 1996).

The Role of Symbols – Eliade's Hierophanies

According to Mircea Eliade, a hierophany is 'the act of manifestation of the Sacred' (Eliade, 1959, p. 11). In other words, a hierophany manifests itself in human life as an experience of the Sacred, which he understands as something totally different from what occurs in one's everyday life. Hierophanies are mediated by the symbols originating in the human psyche and that reveal the most secret meanings of life and death. Through these symbols, people come to understand the universal principles guiding any important human experience beyond the immediate and obvious dimension of one's life. Every symbol that transmits a hierophany remains a part of the material world as we know it, but at the same time it is endowed with a metaphysical meaning, thus acquiring the quality of sacredness (Eliade, 1959).

According to Eliade (1959), although contemporary people tend to be less religious, these symbols continue to be perceived by their unconscious self and sometimes become substitutes for religion. People continue to live their religiosity without even being aware of it. Their unconscious spirituality helps them find an entrance into a space of potential meanings, enabling them to address the most important issues of their lives. Eliade (1959) says that religion has been eclipsed into the darkness and depth of the human unconscious. One can become attuned to this dimension, though not without considerable effort. Meaning can only be found when there is a communication between the various spheres of our life. This communication happens with the help of symbols, and once this is successful, we can experience the world as cosmos rather than chaos, and our life as saved rather than disintegrated. Unfortunately, our modern society continues to be desacralized and many ancient symbols have become meaningless. The cosmos or creation appeals less and less to our sense of awe and contemplation since science seems to be unraveling much of what humanity once held as mystery (Eliade, 1959).

The other danger of our time is that the symbols that once were limited to very unique occasions are now being carelessly overused and deprived of their profound meanings. Eliade (1957) calls this infantilism in that these symbols become a part of the profane dimension. Thus, we integrate symbols into everyday life, so that we can have access to sacred qualities on demand, without respecting the timing and the context of the sacred mystery.

Essential Elements of Effective Rituals

For Durkheim (Durkheim & Cosman, 2001), ritual is likened to a cement that holds society together, a way for people to find their place in society and to define their relationship with the Sacred. Rituals imply intentional actions as participants have an awareness of why they are participating. Their actions are not random. According to Van Gennep (1960), rituals contain phases such as separation, liminality, and aggregation. First, one has to step out of ordinary life. This could be a planned or a spontaneous action. Second, in effective rituals, there is an imagined passage over a threshold, known as a liminal state, meaning an alteration of time and space. In this state, there is an enactment of the crisis (called mimesis) to confront everyday life routines and to redefine them through symbolic acts. Finally, one has to be reincorporated into the ordinary world. In communities, participants of rituals are equal, each practicing a form of humility that recognizes the authority of the group. In this way, through the bonds of community, rituals can strengthen participants facing difficult situations. According to Claude Lévi-Strauss (1977), the meaning of rituals resides to some extent in their choice of language meant to refer to myths present in human history. The difference between a myth and our profane language is that the myth uses a higher level of complexity (Lévi-Strauss, 1977).

For rituals to be effective, they have to include the following dimensions: mindful preparation, focused participation and attention, liminal space and time, multivocal symbolism, performative words, dramatic embodied action, engagement of one's shadow, and a witnessing community. Rituals also have also to take into account the personal maturity of the participants and should never be forced upon anyone. In its essence, a ritual is an action or actions accompanied by words that are brimming with meaning and that contain our most cherished values. Each ritual involves our bodies and the presence of the witnessing community. In summary, there are four elements for a ritual to be effective: (1) preparation of the soul for something significant to happen; (2) separation from society; (3) ritual action; (4) reincorporation and confirmation of the effects of the ritual by the witnessing community (Clarke, 2011).

For the most part rituals are not overly complicated and their simplicity captures and expresses basic truths of life using image or symbol, action and word. Rituals are also honest because they encourage participants to face the realities of suffering and loss as well as hopes and dreams for their futures. Rituals are public, inscribed into relationships with other people who witness, support, and affirm them. Finally, rituals are sacred, because they speak to a timeless dimension of our existence, to our deepest levels of emotion and meaning, as well as to our quest for transcendence. Unfortunately, rituals have not been systematically examined in regard to their effects in psychotherapy. Some clinical accounts suggest that rituals have the potential to be a vehicle of transformation in psychotherapy, especially when other tools become ineffective (Pargament, 2007).

Time and Space

Rituals involve an unusual and distinctive sense of time and space. A sacred space needs to be created in which the ritual can take place. Rituals also involve a sense of connecting with the timeless, or at least with long-established tradition. Though rituals occur in a particular time and place, there is characteristically a sense of connecting with something beyond time, or an awareness that the Sacred is breaking into the ordinary time and space of the created order and human experience, and transforming it. At best, the ritual becomes an experience of unbroken continuity involving rapt concentration and an obliviousness to the passage of time.

This awareness, which ritual fosters, helps explain why rituals are particularly important in religion (Watts, 2017). The actions in a ritual (utterances and deeds) are performed in specific places, at specific times, and are undertaken with appropriate seriousness. They involve the physical, sensory, and cognitive experience of the participants, called liminal space. In this transitional state, the participants leave their familiar world and immerse themselves in a vulnerable and dangerous space outside the social order. It is often a short-lived period when the social conventions and structures of everyday life are cast aside to facilitate altered states of consciousness and a sense of transcendence (Idler, 2013). According to Eliade, rituals often take place in special, sacred places (Beane & Doty, 1975). When it comes to initiation rituals, it is crucial that they include the following steps: 1) going to a place set apart from ordinary life, 2) experiencing a liminal phase with an ambiguous transitional status, 3) reaggregating to society with a new status (Griffith, 2010).

In a ritual, we can experience a liminal space that links our past, present, and future and find an expression for feelings that are difficult to put into words. Because rituals appeal to our senses, we can express ourselves (or our souls) through our bodies by symbolic actions such as sand-play, theater, or psychodrama, or even symbols taken from our everyday life. These can be inspired by nature (water, fire, or earth), or can be souvenirs or objects that have a special significance to the person who uses them. Effective rituals help us move forward and resolve our life problems, because they embrace liminal space and paradoxical truths. In a ritual, we are enabled to hold the tension of life's opposites until our soul finds a new creative balance between them. Effective rituals have to be time sensitive. What has worked well in the past does not necessarily work in the present time. Moreover, a good ritual has to include the shadow aspect of one's personality. Herein lies the difference between a ritual and a ceremony. During a ceremony we do not refer to anything pertaining to our shadow. An example of such a ceremony is found in the contemporary way of celebrating weddings (Clarke, 2011).

Many religious rituals have a cyclical character and are connected to the cycles of life. Some rituals are performed very frequently, some with medium frequency, and some take place only once a year or once in a person's life. For example, in Christianity one can be baptized only once, but one can be a godparent several times. Some rituals are very much time-bound like a Jewish bris that must occur on the eighth day after birth, or a Jewish burial that must take place within the 24 hours after someone's death. Initiation rituals, such as rites of passage from adolescence to adulthood, are less precisely timed. Finally, one-time-only rituals are intimately associated with the extremes of life, marking its beginning and end. These one-time rituals are usually highly sensory and they may go on for days at a time (Idler, 2013). Calendrical rituals occur regularly according to the circularity of nature, such as the movement of the Earth around the Sun, and are associated with the lengthening and shortening of daylight. Another point of reference for rituals are agricultural cycles related to planting and harvesting. In this context we can name the most important holidays of all major world religions: Ramadan (Islam), Yom Kippur (Judaism), Easter (Christianity), Diwali (Hinduism), and Wesak (Buddhism). These annual holidays frequently interrupt the regular calendar and provide occasions for travel and extended family gatherings (Idler, 2013).

Physical Action

Rituals privilege physical actions defined by movement, directionality, and positioning over the spoken word. They can be understood as bodily movements through which the participants of the ritual express their deepest convictions about the world; although distinctive words may be important if not critical elements of ritual performance, they still remain dependent on the bodily movements that make it up. Spatial movement and gestural performance present in a ritual position it close to drama and theater (Parkin, 1992). The elements of rituals may involve kneeling, singing, dancing, speaking responsively, the laying on of hands to bless others, or praying in unison (Idler, 2013).

In this context David Parkin (1992) states: 'Ritual is formulaic spatiality carried out by groups of people who are conscious of its imperative or compulsory nature and who may or may not further inform this spatiality with spoken words' (p. 18). Some ritual actions such as drumming, singing, dancing, gesturing, and speaking in unison may amplify the effects of rituals on both individual and group levels. Group-driven tempos of some rituals are felt physically. For example, a drum rhythm may approximate the pace of heartbeats; singing with a regular cadence can influence the respiration of participants so that their inhaling and exhaling resembles the breathing of a single organism (Idler, 2013).

Witnesses

A ritual cannot be effective if it is not witnessed. This can be conceptualized in many ways; we can be witnesses to our own experience or to the experience of others, we may be aware that others witness our experience, and, finally, we can be a formal witness to an event such as a wedding. There are two dimensions of life where ritual and witness are closely related: religions and faith, and the legal or judicial realms. Religious traditions bear witness to certain aspects of faith. For example, liturgical traditions such as those practiced in the Catholic and Episcopal churches (the Eucharist), bear witness to the life, death, and resurrection of Jesus Christ. The elements of these rituals are prayer, chant, and other practices that engage the human senses; these are acts witnessed by the faith community in order to experience the depth of the ritual meaning. Rituals are ways in which we can bear witness to life experiences and to the challenging emotions that they trigger: fear, rage, grief, shame, guilt, and so on. No wonder that engaging in ritual requires courage, for at its core, ritual acknowledges and expresses something essential and oftentimes difficult for us to verbalize. At the same time, participation in rituals can move us forward and provide a sense of stability by sustaining continuity, discharging emotions, shaping identity, and restoring or developing important connections. Being a witness to a ritual is a sacred task because it validates a meaningful experience whether this be loss, success, or transition (Nelson-Becker & Sangster, 2019). The presence of other participants and their synchronized actions lead the participants to lose their sense of a separate self, while providing a sense of unity with the group (Marshall, 2002). In certain rituals, for example, the Jewish Seder or Muslim Eid al-Fitr, children are given a special role to play. Many annual holidays provide an opportunity to tell and retell children the central stories of the faith and to include them in rituals (Idler, 2013).

In this context, Emmanuel Levinas proposed an approach where suffering is meaningful only to the one who witnesses the suffering of the other and not to one who is suffering. He called this approach the 'inter-human perspective' in which the one who is a witness to the suffering is obliged to negotiate its meaning. The witnessing person should not be indifferent to the one who is suffering and has to take responsibility for the other while making a gesture of healing and helping this person gratuitously (Levinas, 1988).

Therapeutic Dimension of Rituals

Rituals are making their way into therapeutic practice as they open up a healing space within a therapeutic alliance. In this context, rituals can stimulate a therapeutic relationship emotionally through safety and confidentiality, construct a healing venue, provide a conceptual framework to understand and treat the client's symptoms; rituals can also initiate a procedure (ritual) that involves active participation by both therapist and client in order to further the healing process. Rituals thus demonstrate their potential for therapeutic practice as they break down former unsuccessful life patterns and assist clients in their transition toward a healthier understanding and behavior. Among the many therapeutic functions of rituals, we can observe that they (1) provide a language for expressing emotions and ideas; (2) give a sense of stability; (3) integrate people within a community both in times of joy and of loss; (4) help in transitions and lead into new dimensions of living; (5) provide a link with tradition; and (6) assure emotional support (Nelson-Becker & Sangster, 2019).

In the therapeutic setting, rituals are of help when words are simply not enough. Of course, words are necessary to make the ritual meaningful, but actions are even more important. In some cases, therapists can call upon already established rituals taken from their client's spiritual tradition to facilitate therapeutic change, but when rituals are performed mechanically, they often lose their significance and do not enable change (Pargament, 2007). Rituals have a great potential for changing and transforming our lives. Their greatest significance pertains to our affective or emotional dimensions. Sometimes we feel emotionally trapped in certain situations and we do not see any satisfactory way out. Rituals can be helpful in reorienting our lives, reconnecting us with what is most essential to who we are in the deepest parts of ourselves. Through rituals we can find orientation and meaning to our challenging situations and be empowered to take appropriate action.

> Cosmologically, rituals can offer a clearer connection with the universe and give meaning to one's life. Anthropologically and sociologically, rituals support communal relationships and social identity. Psychologically, rituals serve to offer an inner cohesion and expression of an internal dynamic. Therapeutically, rituals can be healing and reconciling aspects of individual and communal nurture. Spiritually, rituals can offer the possibility of broadening one's soul understanding and relationship to the Divine.
>
> (Clarke, 2011, pp. 129–130)

Without ritual it is very difficult to find the paths of transformation that will help us in our journey from one place in life to another. Instead, it becomes difficult to find our way through difficult life challenges such as widowhood or unemployment. We become weighed down by emotions such as anger or sadness, and may develop behavioral patterns such as constant work or social isolation. Without the power of ritual, we are less capable of marking the sacred moments in life (Pargament, 2007). Nonetheless, rituals are not a magic solution to all our problems.

Normally, rituals are unique to a given group of people or to an individual in a specific situation. Every one of us has been touched by painful life situations such as the death of loved ones, personal failures, or health problems. We need good rituals to overcome these situations (Clarke, 2011).

From a neuropsychological perspective, Eugene d'Aquili and Andrew Newberg suggest that the rhythmic and repetitive aspects of rituals contribute to altered states of consciousness (d'Aquili & Newberg, 1999). Though there is transformative power in rituals and almost every religious ceremony focuses on personal transformation, one pays less attention to their transformative impact in regular church services. Religious rituals can provide an opportunity for transformation of the self and for resolution of conflicting positive and negative feelings. For example, the Christian sacrament of Holy Communion, with its multiple layers of symbolic significance, takes the participant through a sequence of stages, from an initial sense of unworthiness to union with Christ (Watts, 2017). Jim Clarke (2011) explains this transformative function of rituals in the following way:

> Life transitions are like doorways, inviting the individual or group to pass over into another space. Rituals are like keys that unlock these doors and facilitate crossing the thresholds. The crossing-over is actually powered by the ritual event. Ritual gives context to our place in the mystery of the cosmos-it frames the meaning of a person's present situation and addresses the desire to understand the paradox of reality, especially the wounding nature of life. Ritual can offer healing, reconciliation, and balm to life's painful struggles.
>
> (p. 8)

The signs of a successful transition ritual are a feeling of being grounded, a perception of increased creativity, and the discovery of our place in this world. The rituals of passage should ensure that we attend to our major life events in an appropriate way, which includes their psychological, social, and spiritual dimensions (Clarke, 2001). When we fail to do so, it opens up an abyss that drains our psychic energy, brings about confusion in our relationships, and distorts the course of our lives. This is where the ghosts of unfinished business hover. The proof of a successful ritual lies in its transformative capacity (Grimes, 2002)

Rituals foster personal transformation. A framework of meaning attached to a ritual enables personal bereavement to be lived within a transpersonal framework of meaning. This often occurs in funeral rituals. Psychologically, effective rituals are both engaging and transformative but should not be overly transparent. They need to employ symbols that have enough depth to point us to a reality beyond our lives. In order to have a powerful psychological impact, rituals have to create a balance between a certain predictability in their structure on the one hand and creativity on the other; they should not be overly banal or vague. If people fail to engage in a ritual, it becomes empty and serves no function (Watts, 2017).

Rituals play a very important role when it comes to dealing with death. They offer an acceptable framework in which to express such difficult feelings as sadness, grief, fear, dread, guilt, and anger. Mourning rituals provide people with a structured way of remaining connected with the departed, thus preventing people from experiencing confusion, isolation, and hopelessness. Since we cannot avoid losses in our lives, we need rituals that help us heal, reconcile, and mourn our losses so that we can integrate these into the fabric of our human journey. We also need to integrate the dark aspects of life rather than denying their existence. Rituals provide us with a safe space in which to face them (Clarke, 2011).

Rituals have a potential to help us in initiating emotional catharsis, defining our identity, building community, and finding meaning in life transitions. But the most important role that rituals can play is restoring our sense of sacredness by placing the conditions of our lives within a universal life context and teaching us the greater truths about existence. It does that by integrating both continuity and change in our lives, by helping us move from one phase of life to another. Rituals also remind us that despite the changes that we are undergoing, some things remain constant; they confront us with the realities of change and loss while celebrating the preservation of our memories, relationships, communities, identities, hopes, plans, and dreams (Pargament, 2007).

Authentic rituals are transformative because they incorporate liminal space and time as well as the human shadow. They give meaning and direction to our lives and should become an integral part of our human journey, leading us to full maturity and to the integration of the different elements of our personalities. Rituals can serve to increase the enrichment of our communities; they bring order to our lives, bridge conscious and unconscious layers of our existence, and facilitate our development. They can also help us consider, accept, and reconcile ourselves with our own losses (Clarke, 2011).

Rituals are the vehicles of meaning transmitted from generation to generation. They have the capacity to create order out of chaos, to integrate beliefs and actions, and to bridge the gap between subjectivity and objectivity. This happens, for example, when people sing a song from their youth together, blending their melodies into one voice that unifies the group. The mere fact of performing rituals carries meaning and offers stability through familiarity and a sense of legitimacy. Rituals also provide support in calamitous events such as school shootings, bombings, and natural disasters. At such times, communities join together to find solace, to remember those who have died, and to regain a sense of meaningfulness and purpose in the face these overwhelming events (Nelson-Becker & Sangster, 2019). Rituals not only help construct meaning but can fuel the capacity to transcend the situation by bringing rest, refreshment, hope, and a needed change of perspective (Wong, 2012). Through supporting meaning-making processes, rituals contribute to establishing an ordered and coherent world (Seeman, 2004).

Some Practical Examples

In contemporary society, there is a significant cross-cultural exchange of rituals originating in different religions: Christians sometimes participate in a Passover Seder, Jews practice Buddhist forms of meditation, and mixed-faith families create new rituals (Pargament, 2007).

Rituals originating in a given culture are interconnected as they all share common features (Cartry, 1992). Normally, we see rituals as symbolic performances that unite the members of a given group, address their common values, and confirm a world of meanings shared by all of them alike, thanks to the use of comprehensive symbols. On the other hand, when rituals are espoused by outside participants, they can become a way for these people to express their aspirations for cultural change. Parkin (1992) also suggested that rituals can have trans-community goals and become a vehicle of competition between different groups. He addresses as well the contemporary traditions associated with Christmas in the Western world. Commercial advertising not only incites people to buy presents for each other but permeates every other aspect of the holiday season: festive office and family get-togethers, greeting cards, Christmas trees or decorations, and holiday vacations. Even Sikh and Hindu families in England have recently begun to celebrate their own Christmas rituals. Thus, Christmas rituals now include Christians and non-Christians, adults and children, consumers as well as marketing experts (Parkin, 1992). This demonstrates that ritual performances, symbols, and meanings are often directed not only toward the community of origin but also to persons who do not share the same background (Baumann, 1992).

Avidan Milevsky and Michael Eisenberg (2012) presented an informative case study of a ritual involving Maya, a 16-year-old Jewish female whose younger sister was adopted as an infant. The sister's biological mother resurfaced and offered to take back her child. Although this was not an easy decision to make, the adoptive parents agreed to transfer her back to the biological mother. Maya was very disturbed by this fact and experienced a profound sense of loss. She was also afraid that something bad might happen to her sister in her new setting.

In order to address Maya's concerns, the therapist suggested organizing a departure ritual that would include the recital of the traditional Jewish traveler's prayer, which is a petition for a safe journey. This ritual would focus on the journey Maya's sister was about to embark on with her biological family. The family used this prayer:

> May it be Your will, God and the God of our ancestors, that You lead her toward peace, guide her footsteps toward peace, and make her reach her desired destination for life, gladness, and peace. May You rescue her from the hand of every foe, ambush along the way, and from all manner of punishments that assemble to come to earth. May You send blessing in her handiwork, and grant her grace, kindness, and mercy in Your eyes and in the eyes of all who see her. May You hear the sound of our humble request because You are God who hears prayers and supplications. Blessed are You, Adonai, Who hears prayer.
>
> (Milevsky & Eisenberg, 2012, p. 338)

The ritual was conducted in-session with the family and therapist, and Maya recited the traveler's prayer. During the follow-up session Maya reported that the experience was a turning point for her in accepting that her sister was moving away from home (Milevsky & Eisenberg, 2012).

For immigrants who have left their homelands, rituals can also be an important means of integration into their adopted country. Participating in customary rituals helps them decrease loneliness and find their way in a foreign land and lifestyle. Well-grounded rituals can help people return to a meaningful life as they play a supportive role when meaning is threatened; they can also be instrumental in helping participants create meaning from suffering (Nelson-Becker & Sangster, 2019).

For American combat veterans, rituals, especially those originating in Native American culture, have turned out to be very effective in helping these soldiers return to civilian life, even as they endure feelings of numbness, terror, hyperarousal, and rage, all common aftereffects of active combat and signs of PTSD. Taking part in these rituals helped veterans assume their new roles in society while also acknowledging their accumulated wisdom and experience (Pargament, 2007).

There is also a pressing need to create new rituals. We are well acquainted with rituals marking important events in a religious life such as welcoming a child into the community through baptism, consecrating a church or holy ground, uniting couples in marriage, and attending funerals. However, we are lacking rituals that extend to other important losses and events. Some such rituals are now emerging. For example, a ritual has been established to mourn a stillborn child. It includes ritualistic actions such as naming the child and burying their remains and clothing. This ritual allows families to process their loss and grief in order to obtain a bit of strength and comfort in their pain. Another example is a ritual addressing the losses resulting from divorce. It involves the couple burning their marriage license together, then burying its ashes along with their wedding rings to stress the finality of the divorce. One of the promising fields in this area is the development of new rituals for seniors that would encourage them to celebrate accomplishments, to accept physical, mental, and material changes in their life situation as well as to grieve losses associated with the aging process, while finding meaning for their lives and hope for the future (Casey, 2012).

Seniors comprise a very important and growing social group and need well-developed rituals to help them cope with the loss of identity and mobility that accompany retirement and subsequent aging. For example, a driver's license gives us freedom and control over our lives; losing it marks a very important and often painful transition in life. We can imagine creating a ritual in which seniors who have recently lost their driver's license, could burn their license (or a copy of it) and bury the ashes, helping them ritualize and bring a certain amount of closure to such an important loss. This ritual would create a formal farewell not only to the license itself but the freedom and control driving once represented. It would also allow seniors to begin to accept their new reality and to grieve the loss of the former one. Another possible ritual for seniors would be the welcoming of a new member to their retirement community. The many important losses associated with the aging process could each give birth to a ritual: loss of a vehicle or driver's license, loss of one's home and independent living after having to move to an assisted living facility and later to a long-term care home, loss of physical mobility, hearing, or eyesight. No ritual can diminish the seriousness of these losses, but could help the experience unfold in a more holistic manner and allow the grieving process to begin. Nonetheless, more extreme situations such as losing contact with one's family because of immigration or whatever reason might not be an appropriate time for a ritual creation. In such cases, some form of professional help may be necessary. No doubt, rituals have their limitations and should not become a substitute for professional care when this is necessary (Casey, 2012).

The COVID-19 pandemic deprived many persons of traditional rituals such as funerals, which normally create a space for expressing grief after the death of a loved one. Without such rituals families are not able to appropriately express the emotions linked to their loss. This shows how important rituals actually are to cope with life's most dramatic events (Pargament & Exline, 2022).

Conclusions

An appropriate practice of rituals can lead to better mental and societal health. In the past, this was done primarily within a religious framework. Today, we need to reclaim the wisdom hidden in rituals on both a personal and a communal level. Rituals need to become a new part of our culture. If not, we risk sustaining the division between the material and spiritual realms and its consequences, notably an increase in violence at every level of society (Clarke, 2011).

One cannot omit ethical considerations regarding the therapeutic use of rituals. Clinicians working with rituals have to respect a client's cultural boundaries and beliefs as sensitivity to the client's spiritual worldviews is essential. Ritual work can provide a very powerful experience for both the counselor and the client. Hence trust and respect between the two are a fundamental principle to be observed. This means developing an attitude of creative collaboration that empowers clients and invites them to participate in the construction of therapeutic rituals. In some cases, there is a danger that a ritual may become more of a hindrance than a help in the client's spiritual growth, especially when they are led toward idolatry or immoderate devotion to ritualism. Idolatry means that they misinterpret the meaning of the ritual. Ritualism occurs when the habitually performed ritual becomes devoid of symbolic truth (Basham 2011).

The psychological dimension of how rituals are conducted is often not considered as much as it should be. From a psychological point of view, rituals can aggravate obsessive-compulsive disorders. Freud indicated the analogy between religion and obsessional neurosis (Freud, 1959), but despite the obvious potential for religious rituals to become overly obsessive, his analogy with obsessional neurosis is overstated and too general. Indeed, he does not seem to have done sufficiently thorough research on religious rituals before suggesting this analogy (Watts, 2017). Although Pascal Boyer (2001), as Freud (1959) did previously, demonstrated the analogy between unhealthy ritual practices and obsessive-compulsive disorders, most research underlines the overall positive effects of rituals on mental health (Idler, 2011).

To some extent, rituals can also be seen as methods of reducing anxiety, creating meaning in life, encouraging emotional expression or control, fostering personal identity, and promoting group cohesiveness. For example, Jan Berry (2009) proposes the use of rituals for women during times of transition in their lives, to help them reclaim and shape their identity when they experience painful events. Nonetheless, we have to be careful not to disregard the primary function of rituals, which is embedded in the sacred dimension. Thus, a uniquely social or psychological analysis of rituals will always be incomplete, as these are supposed to connect participants to the world of sacred realities and help people to be touched be the Sacred.

Through the use of special objects, colors, smells, shapes, sounds, and touch, rituals engage people at many levels of their existence (Pargament, 2007). If we used rituals well, we can live more happily and with more enthusiasm, leaving behind fear and anxiety. Rituals cross religious and cultural boundaries and enable us to live in greater harmony and unity with persons and within communities (Clarke, 2001). There is also a huge potential for including rituals in education, where they make room for everyone to actively participate in the learning process (Thompson, 2017).

Discussion Questions

1. Do you have a favorite ritual?
2. Have you ever been invited to participate in a ritual? What was the ritual and the occasion for it? What were your thoughts and feelings before, during, and after having participated?
3. What characteristics (or qualities) should a participant seek to develop in themselves in order to be touched in some way by participating in a ritual?
4. In a small group, explore the creation of a ritual that could be used with a client during a session. Imagine how your ritual could help your client during or after having participated in it.

References

Basham, A. (2011). Ritual in counseling. In C. S. Cashwell & J. S. Young (Eds.), *Integrating spirituality and religion into counseling: A guide to competent practice* (pp. 209–223). American Counseling Association.

Baumann, G. (1992). Ritual implicates 'Others': Rereading Durkheim in a plural society. In de Coppet, D. (Ed.), *Understanding rituals* (pp. 97–116). Routledge, https://doi.org/10.4324/9780203413210

Beane, W. C., & Doty, W. G. (Eds.). (1975). *Myths, rites, symbols: A Mircea Eliade reader*. Harper Colophon.

Berry, J. (2009). Changing lives, changing rites: Women creating rituals of transition. *Practical Theology*, *2*(1), 93–102.

Boyer, P. (2001). *Religion explained: The evolutionary origins of religious thought*. New Basic Books.

Cartry, M. (1992). From one rite to another: The memory in ritual and the ethnologist's recollection. In de Coppet, D. (Ed.), *Understanding rituals* (pp. 26–36). Routledge. https://doi.org/10.4324/9780203413210

Casey, B. (2012). Pastoral care regarding losses for seniors: Creating rituals, personal narratives, and practices to draw seniors closer to God. *Journal of Religion, Spirituality & Aging*, *24*(4), 289–300. https://doi.org/10.1080/15528030.2012.713801

Clarke, J. (2011) *Creating rituals: A new way of healing of everyday life*. Paulist Press.

D'Aquili, E., & Newberg, A. B. (1999). *The mystical mind: Probing the biology of religious experience*. Fortress Press.

Durkheim, E., & Cosman, C. (2001). *The elementary forms of religious life* (New ed.). Oxford University Press.

Eliade, M. (1957). *Patterns in comparative religion*. Sheed & Ward.

Eliade, M. (1959). *The sacred and the profane: The nature of religion*. Trans. W. R. Trask. Harcourt, Brace.

Griffith, J. L. (2010). *Religion that heals, religion that harms*. Guilford Press.

Grimes, R. (2002). *Deeply into the bone: Re-inventing rites of passage*. University of California Press.

Idler, E. L. (2011). Religion and adult mortality. In R. G. Rogers & E. Crimmins (Eds.), *International handbook of adult mortality* (pp. 345–377). Springer-Verlag.

Idler, E. L. (2013). Rituals and practices. In K. I. Pargament, J. J. Exline, & J. W. Jones (Eds.), *APA handbook of psychology, religion, and spirituality* (Vol. 1: *Context, theory, and research*, pp. 329–347). American Psychological Association. https://doi.org/10.1037/14045-018

Kenney, G. C. (2000). *Lessons & lectures in religion*. Kendall/Hunt.

Levinas, E. (1988). Useless suffering. (R. Cohen, Trans.). In R. Bernasconi & D. Wood (Eds.), *The provocation of Levinas* (pp. 156–167). Routledge.

Lévi-Strauss, C. (1977). *Structural anthropology 2*. Allen Lane.

Marshall, D. (2002). Behavior, belonging, and belief: A theory of ritual practice. *Sociological Theory*, *20*, 360–380. https://doi.org/10.1111/1467-9558.00168

Milevsky, A., & Eisenberg, M. (2012). Spiritually oriented treatment with Jewish clients: Meditative prayer and religious texts. *Professional Psychology: Research and Practice*, *43*(4), 336–340. https://doi.org/10.1037/a0028035

Nelson-Becker, H. (2018). *Spirituality, religion, and aging: Illuminations for therapeutic practice*. SAGE.

Nelson-Becker, H., & Sangster, K. (2019). Recapturing the power of ritual to enhance community in aging. *Journal of Religion, Spirituality & Aging*, *31*(2), 153–167, https://doi.org/10.1080/15528030.2018.1532858

Pargament, K. I. (2007). *Spiritually integrated psychotherapy: Understanding and addressing the sacred*. Guilford Press.

Pargament, K. I., & Exline, J. J. (2022). *Working with spiritual struggles in psychotherapy: From research to practice*. Guilford Press.

Parker, H., & Horton, H. S. (1996). A typology of ritual: Paradigms of healing and empowerment. *Counseling and Values*, *40*, 82–97.

Parkin, D. (1992). Ritual as spatial direction and bodily division. In de Coppet, D. (Ed.), *Understanding rituals* (pp. 11–25). Routledge. https://doi.org/10.4324/9780203413210

Scott, J. (2014). Ritual. In J. Scott and G. Marshall (Eds.), *A dictionary of sociology* (3rd ed.), (p. 99). Oxford University Press

Seeman, D. (2004). Otherwise than meaning: On the generosity of ritual. *Social Analysis*, *48* (2), 55–71. https://doi.org/10.3167/015597704782352500

Taylor, L. (2021). A multidimensional approach to understanding religious conversion. *Pastoral Psychology*, *70*, 33–51. https://doi.org/10.1007/s11089-020-00934-1

Thompson, B. (2017). *Teaching with tenderness: Toward an embodied practice*. University of Illinois Press. muse.jhu.edu/book/54278.

Van Gennep, A. (1960). *The rites of passage*. English trans. 1960 by M. B. Vizedom and G. L. Caffee. Routledge.

Watts, F. (2017). *Psychology, religion, and spirituality: Concepts and applications*. Cambridge University Press.

Wong, P. T. P. (2012). Toward a dual-systems model of what makes life worth living. In P. T. P. Wong (Ed.), *The human quest for meaning: Theories, research, and applications* (2nd ed., pp. 3–22). Taylor & Francis.

13 Spiritual Discipline

Introduction and History

At this time, two decades into the twenty-first century, our contemporaries seem to hunger and thirst intensely for all things spiritual. It also appears that they are not finding what they need to quench their thirst, either in an impersonal, competitive work world, or in domains such as higher education, in the sciences, or even in religious centers. Contemporary people express their spiritual desires in many ways: as being rather than doing, relaxing and listening, quieting down and being detached, self-emptying, and letting go as they seek to be filled and replenished with new light and love. They are also concerned with giving their life an ethical and social direction, which leads to beneficial social action, and to exercises of spiritual discipline resulting in dedicated discipleship. As humans, we thrive on some form of structured regimen to enhance not just our inner regeneration but also our outreach to others, in order to include our whole nature (Kerr, 1993).

Various forms of self-discipline originated in ancient times. They were required for athletes training for competition and for soldiers preparing for combat. As well, they were used by philosophers wanting to acquire clear thinking and wisdom. They took on the form of fasting and sexual self-control in the case of priests belonging to the Greek mystery cults. Buddhists, Muslims, and Christians have all incorporated various forms of spiritual discipline into their spiritual practices. One example is the rigorous annual fast during the month of Ramadan in Islam (Perrin, 2007).

Adele Calhoun (2015) enumerates as many as 75 different spiritual disciplines. Many of these involve various kinds of prayer but also some lesser-known disciplines such as writing religious icons or deliberately taking time away from electronic distractions, including the Internet and social media, for a specified period of time each week (Mulholland, 2016). Taken in a broader sense, many everyday-life practices, such as cooking or doing laundry may also become intentional spiritual disciplines for some people (Warren, 2016). Certain spiritual disciplines demand one's active participation, while others involve abstinence; some disciplines are inward, whereas others are outward (White, 2020).

DOI: 10.4324/9781003262145-14

Spirituality can be seen as a 'discipline' to which someone submits. For example, Christians sometimes call themselves 'disciples' of Jesus Christ and the word 'discipleship' comes from the same root as the word 'discipline.' Being a disciple is essentially accepting and living out a certain discipline. For example, in order to be considered a Hindu or a Buddhist, one must submit to a holistic form of spiritual discipline, a pattern of behavior that has evolved over many centuries. In fact, spiritual discipline constitutes the basis for any religion or philosophy that is centered on a holistic approach to physical, emotional, and spiritual well-being within a given spiritual tradition. This was lived out exemplarily by certain saints and wisdom figures, brave women and men, who developed various spiritual disciplines or patterns of behavior, some of which can still be helpful in today's world and are in fact at the origin of certain very popular exercise and diet regimens recommended by health experts (Rolheiser, 2019).

> For many in the industrialized West, spirituality and religion make an appearance through therapeutic or wellness practices, which they might pursue initially without any concern for the broader tradition from which that practice came. [...] for many who employ them, pathways develop from the practice into other spiritual and religious concerns, leading from wellness to exploring ethics or mysticism.
>
> (Stewart-Sicking et al., 2020, p. 3)

We can argue that this growing interest in asceticism is influenced by the shift from rampant consumerism to moderation, self-control, and sometimes even renunciation and discipline. This interest represents a recognizable change in people's sensibilities. 'Asceticism thus helps people find a balance in life between competing desires. When any one desire becomes so absolute that everything else is ignored, life can become a tyranny' (Perrin, 2007, p. 245). This would be true even in the following example. Excessive studying but neglecting the various components of a healthy life such as exercise, eating properly, and maintaining a healthy social life, can be as destructive as not studying at all. The human being is a mix of desires and impulses that are sometimes in competition with each other.

Ancient Christianity had an ambivalent attitude toward worldly possessions. Its critical attitude toward the world has to be seen in the light of other contemporary Hellenistic-Roman movements of contemptus mundi, expressed in various forms and degrees of ascetic behavior. These movements considered the world in its social, political, and economic manifestations as a stumbling block in the pursuit of perfection. Christianity's negative stance toward the world was influenced by the desire of salvation, and for Hellenistic-Roman movements, by the desire for self-knowledge in association with the ordered *kosmos*. Recognizing the significance of fundamental tensions between the world and these movements inspired asceticism in its criticism (Wimbush, 1993).

> In the Christian tradition ascesis means a training regimen. Spiritual training or discipline may be viewed in three stages: purgation or purification, illumination and union. In first stage we are supposed to work with our will and moral behavior. Stages 2 and 3 are about developing intellectual, psychological and spiritual aspects of our lives. Spiritual athlete has to stay focused on the prize they want obtain. This means setting aside all the elements of training that are no more needed and avoid any distraction. Some training elements are too demanding to some people and some are too easy. In spiritual realm it pertains to certain ways of prayer or behaving.
>
> (Williams, 2018, pp. 38–39)

Despite the prevailing understanding of asceticism as an inwardly focused endeavor, simple acts of charity constitute both a manifestation of spiritual maturity and a practice toward that end. It is probably one of the most important of any ascetical practices, as well as the most neglected. It seems that most of us would rather concentrate on the depth of relaxation that we can attain through meditation or prayer, or even how we can alter the quality of our awareness through fasting, jogging, or meditation, rather than simply doing what needs to be done, thus bypassing the major stepping-stone toward spiritual maturity (May, 1987).

Having dedicated a separate chapter to prayer and meditation, we will now present a detailed look at three forms of spiritual discipline, which are silence, solitude, and fasting. Further, we will illustrate how the practice of a spiritual discipline can be helpful in Christian counseling and psychotherapy in general.

Silence

One of the most important elements of spiritual discipline in all traditions is silence (Kenny, 2021). Adepts are encouraged to practice some kind of quiet reflection, be it prayer or meditation. Silence is an essential part of any spiritual journey. 'The discipline of drawing aside from daily life to a quiet place, free from external distractions, is a long-established practice for fostering awareness, cultivating inner silence and developing greater intimacy with God' (Woolley, 2019, p. 1). We cannot grow spiritually and expand our awareness without an intentional practice of silence where, beyond beliefs, we can experience our universal connectedness (May, 1987).

In the late third century, Christian practices of silence were taken up by the Desert Mothers and Fathers living in the deserts of Egypt, Syria, and Palestine. One of the founders of this movement was Anthony the Great; subsequently, Saint Benedict paved the way for Western monastic life to flourish by developing the Rule that bears his name. More recently, Thomas Merton, an American Trappist monk, as well as others who have followed him, have been instrumental in deepening the true meaning of silence through dialogue with prominent Asian spiritual figures (Woolley, 2019). Groups with Christian roots such as Quakers, cherish moments of silent waiting during their services. This form of communal worship has existed for many centuries and is still part of their contemporary experience (Perrin, 2007).

In today's world, there is not much space or time left for silent moments. Since the advent of the radio, and the subsequent development of technology, people have continuously and compulsively filled silent moments with some sort of noise. Nowadays, people who search for silence tend to find it in nature. But even there, noise caused by human activity has increased exponentially and one needs to go farther and farther into the wild to escape from it. Yet, without silence there is no spiritual growth; it is only in silence that we can meet the Sacred, God, and our true self. Silence helps us discover our true identity and connectedness with all that exists.

Silence has different faces. There is a silence full of contentment, which understands and accepts the presence of the other, a silence that heals. There is also a silence that is painful, which stigmatizes the other as an isolated or misunderstood outcast. In counseling, a client's silence is often understood as a sign of resistance with regard to required change or as a way to conceal suffering. However, silence can be an opportunity to discover the best of oneself and the uniqueness of the human person; it can also protect our inner space and promote an inner transformation. For the therapist, this means listening from a place of respect, putting aside fixed theories in order to get to know the truth about the client's subjective world (Jastrzębski, 2018; Ronningstam, 2021). One of the recent examples of spiritual and therapeutic work with silence in the feminist context lies in Alison Woolley's research (2019) that explores ways of using silence as a powerful transformational tool, helping women on their spiritual journeys by creating meaningful relationships with themselves, with the Sacred, with the universe, and with others.

Solitude

From times immemorial, people who wanted to enter deeply into their hearts and discover spiritual realms, distanced themselves from their community. Silence combined with solitude has been considered a condition sine qua non for any serious spiritual work. In the past, great spiritual leaders and charismatic figures spent significant time in solitude preparing for their mission. Often this took place in the desert. The image of a desert gradually became a metaphor for a period of time specifically dedicated to spiritual work done in the context of solitude. As David B. Perrin (2007) explains: 'The stillness of the desert provides times of long uninterrupted silence, allowing the individual to contemplate the mystery of life, the presence of God in that life, and the ways God is mysteriously present in the world' (p. 65). A spiritual desert can also mean a state of mind or heart that is open to the presence of the Sacred even in the middle of a crowded city. Catherine de Hueck Doherty (1975), the foundress of Madonna House Apostolate, named this state of heart 'living the experience of *poustinia*,' following the Orthodox Christian tradition.

Hermeticism, or the practice of removing oneself from society to live in solitude, originated in this type of experience and is known to many spiritual traditions. Some hermits chose a more organized form of contemplative life by establishing communities under one roof called monasteries (Brox, 2019). As mentioned before, this tradition has come to be known through the life and work of one of the best-known monks of the twentieth century, Thomas Merton (2003). Depending on a person's religion, deserts take on many different manifestations, but people willingly spend time in them when they need to reflect peacefully on their life challenges. These practices are often called retreats in silence and solitude. An essential part of these retreats is an accompaniment by a spiritual guide.

A number of recent Christian books on spirituality (e.g., Murphy, 2010; Mathews, 2015; Maseko, 2017) promote both silence and solitude as a way of deepening one's relationship with God. There is also preliminary research on the potential usefulness of solitude in the formation of therapists (VanMeter et al., 2001). This may be indicative of a more generalized popular interest in these topics that is tied in with a modern fascination with Eastern spiritual traditions (Plummer, 2009).

Fasting

One can say that to some extent, silence and solitude are analogous to fasting (Plummer, 2009). Traditionally, fasting has been associated with certain practices that facilitate purification of the spirit, such as during Ramadan in the Muslim tradition and during Lent in the Christian tradition (Pargament, 2007). Fasting is the deliberate abstention from eating for extended periods of time (Idler, 2013). Rick Goldberg (2009) noted that the practice of fasting can be found in all of the major world's spiritual traditions including Christianity, Hinduism, Islam, Judaism, Mormonism, and Buddhism. In Protestantism, the practice is not regulated by ecclesiastical authority. However, fasting is seen by many Protestants as a personal choice, usually accompanied by prayer; it is considered part of a comprehensive spiritual experience. From the physiological point of view, fasting helps purify, detoxify, and heal the body. From the spiritual point of view, it may promote visionary or transcendental experiences (Goldberg, 2009).

Today, in Western societies, fasting practices are becoming so popular that one can even talk about a new secular asceticism, inspired by its religious roots, but nonetheless detached from institutional religion. Unlike its spiritual counterpart, its motivations are mostly related to personal health, but sometimes are transformed into a communitarian protest against our consumer society or the polluting of our planet. This new, secular asceticism takes many forms, from adopting vegetarianism or veganism as a way of living, to engaging in a variety of other life changes that also reduce fossil-fuel usage. It is interesting to note that at the same time, one can observe the disappearance of obvious asceticism in monastic religious life and in religious life general. Where does this new asceticism come from? Contemporary people seem to be increasingly interested in rebalancing and reintegrating body, mind and spirit, in reaction to a world where there is a great deal of imbalance and disintegration. People are attracted to secular regimes of fasting, silence, and hiking in nature in order to seek a new harmony in their lives and to reconnect with their embodied self (Chatteris, 2019).

Modern ascetic movements have returned to rites of purification, now commonly referred to as 'detox diets.' Retreat centers also exist where people can take a leave of absence from everyday life. During their time of retreat, they often limit their sustenance to frugal vegetarian meals and pure spring water. The reconnection with one's body when hunger appears and the sense of lightness without heavy meals is but a natural consequence of the process, whether one believes in God or not (Chatteris, 2019).

The contemporary ascetic movement is supported by science. For instance, a study of cholesterol levels among Bedouin Muslims in Israel found that the day-long fasts followed by traditional evening meals during the month of Ramadan were associated with a significant increase in high-density lipoprotein (HDL, often called 'good cholesterol'); these levels returned to baseline after four weeks (Maislos et al., 1998).

The search for wellness and salvation seem to be linked, although the quest for salvation is not what fundamentally motivates secular devotees of this new asceticism. They are much more immersed in 'the here and now' than searching for the divine. Nonetheless, it seems that the religious roots of fasting cannot be easily ignored (Chatteris, 2019). Having said this, some Christian authors (e.g., Plummer, 2009) underline that although there are undeniable health benefits to fasting, fasting done with one's focus on God, or biblical fasting, introduces an even deeper level of meaning. In this context, fasting is a response to God's love, done with the goal of drawing nearer to God.

Spiritual Boredom

Boredom in spiritual practices is a common experience among those on a spiritual path. When this happens, people naturally wonder what is going wrong, and some may abandon their practice altogether. From the point of view of spiritual theology, boredom may be a result of sin or God-initiated purification of the heart. From a psychological point of view, it can sometimes be associated with a developmental deficit. Throughout the spiritual journey, there are times when spiritual practices feel life-giving and times when they feel dry or just plain boring. Sometimes it seems that something in the exercise is lacking or has changed. Another possibility is that people practicing ascetic ways bring their histories and personalities into their spiritual practices and the boredom that they experience may reveal something worth exploring psychologically. Boredom always ends up appearing in times of prayer and other spiritual exercises, simply because it is an inevitable part of one's spiritual journey. This kind of spiritual experience is interesting for both spiritual theologians as well as psychologists who integrate religion and spirituality into the therapy process. They all have to answer the question as to whether the appearance of boredom is a manifestation of spiritual dryness or of underlying psychological problems (Straw & Gioielli, 2020).

Historically speaking, spiritual boredom was referred to as 'apatheia' (Evagrius), 'acedia' (Thomas Aquinas), 'sensory night' (John of the Cross), or 'sick soul (William James). John of the Cross (1991) saw three possible causes for boredom: a sinful choice or imperfection, a God-initiated purgation, an emotional or bodily indisposition, which in modern terms may be described as a medical disorder. For Aquinas (1964), acedia meant a willed lack of interest in spiritual things as the individual chooses to become disinterested in spiritual endeavors once they do not receive what they seek from such practices. Consequently, the individual may become interested in things that are not of God in order to fulfill their sensory desire. According to Thomas Aquinas (1964), the individual is culpable regarding the boredom due to their lack of effort and subsequent lack of investment into the spiritual realm. In cases of spiritual boredom, the task of the spiritual director is to discern whether a person loves God in the hope of personal benefit or if they are sincerely seeking communion with God.

According to John of the Cross (1991), the 'sensory night' experienced as subjective boredom or dryness is a process initiated by God that brings about feelings of desolation, the felt absence of God's presence. However, its aim is the deepening of a person's relationship with God and the realization that they cannot find their delight in anything other than God. In short, the goal of this purification is to remove the imperfections that exist in our relationship with God. In this way, we can be more solidly grounded in pure love without expecting the delightful experiences that God sometimes provides. Also, Ignatius of Loyola (2000) indicates that God allows times of desolation in order to test a person and see how much they will advance in God's ways, as well as to give the person a true awareness that they cannot attain spiritual perfection by their own means. Through periods of dryness, God reveals the true nature of the human heart, which is imperfect and weak. God also demonstrates that any consolation is a divine gift and not a product of human actions. God's aim, through desolation, imperfection, and weakness is to bring the person closer to a true and intimate relationship with God.

Usually, this spiritual dryness has spiritual roots and needs to be distinguished from a psychological issue. A clear discernment between the two issues can be challenging, especially when the person is experiencing a depressive mood in addition to God's purifying action. In such instances, spiritual directors would need to consult mental health practitioners in order to prevent misdiagnosis and unintended outcomes (May, 2009). One of the possible signs of a psychological disorder could be that the relational deficit influences all of the person's relationships and is not unique to their relationship with God. If a form of boredom is also experienced in many interpersonal relationships, it would indicate that there is a deeper psychological issue at stake. Despite that, there is always an opportunity for the person to grow in their relationship with God, as this situation can be used as a purification chosen by God (Straw & Gioielli, 2020).

According to Thomas Aquinas (1964), there are two possible responses to the experience of boredom in spirituality. First, there can be an increase in anxiety, when a person finds it too difficult to tolerate the boredom and ends up seeking sensory stimulation and other pleasant distractions. It may even take the form of a new spiritual discipline or practice. Secondly, the reaction can be one of depression and despair, when the person gives in to the existential loneliness of boredom and abandons the entire spiritual pursuit (Straw & Gioielli, 2020).

Michael Raposa (1999) suggests that boredom may be the result of a psychic deficit within the person who is confronted with an experience that induces feelings of abandonment. It is especially linked to the awareness of death and the realization that all things will eventually pass away. Experiencing the absence of God in such circumstances only exacerbates this uncomfortable feeling. This awareness of nothingness makes chronic boredom very difficult to accept and requires that we patiently wait for the emergence of something new. When confronted with such an experience, people tend to engage in defensive, distracting behaviors or give in to existential despair (Raposa, 1999).

Sherry Turkle (2015) underlines that boredom is one of the most important elements in child development, because the child has the opportunity to transform boredom into solitude as well as into creativity through the process of looking into the self. Unfortunately, contemporary technology offers all too many means of avoiding boredom and its associated anxiety, both of which could otherwise have been an important element of growth. Technology rescues modern people from attending to those matters that are of genuine concern (Turkle, 2015).

When one looks at developmental psychological deficits, there are two ways to understand boredom. The first is when a person is unable to entrust themselves to the divine, someone who can be loved without fear. It is difficult for them to believe that they do not need to perform for the divine, or worry about what the divine thinks about them. It is crucial for them to reach the stage when they start believing that the divine is present even if it feels absent. Secondly, boredom may indicate that the person is externally oriented to such an extent that they are attempting to guess what the divine wants from them. In such cases, they may try all types of spiritual discipline in order to please the divine. This type of response can lead to despair (Straw & Gioielli, 2020).

To summarize, one can say that in their spiritual development, an individual should be able to give themselves over to the One whom they are not able to control and to ultimately discover that they can be held by that seemingly elusive One. Without having experienced this kind of relationship in childhood, it will be a challenge for them to allow boredom to function as a time of grace during which they wait and search for their deeper desire to emerge. When this occurs, people will naturally use boredom constructively to search out what the other, in this case God, may want. Such a person may first need to experience unconditional loving, holding, and perhaps even boredom in therapy or spiritual direction before they can translate their discoveries into a more mature relationship with God (Straw & Gioielli, 2020).

Spiritual Discipline of the Christian Counselor

Although we intuitively understand the requirement for spiritual discipline in the life of a Christian counselor, these guidelines are to some extent applicable to all therapists. It is important to underline that spiritual training, experiential in its nature, is difficult to acquire in the classroom or through graduate degrees. Rather, it is the end result of private prayer and devotional reflection, engagement in communitarian worship, or quiet times of fasting and solitude. Practicing spiritual discipline should help counselors remain kind and calm in the presence of angry or provocative clients. The professionalization of counseling has led to the myth that all it takes to become an effective counselor is to master certain techniques such as learning how to develop a counselor's demeanor, affective response, and display of empathy. From a Christian perspective, counseling goes far beyond this. Therapeutic relationships that foster healing are not based on techniques, however effective, but grow out of the counselor's inner life (McMinn, 2011).

When therapists embrace some kind of contemplative practice, they will grow in the wisdom that can be found in the world's spiritual traditions. They will better understand the mysterious flux of life, the potential for enslavement found in one's own desires, and the interconnection of all that exists as well as learn spiritual discernment (Stewart-Sicking et al., 2020).

> A counselor cannot simply walk into the office and 'put on' an effective counseling demeanor, even if the counselor uses prayer, Scripture, and other religious interventions during the session. The substance of spiritually sensitive counseling goes deeper than technique; the care, disciplined objectivity, trustworthiness, empathy, wisdom, and insight must come from within.
>
> (McMinn, 2011, p. 15)

The spiritual life of the counselor influences their understanding of therapeutic problems and strategies. Reading and ongoing education are important, but the Christian counselor would also benefit from the practice of spiritual disciplines such as prayer, fasting, and spiritual mentorship; they must get away for times of prolonged solitude and meditation, as well as participate in community worship (McMinn & McRay, 1997; McMinn, 2011).

> Discipline, regular meditation, and scheduled times for reading and journaling are not in themselves assurances of the coming of the Spirit. The Spirit, after all, is not under our control. We cannot manipulate the Spirit to suit our purposes. The Spirit, like the wind, blows according to divine, not human, direction. But we can make ourselves ready and receptive, not knowing when or where the Spirit will appear.
>
> (Kerr, 1993, p. 452)

Spiritual discipline should enhance the integration of the counselor's self and establish a healthy balance leading to appropriate choices that reflect one's most cherished values and help to achieve ultimate goals in life. Unfortunately, while doing so, the counselor may fall prey to a dualistic approach to spiritual discipline, an age-old temptation that sharply opposes flesh and spirit and that can lead to unhealthy exaggerations in certain forms of ascesis (Perrin, 2007).

Spiritual Discipline of the Therapist

Asceticism is one of many natural movements of humanity in the search for authentic human existence. To achieve particular goals for their lives, people are constantly faced with choices that lead them along one pathway and force them to leave others behind. All pathways cannot be followed; people need to make choices if they are to achieve their most important life goals. For example, if a student wants to pass a course at college or university with the goal to eventually graduate, they will have to accept to fulfill the requirements of the course (Perrin, 2007).

For a therapist, spiritual discipline involves the willingness to live out one's life in a consistent manner. More precisely, it requires the disciplined practices of self-exploration and self-acceptance. This kind of discipline helps develop therapeutic relationships where the spiritual core of both client and counselor can be brought together and thus release healing energy. Practically speaking, a therapist's spiritual discipline should include reflection on thoughts and feelings about their physical being, discovering where they become self-rejecting or self-deprecatory. This part of spiritual discipline translates into a compassionate and respectful attitude toward one's own body. What we eat and drink, what we wear, and what activities we pursue matter. Spiritual discipline in this context may take the form of a weekly massage, a daily walk or run, as well as a balanced diet. It can extend beyond a concern for health and appearance into a willingness to listen to our bodies. This can take the form of a daily period of meditative silence in which the body is allowed to share its message with us, or by practicing deep breathing, which calms the body and allows it to uncover its most important truths (Thorne, 2012).

This care may also include physical activity, well-balanced nutrition, inspirational reading, regular time reserved for quiet reflection as well as for spiritual or emotional processing or journaling, and developing hobbies or spending time in nature. One of the most important parts of the therapist's self-care is spending time with friends. Without an intentional dedication to holistic self-care, the therapist risks becoming overburdened and can experience burnout (Stewart-Sicking et al., 2020).

Spiritual discipline is also expressed in one's relationship with others and in putting oneself on the path of love and appreciation of others. Self-acceptance is related to being close to people, to love and to be loved. Another element of spiritual discipline is our use of time and an acceptance of all the time constraints in which we find ourselves as well as in the activities to which we are committed. Spiritual discipline is also expressed in an awareness of the created world to which we belong, including the natural environment of trees and animals, the sun and the rain, but also the work of human hands such as architecture, art, music, and poetry. Our lives will be all the richer if we take time out of our busy schedules to contemplate nature or to read a poem (Thorne, 2012).

For the therapist, spiritual discipline takes the form of an acceptant and empathic response to their own inner world where conflicting and confusing voices may be at play. The therapist needs to adopt an attitude of patience and remain unperturbed by these discordant inner voices and dark places. In doing so, they can learn to acknowledge the troublesome parts of themselves, just as they do with their clients. Developing their own spiritual life may help counselors accept their broken spaces in ways that are redemptive and nonthreatening to their own souls (Langberg, 2006).

A loving connectedness with one's self is a condition for connecting with clients. Also, compassionate solidarity with the suffering of our planet and identification with the beauty of nature as well as the caring for the natural environment should be parts of a therapist's spiritual discipline. Moreover, nurturing the intellectual and aesthetic dimensions of one's life as well as being open to experiencing the precious sense of awe and wonder that naturally flows from spiritual discipline, all this will prepare the therapist to be surprised by the resourcefulness and the beauty of the human being they meet in therapy. Spiritual discipline also means developing the capacity to wait patiently for the hidden human potential to reveal its treasures (Thorne, 2012). Thanks to spiritual discipline, the therapist can develop a wise self that 'provides a view of the deep structure of reality, beyond the illusions and fictions that often cause our suffering' (Stewart-Sicking et al., 2020, p. 29).

Spiritual discipline or asceticism in this context may signify restraining some part of one's emotional expression. Although it does not mean denying the fullness of one's humanity, a capacity to do it in a more charitable manner and an ability to wait in the midst of impulse, are essential elements of the counselor's spiritual growth (May, 1987). In summary, for the therapist, spiritual discipline involves cultivating and maintaining a loving disposition toward oneself. Regularly and systematically practiced, spiritual discipline leads to an attitude of self-love that releases the therapist from exaggerated self-preoccupation and fosters profound encounters with clients that can lead to powerful healing (Thorne, 2012).

Counseling as a Spiritual Discipline

Beyond incorporating various spiritual disciplines into the counseling process as well as into the self-care of the therapist, Kristen M. White (2021) proposes to conceptualize the entire counseling process as a form of spiritual discipline because there are many intentional practices shared by these two approaches. First, there is the practice of meeting regularly with a therapist; this requires the discipline to organize one's schedule and to adhere to it over an extended period of time. Second, as in the case of some spiritual disciplines, the counseling process reveals one's own pain or brokenness and exposes one's human fragility. Moreover, both spiritual discipline and counseling significantly increase one's self-awareness and foster better insight into one's psyche. In fact, this is a condition of both spiritual and human growth. Finally, by conceptualizing the counseling process as a spiritual discipline, counselors may also encourage their clients to use some of the more traditional spiritual disciplines such as meditation or solitude (White, 2021). A similar approach has been developed from a psychoanalytic perspective (Marcus, 2021).

From a Christian perspective, even if one considers the counseling process to be a spiritual discipline, it appears to be insufficient to finalize the process called sanctification, which means conforming oneself more and more to the image of God. This is why in Christian counseling one underlines the role of divine help called grace that helps to bring wholeness or holiness into one's life. Without grace there is a danger that self-examination will become self-absorption (White, 2021).

Discussion Questions

1. Did this chapter change your understanding of and attitude toward spiritual discipline?
2. For you personally, which one of the elements of spiritual discipline are the most attractive and which ones are challenging? Why?
3. Do you think that some degree of spiritual discipline is necessary in order to become a fulfilled counselor? Please explain.
4. What is the role of 'balance' in the client's life as well as the counselor's life?

References

Aquinas, T. (1964). *Summa theologiae: Latin text and English translation, introductions, notes, appendices, and glossaries* (T. Gilby, Ed.). McGraw-Hill.

Brox, J. (2019). *Silence: A social history of one of the least understood elements of our lives*. Houghton Mifflin Harcourt.

Calhoun, A. A. (2015). *Spiritual disciplines handbook: Practices that transform us*. InterVarsity Press.

Chatteris, C. (2019, May 17). The new asceticism. *Spotlight Africa*. https://spotlight.africa/2019/05/17/the-new-asceticism/ Accessed on 10.07.2020.

Doherty, de Hueck C. (1975). *Poustinia: Christian spirituality of the East for Western man*. Ave Maria Press.

Goldberg, R. (2009). The adaptiveness of fasting and feasting rituals: Costly adaptive signals? In J. R. Feierman (Ed.), *The biology of religious behavior: The evolutionary origins of faith and religion* (pp. 190–203). Praeger.

Idler, E. L. (2013). Rituals and practices. In K. I. Pargament, J. J. Exline, & J. W. Jones (Eds.), *APA handbook of psychology, religion, and spirituality* (Vol. 1: *Context, theory, and research*, pp. 329–347). American Psychological Association. https://doi.org/10.1037/14045-018

Jastrzębski, A. (2018). Lecząca, oczyszczająca i integrująca rola samotności w życiu człowieka. In M. Gajewski & Z. Dołęga (Eds.), *Społeczne i osobiste przestrzenie samotności* (pp. 41–52). Oficyna Wydawnicza von Velke.

Kenny, C. (2021). Encountering religious and spiritual silences. In A. Dimitrijević & M. B. Buchholz (Eds.), *Silence and silencing in psychoanalysis: Cultural, clinical, and research perspectives* (pp. 26–40). Routledge/Taylor & Francis Group.

Kerr, H. T. (1993). Spiritual discipline. *Theology Today*, *50*(3), 449–453.

Langberg, D. (2006). The spiritual life of the therapist: We become what we habitually reflect. *Journal of Psychology & Christianity*, *25*, 258–266.

Maislos, M., Abou-Rabian, Y., Zuili, I., Iordash, S., & Shany, S. (1998). Gorging and plasma HDL cholesterol – the Ramadan model. *European Journal of Clinical Nutrition*, *52*, 127–130. doi:10.1038/sj.ejcn.1600526

Marcus, P. (2021). *Psychoanalysis as a spiritual discipline: In dialogue with Martin Buber and Gabriel Marcel*. Routledge/Taylor & Francis Group. https://doi.org/10.4324/9781003162360

Maseko, M. (2017). *The Daniel fast: Biblical and scientific facts*. Wipf & Stock.

Mathews, S. H. (2015). *Christian fasting: Biblical and evangelical perspectives*. Lexington Books.

May, G. (1987). *Will and spirit. A contemplative psychology*. HarperCollins.

May, G. (2009). *The dark night of the soul: A psychiatrist explores the connection between darkness an spiritual growth*. HarperOne.

McMinn, M. R. (2011). *Psychology, theology, and spirituality in Christian counseling*. Tyndale House.

McMinn, M. R., & McRay, B. W. (1997). Spiritual disciplines and the practice of integration: Possibilities and challenges for Christian psychologists. *Journal of Psychology and Theology*, *25*(1), 102–110. https://doi.org/10.1177/009164719702500110

Merton, T. (2003). *New seeds of contemplation*. Shambhala.

Mulholland, R. M. Jr. (2016). *Invitation to a journey: A road map for spiritual formation*. InterVarsity Press.

Murphy, C. M. (2010). *The spirituality of fasting: Rediscovering a Christian practice*. Ave Maria Press.

Pargament, K. I. (2007). *Spiritually integrated psychotherapy. Understanding and addressing the sacred*. Guilford Press.

Perrin, D. B. (1997) Asceticism: The enigma of corporal joy in Paul Ricoeur and John of the Cross. *Pastoral Sciences*, 16, 135–162.

Perrin, D. B. (2007). *Studying Christian spirituality*. Routledge. https://doi.org/10.4324/9780203944776

Plummer, R. L. (2009). Are the spiritual disciplines of 'silence and solitude' really biblical? *Journal of Spiritual Formation and Soul Care*, *2*(1), 101–112. https://doi.org/10.1177/193979090900200106

Raposa, M. L. (1999). *Boredom and the religious imagination*. University Press of Virginia.

Rolheiser, R. (2019, January 28). Spirituality and spiritualities. *Voices*. Available at: https://grandinmedia.ca/spirituality-and-spiritualities (Accessed on 7 September 2020).

Ronningstam, E. (2021). Cultural function and psychological transformation of silence in psychoanalysis and psychoanalytic psychotherapy. In A. Dimitrijević & M. B. Buchholz (Eds.), *Silence and silencing in psychoanalysis: Cultural, clinical, and research perspectives* (pp. 105–127). Routledge/Taylor & Francis Group.

St. Ignatius of Loyola. (2000). *The spiritual exercises of St. Ignatius* (L. J. Puhl, Trans.). Vintage Books.

St. John of the Cross. (1991). *The collected works of Saint John of the Cross* (Rev. ed.; K. Kavanaugh & O. Rodriguez, Trans.). ICS.

Stewart-Sicking, J., Fox, J., & Deal, P. (2020). *Bringing religion and spirituality into therapy: A process-based model for pluralistic practice*. Routledge.

Straw, B. D., & Gioielli, C. D. (2020). Spiritual practices are boring: A psychoanalytic understanding of spiritual ennui. *Pastoral Psychology*, *69*, 509–522.

Thorne, B. (2012). *Counselling and spiritual accompaniment: Bridging faith and person-centred therapy*. John Wiley & Sons.

Turkle, S. (2015). *Reclaiming conversation: The power of talk in a digital age*. Penguin Books.

VanMeter, J. B., McMinn, M. R., Bissell, L. D., Kaur, M., & Pressley, J. D. (2001). Solitude, silence, and the training of psychotherapists: A preliminary study. *Journal of Psychology and Theology*, *29*(1), 22–28. https://doi.org/10.1177/009164710102900103

Warren, T. H. (2016). *Liturgy of the ordinary: Sacred practices in everyday life*. InterVarsity Press.

White, K. M. (2020). Conceptualizing therapy as a spiritual discipline. *The Journal of Psychology and Christianity*, *39*(2), 91–103.

Williams, J. P. (2018). *Seeking the God beyond. A beginner's guide to Christian apophatic spirituality*. SCM Press.

Wimbush, W. L. (1993). The ascetic impulse in ancient Christianity. *Theology Today*, *50*(3), 417–428.

Woolley, A. (2019). *Women choosing silence: Relationality and transformation in spiritual practice*. Routledge. https://doi.org/10.4324/9781351273602

14 Sin, Confession, and Reconciliation

Introduction

Sin is probably one of the most misunderstood of theological terms. It has to do with spiritual suffering associated with stagnation or enslavement. For many professional counselors, this theological vocabulary remains deeply problematic. It feels old-fashioned, piously moralizing, and carries too much historically marked emotional baggage (Stewart-Sicking et al., 2020). Nevertheless, there are self-destructive forces in the human personality that one can refer to in the Christian tradition as original sin, understood as an age-old and inherent inclination for evil resulting from the breaking of communion with God, with others, and with the whole of creation (nature). The end result is a kind of mental tension or an existential struggle between good and evil, oneness and division, between serving others or giving in to selfish tendencies. This primordial injury to human nature is inherited in different ways. It can be through a genetic inheritance (illness), a dysfunctional family, traumatic events, a pathological growth environment, and, in religious language, rebellion against God's plan (God's commandments). Whatever the reason, the effect remains the same: human propensity to fault and evil (Montgomery, 2009). Alvin Plantinga (2000) compares sin to a contagious virus that spreads through society.

The woundedness of human nature can be defined as the sum of its disordered reflexes, impulses, and proclivities. Along with all the goodness of human nature, humans come into the world with innate weakness and a tendency toward evil. This inborn woundedness is aggravated by other injuries resulting from experiences in our personal life, which often begin in childhood and that become part of our history. This original wound within human nature is marked by both personal sin and those of others against individuals and collectives alike. Karen Horney (1991) speaks about the power of feelings of self-hatred and their devastating intensity, which are one of the greatest dramas of the human psyche. When someone tries to reach perfection, which is an unattainable absolute, they begin the work of self-destruction. These self-destructive behaviors, manifested in poor choices, begin to create hell within their life (Horney, 1991). According to Pargament

DOI: 10.4324/9781003262145-15

and Exline (2022), it can be called moral perfectionism, which is based on the fear of falling short.

Sin comprises three dimensions: human actions as concrete transgressions, the capacity of fault, and the consequences of these. Sins are individual and collective acts whereas sinfulness is part of human nature. Because both affect every human being, this realization should incline therapists toward empathy. Clients are often wounded by their own sins in addition to the sins of others. From the Christian perspective, both the therapist and the client are broken and fallen human beings. We all have sinned and have experienced the sins of others. Theologically informed empathy does not minimize sin but recognizes that we are all in the same sorry state and have a great need for redemption, relief from what causes harm to self and to others (McMinn, 2008). 'In the world's religions we can find an abundance of redemptive resources – forgiveness, grace, compassion, confession, atonement, making amends – that appear to be tailor-made to the challenge of redeeming people from their offences and limitations' (Pargament & Exline, 2022, p. 250).

Sin seems to be inscribed into the very fabric of human life. Even if love expresses the most noble and best facets of human nature, it is rarely completely pure and is almost always contaminated with self-interest or self-absorption. Naturally, the human heart cries out for justice in the face of racism, agism, sexism, and oppression, but even then, it is easy to harbor a smug sense of self-righteousness or superiority, especially toward those who care less about justice (McMinn, 2008). A psychiatrist and spiritual director, Gerald May (1993) gives a very persuasive firsthand report:

> I studied and practiced psychiatry for a quarter of a century; I know how the human mind can fool itself and how selfishness can masquerade as righteousness. I worked in a prison with people convicted of repeated crimes of physical violence, and I was in the military for the majority of the Vietnam war, so I have no doubt that evil exists and that we humans are capable of absolute destructiveness. And I have spent enough time in silence to know that my own impulses, perceptions, and additions often lead me astray. I believe in sin, not only as making mistakes or being compelled by addiction, but also as hard, calculated meanness.
>
> (pp. 62–63)

We need both theology and spirituality to understand the question of sin. Theology without spirituality may end up as nothing more than a dry intellectual quest. On the other hand, spirituality without the guidance of theology risks becoming a journey without a clear direction.

Original Sin and Personal Sin

Original sin is expressed psychologically through living at the level of mental illusions and unreal idealizations, or in focusing on one's own ego. By discovering the unconscious, psychology has allowed us to look at human spirituality in a new way. This understanding of the human condition would bring us closer to the psychological approach to original sin (Keating, 1999).

If we are truly honest with ourselves, we cannot deny the experience of a certain sphere within ourselves, which can be called 'darkness' or 'shadow.' It may be a mixture of chronically negative feelings: dissatisfaction, abandonment, anger, sadness, depression, disappointment, stress, feelings of inferiority, guilt, jealousy, and envy. We usually attribute the genesis of these feelings to the circumstances of our lives and to the difficult events that we are confronted with. And yet, it is easy to overlook the fact that this darkness can also come from within us. It is so deeply ingrained that it can easily escape our conscious perception. It is at the root of all of our unhealthy tendencies, but because these inclinations are often unconscious, we may not even be aware of them. And when we are, our response is either to feel powerless or not to feel responsible for them. This is sin in the deepest sense; it separates us from one another and from God. In Christian theology one calls these tendencies 'original sin' (Jastrzębski, 2014a).

This theological perspective can shed some light on the brokenness in this world as well as the prevalence of mental distress. For example, a number of psychological theories have been developed in relationship to co-addiction or dysfunctional families. Research based on these theories shows that, at least in the Western world, up to 95% of the population may be affected by some mental disorder (Keating, 1999). From the psychological point of view, we may add that the root of evil is an illusory self-image (Thorne, 2012).

Christianity also speaks of personal sin, which is a manifestation of original sin. It consists of all voluntary thoughts and deeds that are not life-giving. However, it is only a part of human sin, and the less important part at that. We can regret the deeds, confess them, and thus obtain release from the guilt associated with them.

> It is around this area of personal choice that religion most directly addresses the relationship between attachment and sin. Though we may have no choice whatsoever about our basic desires or fears and very little choice about the strength of our attachments, we do have something to say about how far we go in pursuit of those attachments, how much we will harm ourselves or others or set ourselves up as gods to try to get what we want. In religious terms, there is a basic condition of sinfulness about which we have no real option, but we can maximize or minimize it by the kinds of choices we make between willingness and willfulness are every moment of our lives.
>
> (May, 1987, p. 233)

The Christian doctrine regarding original sin challenges the psychological conviction regarding the goodness or neutrality of human nature as developed by humanists (Carl Rogers, Abraham Maslow). Even when people are exposed to their misbehavior, they tend to justify it in thousands of rational ways rather than feel sorry for it. They justify themselves by putting the blame on bad reinforcement patterns, poor parenting, misbalanced neurotransmitters, or inadequate self-esteem. Surely, these problems play a role, but they do not take into account the full weight of moral value in human actions. In a sense, all these issues contribute to aggravating the sinful condition of our world. For that reason, counseling should not be a place to promote cheap grace by suggesting that God really does not care about the bad things people do. Sin should not be minimized but rather needs to be uncovered in the context of a safe relationship, paving the way for repentance, which at times can be a very emotional experience (McMinn, 2008).

The paradigm for human sin is willful self-determination that increases one's sense of separateness, a destructive alienation of oneself from the divine and from other people. This separateness is a mistake. Sin occurs when personal willfulness becomes so important that one forgets or denies the beauty of one's true nature, which is grounded in the divine power that created and sustains the cosmos. Sin is much more related to the turning of oneself away from the ultimate Truth and course of the universe, the setting oneself apart as an autonomous and separate being. Sin can be thus seen as a striving for self-importance at the cost of others (May, 1987).

Sin and Defense Mechanisms

One of the basic psychological reactions to human sin is defense mechanisms. In the earliest years, children learn to cope with all kinds of life situations. This learning process is not always easy because they quickly figure out that certain emotions should not be expressed. Consequently, they gradually develop habits and strategies that enable them to dull these unwanted emotions to some extent or even to anesthetize them completely. This occurs through suppressing, blocking, or projecting these emotions onto other people and imagined creatures. The world of human feelings is so complex that mechanisms developed in childhood have a tendency to persist into adult life, thus confusing human motivations and causing irrational decisions that are objectively considered to be morally wrong (sin).

Defense mechanisms provide a way for people to deal with their problems, but do not offer authentic solutions. They plunge people into a world of infantile imaginations, preventing them from accomplishing the necessary work on their personal development. One of the more common defense mechanisms is rationalization, particularly developed and effectively used by intelligent people. Rationalization is a kind of self-justification that can be used relatively easily to justify sin. Another defense mechanism is spiritual bypass, as discussed in Chapter 9.

For example, if a client is struggling with an addiction, they cannot rely on their own judgment, because the mind's tricks are too cunning. Individuals need independent help from other people to move beyond their state of 'being stuck.' For full recovery from sin, we have to become aware of the defensive mechanisms; this process normally takes place during psychotherapy. Unfortunately, being aware of these mechanisms is not sufficient to overcome them as these often overpower our good will. This leads to even greater suffering when we realize the challenges that true liberation from sin entail. Psychologically speaking, this is characterized by a disconnect between the idealized idea that we have of ourselves and the reality of who we actually are. Bridging this gap requires a substantial amount of mental energy, which cannot always be mustered. This realization can be accompanied by feelings of guilt. In healthy individuals, guilt normally provides a motivation to compensate for the wrongdoing, but in a pathological situation, there is an exaggerated tendency for self-blame. Pathological guilt is the result of a poor, immature emotional self-assessment. It may also occur in people with perfectionistic or narcissistic tendencies. And although there will always be a gap between the ideal self and real self, if it is too great, it will always lead to an unreal sense of guilt, which is quite difficult to deal with in therapy (Jastrzębski, 2014b).

Perhaps our contemporary preoccupation with self-esteem is nothing more than a widespread defense mechanism that protects us from the awareness that we are sinners living in a corrupt world. We have used this mechanism very effectively since its alternative, which is admitting our sins, seems all too menacing. But is not acknowledging our problem a manifestation of true freedom? In the Christian approach, sin can be confronted humbly and with empathy, in a way that privileges genuine spiritual growth over guilt and shame. This may include silence at strategic moments, challenging inconsistencies in the client's narrative, and requesting clarifications to better understand whether the client's views are right or wrong. In the final analysis, understanding and fostering change in one's inner life is far more important than concentrating exclusively on changing one's behavior. In this context, humility does not mean self-abasement but rather a realistic opinion of oneself (McMinn, 2011).

Confession and Its Existential Dimension

For many believers, a failure to live according to their cherished values, known by some as God's commandments, is very significant because it changes their perspective from a secular one, where we talk about a mistake or an error, to a spiritual one, where we use the language of transgression or sin that normally elicits feelings of shame and guilt (Pargament & Exline, 2022). Some empirical evidence shows that these feelings actually help people repair their wrongdoings (Fisher & Exline, 2006).

Many spiritual traditions propose a number of ways that enable their adherents to ask for forgiveness, to make amends, and to atone for their transactions: the Yom Kippur service in Judaism; *tawbah*, asking forgiveness from God in Islam; and repentance verses in Buddhism (Pargament & Exline, 2022). In Christianity, there is a long tradition of confessing sins and asking for God's forgiveness. This process requires humility and readiness to repent and is helpful when one is working with the sins of a believer. Its primary aim is not to fill the believer with shame, but to help them turn from their self-deceiving ways and to seek a better way of living. Ultimately it is God who desires reconciliation with the believer and who calls the sinner to confess their sin in order to restore their relationship with God (McMinn, 2008).

In an existential perspective, sin can be understood as unfaithfulness to God's project for humankind. In the Bible, God invites us all to love creation, each other, and the human community as well as our own self. Thus, sin is not fundamentally the breaking of rules. From the existential Christian point of view, sin is seen as a destruction of the fundamental Christian attitude of loving-kindness whereas a particular sin is an expression of this attitude. Consequently, the process of reconciliation must include the whole of creation, the community, God, and oneself (Perrin, 1998).

In some Christian traditions, people who wanted to confess their sins and obtain forgiveness met with a priest. After hearing the confession, the priest usually suggested some form of penance to help the person acknowledge the weight of their sins. And then the priest would offer the most important and free gift: reconciliation with God. Today many prefer to go to the psychotherapist. It is more appealing to be reassured that our behavior is understandable and that it can be justified in some way or another: by our parent's conduct, our boss' need for control, or perhaps by some chemical imbalance in the brain (McMinn, 2008).

It seems that one form of confession has been exchanged for another. We would rather see a counselor for an emotional problem than a pastor or priest for a spiritual one. Perhaps this is because the priest deals directly with the immediate moral problem, whereas the counselor explores the psychological context in order to explain why the given problem occurs. Both intend to change behavior, but the approaches differ. In confession there is moral evaluation, whereas in counseling, moral neutrality. This is where the sin-versus-sickness dichotomy originates. Simply put, priests attribute problems to sin, and counselors to disorders. But maybe the truth lies somewhere in the middle and that both sin and sickness contribute to dysfunctions in human behavior. Because of this, moral discourse could be included in some counseling situations. In fact, through every word and gesture, therapists communicate something about how life is or how it ought to be, thus becoming practitioners of moral philosophy (McMinn, 2011).

Reducing all human problems to psychological issues deprives us of the meaningful spiritual riches of redemption. Without allowing people to use the language of sin, we concentrate on symptom relief and rob them of the opportunity to embark on the journey of repentance and change (McMinn, 2008). With the popularization of psychology, good ideas have been misused. Although therapists should free people from excessive burdens of guilt, too often they also try to free people from appropriate guilt. As a result, although many competent psychotherapists do not accept the prevailing dogma of guiltless individualism, popular psychology promotes self-sufficiency while undermining spiritual development. Because of this, many people associate psychology with irresponsible freedom and self-centeredness (McMinn, 2011).

The sacrament of reconciliation in the Roman Catholic tradition can be seen as a new beginning as it provides purification and healing through a confrontation with human fragility and transforms chaos into cosmos, to use the ancient philosophical concept. In this reconciliation process, human reality is seen as it is: both good and evil at the same time, containing the natural tension between these opposites. In an existential sense, this sacrament helps people deal with the limits of their lives and transform them into a meaningful human existence (Perrin, 1998).

It would be misleading to reduce psychological problems to simplistic cause-and-effect algorithms. We humans are a far more complex world, which is distorted by our own sins as well as the sins of others, all of which contribute to an unjust world order. How marvelous it would it be if we were able to work together in merciful fellowship, helping one another to make things right. Of course, this would require an acceptance that spiritual estrangement is as important a cause of existential loneliness as psychological issues. Repentance and forgiveness are key to going beyond our self-serving pursuits and discovering that our greatest hope is much greater than our simple well-being (McMinn, 2008).

> I have witnessed the cleansing power of confession and the beauty of healed relationships many times in my years as a psychologist. Each time I am deeply moved by the splendor of grace; it resonates with some unnamed primordial cadence in the human soul. Those who are able to confess and forgive are often transported beyond the limits of what they thought possible, and the healing that ensues takes my breath away: expression of remorse, tears of loss and joy, and the beautiful gift of humility. If it were not for repentance and forgiveness, every person and every relationship would eventually accumulate into a mountain of bitterness and resentment.
>
> (McMinn, 2008, p. 157)

Working with sin and guilt is not limited to the Christian tradition. For example, in a Muslim context, Hamdan (2007) assisted his client Fatima in eliminating her excessive guilt by means of several psychotherapeutic and spiritual exercises. First, Fatima was helped to cognitively acknowledge her mistakes as part of being human. Based on Islamic beliefs, the therapist reminded Fatima that Allah forgives people who sincerely want to avoid sins in the future. The most important element of therapy was the spiritual exercise of repentance, called *tawbah* in Islam (Hamdan, 2007).

According to Hamdan (2007), the process of repentance should involve specific steps: immediately stopping the sinful action, seeking forgiveness from Allah, regretting the sin, and resolving not to return to it. Finally, if possible and appropriate, there should be an attempt to make retribution for the wrong done. The process of repentance may be expressed through a ritual prayer for repentance called the *salat al-tawbah*. These steps of reconciliation are very similar to the conditions for a confession in the Catholic tradition.

In a more existential approach to the Catholic rite of confession, Perrin (1998) proposes a model of the healing process that is composed of several elements: becoming truly aware of one's transgression, accepting one's authorship of the deed, being able to appropriately verbalize one's sense of guilt, undertaking some form of amendment of the harm caused by oneself, and finally, being able to accept forgiveness and reconciliation as well as believing in the possibility of one's improvement and transformation or new beginning.

> Appropriate guilt expressed to another person is an indicator that one has truly experienced the crisis inflicted in one's life through failed relationships. This verbalization is an encounter with the past fault which in turn allows the individual to take a certain distance from it. The penitent is thus free to let go and move on. A new beginning moves him or her to a purification of self and liberation toward a better future. The necessity of a 'new beginning,' [...], is an existential necessity for authentic life.
>
> (Perrin, 1998, p. 118)

The idea of confession has become less and less popular in contemporary Western society. Even for Roman Catholics who for centuries have cherished the sacrament of penance, the practice of confession has declined. On the other hand, the demand for counseling has increased (McMinn, 2011). Despite the contemporary reluctance toward this practice, the Roman Catholic views of confession and penance still have merit. Regular confession invites the penitent to confront sins that are easily overlooked or minimized in everyday life. Often, people who regularly confess their sins take them more seriously than those who do not and accepting a penance for them can increase their moral sensitivity. Some theological views may lead to a lack of concern about sin because of the conviction that we will always be forgiven. It is penance that counters this tendency by letting one experience the consequences of sin. The beauty of the Roman Catholic sacrament is that the burden of guilt is unambiguously lifted as formal absolution is granted, which for some people is profoundly liberating (McMinn, 2011).

In the Christian tradition, confession is neither a technique nor just an occasional expression of remorse. Rather, it is an attitude toward life that helps people to learn to live humbly, admitting their weaknesses to one another and drawing support from a safe spiritual relationship and from God. In fact, human nature is characterized by a longing to confess one's moral shortcomings and by the need for forgiveness. At its best, confession becomes a way of life and a path to holiness (McMinn, 2011). Confession should be a tool for deepening the integrity of human life. This is what the purpose of the Sacrament of Reconciliation really is: to help believers grow in their humanity. It is not a mere eradication of sins but rather a way of developing a community of persons reconciled by love and charity (Perrin, 1998).

Reconciliation

Among spiritual challenges, struggling with forgiveness and reconciliation is a separate issue that has gained some attention in psychological research. Although we will not treat this exhaustively, we need to include at least major points of reference pertaining to it. Some research indicates that forgiveness can be of benefit for one's mental health and marital satisfaction. On the contrary, resorting to defensive responses or even to fantasies of revenge has been associated with poor metal health and psychopathology. There is some evidence that repentance may be associated with mental and physical health benefits. Both forgiveness and repentance appear to lead to healing of emotional and relational wounds (Exline & Baumeister, 2000).

We are always free to decide how we wish to respond to the conditions that define our life. We can strive to become less attached to objects, less self-important, and more open to reconciliation and to the fact that we are united with all humanity. But we can also align ourselves with our separateness and willfulness. All major world religions underline the possibility of this choice (May, 1987).

Thanks to honest work on our sins, our relationships with others can become a channel for redemption and sanctification just as before they promoted sin and destruction. In this context, effective counseling is not so much about applying particular techniques as creating healing relationships. From early psychodynamic traditions to certain contemporary approaches, some authors suggest that therapeutic relationships are the true vehicle of healing rather than the various techniques taught to therapists during their clinical formation. As it turns out, putting the emphasis on the relational dimension of the therapeutic process has marked the entire history of counseling (McMinn, 2011).

Christian theology states that this reconciliation has already been accomplished through Christ, and Christians are invited to acknowledge it as a gift already given. Jewish theology explains reconciliation as atonement for unfaithfulness to the covenanted relationship with God, where there is more room for human collaboration in this process. In Hinduism and Buddhism, sin is linked to the dualistic view of self and the world. Every attachment brings about a bad karma negatively influencing one's present and future lives as well as those of others. Reconciliation here means reaching the state of enlightenment, which is abandoning the dualistic view (subject versus object) of the world and accepting one's fundamental unity with the rest of creation. Final liberation from evil occurs when one is released from the endless cycle of birth and death. This is also called the state of nirvana (May, 1987).

In Western culture, confession is perhaps the most common reconciliation ritual. It is practiced by most religious groups in America as well as in 12-step programs, support groups, and counseling. Spiritual confessions may be public or private, and always have two important components: an acknowledgment of having committed a spiritual violation and a request for forgiveness. These two elements are usually followed by acts of penance and restitution. The experience of catharsis involved in confessing sins is certainly helpful in and of itself as it is tied to a number of physical and mental health benefits (Pargament, 2007).

> Reconciliation moves toward finding peace with oneself. It is a 'profound therapy' for one's mistaken attitudes about life. It seeks to go deeper than the sinful act, that is, it seeks to go where the delusion about life exists. Reconciliation with oneself forms part of the dynamic of reconciliation with the wider community. Acceptance of the pardon offered by God is also essential, for this is where there exists Christian hope and a new future. Reconciliation with the cosmos is no less real. Since the human person has his or her home in the world, that person must assume as well a caring and loving attitude toward that world gifted by God.
>
> (Perrin, 1998, p. 114)

In both its theological and its spiritual context, forgiveness is a life-giving and transforming experience. Removing the spiritual context from forgiveness and making it just a clinical technique misses the essence of forgiveness. Emphasizing only its role of reducing negative emotions may perhaps lead people away from resentment or hatred, but it can leave them in cold neutrality and it is not the true fruit of forgiveness (McMinn, 2011).

A spirituality of reconciliation is for everyone. Challenging life situations often require some form of reconciliation in order to develop the full potential of human life for infinite happiness, joy, and hope. In this sense, salvation can be best conceived as a new and more authentic mode of being human rather than as a salvation from sin. Thus, encountering the limits of our lives in the chaos that often accompanies them, we can also discover the potential for developing a more meaningful order (cosmos) of our lives (Perrin, 1998). 'Redemption does not mean overlooking or condoning transgressions, but rather involves finding some compassion and forgiveness for oneself to balance or soften the harshness of personal judgments and responses to these offences' (Pargament & Exline, 2022, p. 255).

A life that does not acknowledge the need for repentance does not help people understand why life is so difficult, relationships so complex, and meaning so hard to find. The Christian proposal is challenging but honest. We experience all this pain because of the profoundly contaminating effects that sin has in our lives. When we see things more realistically, the simple beauty of our spiritual journey comes to the foreground. As long as we look for an easy life, we are bound for disappointment and discouragement. Only by accepting the inevitability of life's challenges such as doubt and fear do we free ourselves to be surprised by joy (McMinn, 2008).

Spiritual Healing

Spiritual healing is a religious practice that raises many interesting questions. Relatively little empirical research on this phenomenon has been carried out so far, though Fraser Watts (2011) has come up with some psychology-based comments. Spiritual healing refers to healing that comes about through certain spiritual practices. We have already mentioned in Chapter 11 that regular prayer can have health benefits. By spiritual healing we refer to a special gift of healing that involves a person's spirituality. In Christian terms, spiritual healing can refer to healing that comes about through the action of a transcendent Spirit, the Holy Spirit. This is what most Christian practitioners of spiritual healing assume (Watts, 2017).

The Bible recounts the life of Jesus, someone who healed all diseases and weaknesses among the people (Mt 4:23). After the death of Christ, the apostles continued his mission. For example, Peter and John heal a lame man at the gate of the temple (Acts 3:1–11). In the Christian understanding, Jesus saves the whole person in their spiritual, mental, and physical dimensions. It is more than medical assistance (Catalan, 1991). God's grace touches and heals without ignoring any dimensions of human existence. Extracting individual elements of the human being's structure as we do in psychology is hermeneutically fertile, but this carries the risk of singling out only one of the dimensions of human life and can actually lead to reductionism (McNeill, 1998). Both disciplines of theology and psychology can end up with a completely different understanding of the same reality.

From a faith perspective, healing can simply mean conversion. Many disorders that occur in the human psyche are the result of sins, disobedience to God, and bad choices; full recovery can only take place through conversion. In this case, psychological help will not do much. As a rule, psychotherapy does not lead to conversion. In the Christian view, only Christ can bring about the genuine transformation of a human life, integrally touching the entire human person and changing them from within. Religious faith, which is expressed through prayer for healing, can have a very powerful psychotherapeutic effect, but this is not its primary role. Its purpose is not to resolve psychological problems but to save and sanctify the person.

Spiritual life for contemporary people seems to be something outdated and irrelevant, because many have already been cut off from their spiritual roots. Instead, new forms of therapy and new religious movements have taken its place in an attempt to answer the problems of our time. An empty space always needs to be filled. People may turn to alcohol, sex, or drugs in an attempt to deal with this emptiness. Sometimes they may open themselves up to substitutes for spirituality such as occultism and esoterism, or even to the action of evil spirits. Spiritual healing is not the equivalent of psychological well-being, nor is it a substitute for successful self-actualization in the understanding of humanistic psychology. In the Christian view, healing through the power of the Holy Spirit gives believers more than any therapy can, but also imposes many more demands on them – above all, accepting the mystery of unavoidable suffering. For the reasons mentioned above, combining psychotherapy and faith interventions may potentially lead to misunderstandings and tensions. Although the benefits ensuing from both approaches may sometimes converge to some extent, medical and spiritual interventions are of a different nature (Jastrzębski, 2014c).

We are aware that within Christian spirituality, one is allowed and even encouraged to ask God for the healing of another person or of oneself (Dein et al., 2012). Although modern science does not accept the existence of spirits, people continue to report such experiences as Marian apparitions, visionary accounts of Jesus, weeping statues and icons, miraculous healings, and charismatic encounters with the Holy Spirit, often expressed in manifestations such as speaking in tongues or being 'slain in the Spirit.' Moreover, the Catholic Church, through the work of the Congregation for the Causes of Saints, continues the medical investigation of healing miracles, inviting some of the most eminent doctors and scientists in the world to undertake the study of such cases. This kind of investigation is an integral part of the canonization process. Before canonizing someone as a saint, there must be a healing that cannot be explained in a scientific way such as an instantaneous and permanent physical healing. It has also to be connected to the intercession of the candidate for canonization, for whose intercession the suffering person was praying (Orsi, 2016).

Practicing spiritual healing assumes that a spiritual force of healing exists beyond the healer, although there are various ways to conceptualize this. Normally, it is also assumed that healing is a gift or a charism that can be developed and that it is a holistic process that touches the whole person. It goes beyond the simple relief of symptoms and often requires spiritual or personal change (conversion) for healing to occur. In some healing practices people are encouraged by their healers to expect an immediate result, while other healers do not have clear expectations and leave the possibility open for a 'miracle' to happen. From the psychological point of view, it is clear that strong expectations are often associated with a placebo effect. Trust in the healer may also play an important psychological role. Furthermore, from a psychodynamic perspective, there exists a phenomenon termed hysterical conversion syndrome, popularly called a flight into illness. In this case spiritual healing may be efficient in helping people free themselves from this psychologically based disorder. Spiritual healers as well as the people seeking their help usually consider that healing is an event that defies natural explanation, though this does not exclude a scientific description of the natural processes by which healing is mediated. Adding a theological perspective can enrich the understanding of such phenomena (Watts, 2017).

In some spiritual traditions such as Buddhism, Taoism, and Chinese medicine, health is seen as a balancing act between mind, body, emotions, and spirit. The interdependence between each of these domains is under research. In these traditions, health and maturity are considered to be the natural result of the integration of mind, body, emotions, and spirit, as well as living in satisfying community with others. There is also the assumption that if we suffer on one level, our whole being suffers as well. Research is beginning to confirm these Eastern convictions. On the other hand, Western healing practices have a long history of fragmenting the human being into distinct parts and developing specializations for each area separately so that physicians attend to the body, psychotherapists the emotions and mind, and religious leaders attend to the soul. Historical spiritual figures such as Jesus Christ and the Buddha are good examples of fully self-actualized and spiritually mature individuals. Having said this, some people nowadays also exhibit the characteristics of spiritual maturity; they are grounded, radiate unconditional love, and are able to live either connected to others and in solitude as well (Cashwell et al., 2007).

Conclusions

Sin, reconciliation, atonement, and redemption are concepts considered to be strictly theological and of no use for counseling. And yet experience in the counseling room demonstrates that, at least at times, entering into religious or spiritual conceptualizations of the clients can foster and actually enable the process of recovery and healing. Psychotherapy can play a redemptive role and help people reconcile themselves with their divinity, eternal destination, and ultimately make peace with God and others. Such a powerful tool should not be easily neglected. Taking some time to get to know spiritual channels of healing used for centuries in various spiritual traditions may potentially enhance professional efforts of counselors trying to help their clients become whole and grow as fellow human beings.

Discussion Questions

1. What was your first reaction when you heard the word 'sin'?
2. Have you ever experienced true reconciliation or atonement?
3. What are the major insights of this chapter that are new for you?
4. Do you think that you will be able to work with the concept of sin when your client asks you to do so?

References

Cashwell, C., Bentley, P., & Yarborough, J. (2007). The only way out is through: The peril of spiritual bypass. *Counseling & Values, 51*, 139–148. https://doi.org/10.1002/j.2161-007X.2007.tb00071.x

Catalan, J.-F. (1991). *Expérience spirituelle et psychologie*. Desclée de Brouwer.

Dein, S., Cook, C., & Koenig, H. (2012). Religion, spirituality, and mental health: Current controversies and future directions. *Journal of Nervous & Mental Disease, 200*, 852–855. https://doi.org/10.1097/NMD.0b013e31826b6dle

Exline, J. J., & Baumeister, R. F. (2000). Expressing forgiveness and repentance. In M. McCullough, K. Pargament, & C. Thoresen, Eds. *Forgiveness: Theory, research, and practice* (pp. 133–155). Guilford Press.

Fisher, M. L., & Exline, J. J. (2006). Self-forgiveness versus excusing: The roles of remorse, effort, and acceptance of responsibility. *Self and Identity, 5*(2), 127–146. https://doi.org/10.1080/15298860600586123

Hamdan, A. (2007). A case study of a Muslim client: Incorporating religious beliefs and practices. *Journal of Multicultural Counseling and Development, 35*, 92–100.

Horney, K. (1991). *Neurosis and human growth: The struggle toward self-realization.* W. W. Norton.

Jastrzębski, A. (2014a). Człowiek grzeszny powołany do doskonałości. *Zeszyty Formacji Katechetów, 1*, 33–46.

Jastrzębski, A. (2014b). Psychologiczny wymiar grzechu. In M. Pyzik-Turska & P. Stepnowska (Eds.), *Święty Kościół grzesznych ludzi. XLVI Tydzień Eklezjologiczny* (pp. 118–126). KNT KUL.

Jastrzębski, A. (2014c). Pomoc psychologiczna a modlitwa o uzdrowienie wewnętrzne. *Roczniki Teologiczne, 61*(5), 79–98.

Keating, T. (1999). *The human condition.* Paulist Press.

May, G. G. (1987). *Will and spirit. A contemplative psychology.* HarperCollins.

May, G. G. (1993). *The awakened heart.* HarperOne.

McMinn, M. R. (2008). *Sin and grace in Christian counseling: An integrative paradigm.* IVP Academic.

McMinn, M. R. (2011). *Psychology, theology, and spirituality in Christian counseling.* Tyndale House.

McNeill, J. J. (1998). Psychotherapy and the spiritual journey. *Journal of Religion and Health, 37*(4), 333–344.

Montgomery, D. (2009). *Compas therapy: Christian psychology in action.* CompasWorks.

Orsi, R. A. (2016). *History and presence.* Belknap Press.

Pargament, K. I. (2007). *Spiritually integrated psychotherapy: Understanding and addressing the sacred.* Guilford Press.

Pargament, K. I., & Exline, J. J. (2022). *Working with spiritual struggles in psychotherapy: From research to practice.* Guilford Press.

Perrin, D. (1998). *The sacrament of reconciliation: An existential approach.* Edwin Mellen Press.

Plantinga, A. (2000). *Warranted Christian belief.* Oxford University Press.

Stewart-Sicking, J., Fox, J., & Deal, P. (2020). *Bringing religion and spirituality into therapy: A process-based model for pluralistic practice.* Routledge.

Thorne, B. (2012). *Counselling and spiritual accompaniment: Bridging faith and person-centred therapy.* John Wiley & Sons.

Watts, F. (2011). *Spiritual healing: Scientific and religious perspectives.* Cambridge University Press.

Watts, F. (2017). *Psychology, religion, and spirituality: Concepts and applications.* Cambridge University Press. https://doi.org/10.1017/9781107360549.009

Index

For Product Safety Concerns and Information please contact our EU representative GPSR@taylorandfrancis.com
Taylor & Francis Verlag GmbH, Kaufingerstraße 24, 80331 München, Germany

www.ingramcontent.com/pod-product-compliance
Ingram Content Group UK Ltd.
Pitfield, Milton Keynes, MK11 3LW, UK
UKHW022017180926
475701UK00005B/886
* 9 7 8 1 0 3 2 2 0 0 1 8 7 *